How ~~not~~ To Speak English

Vinay Sethi

How Not To Speak English
First Edition: November, 2015
Reprint : December 2016
© Vinay Sethi
Author's email : vinset19@gmail.com
All rights reserved. No part of this book will be reproduced, used or stored in any form without the prior permission of the Publisher.

ISBN 978-93-83572-74-8

Published by:
Vishwakarma Publications
283, Budhwar Peth, Near City Post,
Pune- 411 002.
Phone No: 020 20261157 / 24448989
Email: info@vpindia.co.in
Website: www.vpindia.co.in

Cover Design & Typeset and Layout Credits -
Abhishek Darekar - Vishwakarma Publications

Foreword

English is often experienced as a dampener of spirits by those who have not spoken or learnt it correctly in their formative years and have to use it perforce in their professional lives. When their inevitable mistakes in English are pointed out, such people get defensive or resentful, seeing this as more evidence of how this supposedly alien language is not for them. However, the truth is that English has been on the Indian sub-continent for more than three hundred years and enough people speak it in our country today for us to accommodate it as one of our own languages. We need to lose the fear of English and accept it as one of the most versatile and functional languages of the world, enabling communication across developed and developing countries. The more naturally we speak English, the better it will be for our personal and professional progress.

Vinay Sethi brings this book for those who are often unaware of their mistakes, yet keen to correct them in order to become more effective speakers and writers of English. Vinay has a love for the language that was very much in evidence when I first met him in our years together in St. Xavier's College, Mumbai. In those days, he wrote short stories written with quirky humorous twists that appealed hugely to us, his readers and listeners. Since then he has worked for many years in teaching and training. These experiences have given him an eye and ear for spotting stumbling blocks where people usually falter, and how they can be helped by explaining the correct usage or meaning.

I am sure *How Not To Speak English* is going to win a huge following among students and professionals and all those seeking a deeper understanding of and an intimate relationship with the language, beyond a mere nodding acquaintance. As an author, having written many books in English based on interviews I conducted in Hindi and other regional languages, I have a soft corner for this book, which I perceive to be a powerful instrument of much needed empowerment for many of my fellow Indians.

- **Scharada Dubey**

Preface

This book is for my mother, Mrs. Kamla M. Sethi, who, in her thirties, passed away in Bombay on the eleventh day of February, nineteen hundred and seventy-three.

My mother did not know much English nonetheless, maternal intuition had made her proudly conscious that I was profoundly passionate about the language.

She was fascinated and intrigued by the many new and difficult-sounding words that I brought home often from school (Don Bosco's-Matunga). She regularly made me read and speak these words out aloud so that both of us could try to get their pronunciation correct and understand better their meaning. One such word was *paraphernalia*.

The only paraphernalia essential to acquiring a sound grasp over English is application, diligence and a mother's love. Crucial to human development, a mother's love by itself, toward the acquisition of a skill is of minimal use. Conversely, a combination of application and diligence, when unaccompanied by a mother's love, is misfortune. The three together can make a child not only study English well, but also speak it with flawless fluency.

A mother's love can inspire and correctly orient the judicious exploitation of the attributes of application and diligence toward academic and, closely connected with it, economic success.

This book is therefore, for each and every mother who wishes to bask in the glory that her child, irrespective of age, by purposefully reading this book, is going to achieve.

– **Vinay Sethi**

Introduction

This book is about the perceptions, attitudes, inclinations and associations of ideas we Indians employ with regard to English. Grammar *per se*, is also its mainstay.

In India, English is highly coveted but studied with application and diligence by only a select few. Rules of English grammar, replete with exceptions, make them difficult to follow. Furthermore, inherent flexibility in its syntax leads to innumerable variations of English. These variations, given innate Indian apathy, blissful ignorance and unshakeable indolence, get misconstrued to be correct and proper. Smattering therefore gets identified as fluency. To learn English well, it is vital for us as Indians, to consciously halt subconscious transliteration of every sentence from non-English Indian languages into English and vice versa. This vicious circle must stop. Only standard English-English dictionaries (not the pocket-sized ones) must be used. Additionally, if you've learnt, but aren't confident of your English skills, the best way to improve upon them, is by beginning to unlearn English. For unlearning to begin, you must know how *not* to speak English. Knowing how *not* to speak English will definitely lead you to realize how to speak correct English.

The purpose of this book is to acquaint the earnestly interested reader with English grammar in a simple manner. This acquaintanceship will enable the avid reader develop a fruitful relationship, getting the essential nudge toward correctness. It would also be in keeping with the spirit of this book if readers treat English as a language and not as only a subject to be studied in schools as has been the norm all over India for so many years. It will also help a great deal if English is regularly used outside of academic confines. This book is certainly not a substitute to prescribed textbooks, it being a supportive non-academic endeavour.

The motive behind the absence of exercises in this book is not ulterior, with the Lessons having been written more in an informative than instructive manner. Readers are therefore enjoined on creating their own exercises. Assimilation of information within these Lessons is a confidence building measure toward interactions involving English. Utilizing information contained within this book will result in high-scoring academic performances. It will also ensure elimination of nervousness when indulging in exchanges involving English.

It is downright impossible for an individual to be fluent in a language and be using its grammar incorrectly. The key to fluency in English begins with concentrated reading. You may read these Lessons at random, or, when in need of information on a particular topic of interest, look it up in the **search guide** to get to its exact location. Those who wish to obtain information on topics not covered in this book may contact me and I shall try my best to professionally enlighten them, and in the process, enrich myself. I am open to correction and if readers feel that I have erred in a particular Lesson they are welcome to contact me. I shall duly acknowledge the correction, if and when convincingly pointed out, with the concerned reader's name in the next edition.

Of the many who have contributed to the creation and success of this book two names that stand out are Asawari Joshi and Eunice de Souza. I am highly indebted to the former, for her insights and also for suggesting the title for this book. To the latter I owe the prowess I possess over imparting sound education to genuine and keen learners of English. For any teacher who wishes to teach it well, it is imperative to have been taught English by Eunice de Souza, who instinctively knows how to painstakingly turn the art of teaching as well as that of writing, into a highly skilled craft.

— **Vinay Sethi**

How Not to Speak English

LESSON 1

Making mistakes is your birthright, repeating them is suicide.

A lot has been written and said about English having become a universal language today. Most of us are keen on displaying our English-related skills, but very few of us take the trouble to actually work on and practise speaking this wonderful language correctly. Many Indians even today associate skills related with English to be more accent-oriented rather than grammar-oriented. English grammar, with its mind-boggling number of exceptions, is not easy to master. However, if you keep certain general rules in mind and apply them with care when you speak and write English, then the language is easier to grasp. For correct English to become part of your subconscious, it is essential that you speak English as much as possible.

To make English very easy for you to speak here is the first lesson:

'To' – Wrong Usage

'To'

This word is very often incorrectly inserted and mistakenly omitted from where required. When you read the following sentences, you will find that you have sometimes committed these errors. All incorrect sentences with their errors are in italics, The correct sentences, without errors are in bold. However, italics have been used for some words in the middle of correct sentences in order to emphasize them or highlight them. Thus, only full sentences in italics are examples of incorrect usage.

    1) *I am going to home.*
    2) *S/he is going to home.*

With the word 'home', the use of 'to' is unnecessary. When it is your own home, 'to' is not used. When you go to somebody else's residence, then the word 'house' is used. We use 'to' with 'house', e.g.

    1) **I am going to my friend's house.**
    2) **I am going to my uncle's/aunt's house.**

When we speak of some persons going home, then we mean that these persons are going to their own residences and not to anyone else's, e.g.

    1) **'Are you going home late today?'**
    2) **'We are going home early today.'**
    3) **'They have all gone home.**

And to correct the first two incorrect sentences:

    1) *'I am going to home.'*
    1) **'I am going home.'**
    2) *'S/he is going to home.'*
    2) **'S/he is going home.'**

We will continue with some more mistaken uses of the word 'to' in our next lesson.

LESSON 2

'To' – Incorrect Omission

In the previous lesson, we saw how 'to' is incorrectly inserted. Now, we will see how 'to' is mistakenly omitted. Many Indian speakers of English do not use 'to' with the verb 'say' or its past tense form 'said'.

    1) I said him that he should work hard.
    2) She said her that she should obey her parents.
    3) You had said me to return your book today.
    4) They say us "Good Morning!" every day.

With 'say/said', the use of 'to' is very important. When 'to' is used with 'say/said', it clearly indicates the person at whom the utterance is/was directed. It also makes it clear that the communication is/was complete. This is because 'say/said' has a slightly different meaning as compared to 'tell/told'. With 'tell/told', we generally provide information. The word 'to' with 'tell/told' is not used and it must always be avoided e.g.

    1) I told him not to disturb me.
    2) They are always telling me to be neat and clean.
    3) Could you tell me why you are late?

Returning to 'say/said', it is extremely important that 'to' must be inserted, otherwise the speaker will be considered to be making a statement in the direct speech e.g.

    He said, "I am the greatest."

When 'to' is not used with 'say/said', the indirect/reported speech form of the above sentence above can be wrongly interpreted as:

He said me that he was the greatest.

The formation of this sentence, when spoken, sends the wrong message across that this sentence meant:

He said, "Me, that he was the greatest".

The above sentence, as you can see for yourself, has no meaning and the correct sentence is:

He said to me that he was the greatest.

As shown above, because of the correct use of the word 'to', the correct meaning has been communicated.

Once again, please remember the sentences in italics are incorrect, and those in bold are correct.

Now, coming back to the first three incorrect sentences, please note them corrected in bold and resolve to say them or any other which you make with the verb 'say/said' correctly:

1) I said him that he should work hard.'
1) I said to him that he should work hard.'
2) She said her that she should obey her parents.'
2) 'She said to her that she should obey her parents.'
3) 'You had said me to return your book today.'
3) 'You had said to me to return your book today.'
4) 'They say us "Good Morning!" every day.'
4) 'They say to us "Good Morning!" every day'

or

'They say "Good Morning!" to us every day.'

For serious students of English grammar, it will be helpful to remember that, when 'to' is followed by a Noun/Pronoun, it becomes a Preposition e.g. 'to Ramesh' etc /'to him/her' etc; when 'to' is followed by a Verb in its Present Tense form, it combines with that Verb to form the Infinitive, e.g. to+give = to give.

LESSON 3

'To' – with 'listen'

As seen earlier, the word 'to' is mistakenly omitted by many students, when speaking English. When asked about our hobbies, we generally say:

1) 'I listen music.'
2) 'I love listening music.'

The use of the verb 'listen' (and its forms) without 'to', is incorrect. We can use the Verb 'hear/heard' without 'to' because hearing is an involuntary activity, e.g.

'I can hear the music being played loudly next door.'

The use of 'hear' without 'to' is correct because your neighbours have voluntarily put on the music for themselves. You get to hear it because of its loudness. You have not put the music on. In all possibilities, you would want it switched off or the volume lowered.

Similarly,

1) 'I can hear the traffic.'
2) 'Have you heard the latest gossip?'

However, with the verb 'listen', 'to' must always be used. Looking at the first two incorrect sentences:

1) 'I listen music.'
1) 'I listen to music.'
2) 'I love listening music.'
2) 'I love listening to music.'

There are a number of Verbs that take 'to' and a few others that do not take 'to'. You should always understand and practise Verbs which take 'to' and remember those that don't. Continuous practice of the correct combination will ensure you are communicating using correct English.

LESSON 4

'Myself', 'Himself', 'Herself' and 'Themselves'

'Myself, Vijay Singh!'
How many times have you heard this sentence as the beginning of an introduction? I am sure, on a number of occasions. Howsoever, it is incorrect. Whenever introducing yourself, formally or informally, the word 'myself' must never be used at the beginning of a sentence. It is proper to say:

'I am Vijay Singh'
Or
'My name is Vijay Singh.'

When you type "myself", "yourself/yourselves",

"himself/herself", "ourselves/themselves" on your computer, the red line underneath each one of them clearly indicates some kind of error. These words are Reflexive or Emphatic Pronouns and should be used only with the Root/Personal Pronouns e.g. I-myself; we-ourselves; you–yourself; (singular); you(all)-yourselves (plural); he-himself; she-herself; they-themselves. When you look at the following sentences, you will understand the method of using Reflexive/Emphatic pronouns correctly:

1) I hope you enjoyed the food, I cooked it myself.
2) S/he hurt herself/himself while jumping into the pool.
3) Did they enjoy themselves at the party?
4) We need to ask ourselves several questions.

Therefore, use of the word 'myself' at the beginning of a sentence is clearly incorrect and conveys a poor grasp of English. We must never use a Reflexive/Emphatic Pronoun at the beginning of a sentence.

LESSON 5

'They're' – The Contraction of 'They are'

Speakers of English find three similar-looking and similar-sounding words very difficult to use - (a) they're (b) there &(c) their. The fact is, each one possesses its own identity. Let us take the first one, 'they're'. The word 'They're' is a contraction/shortened form of 'they are'. When we use 'They are .....', the two words, 'They' and 'are' get separately and distinctly pronounced. When combined into one word together, they become together, a contracted form, 'They're', wherein the letter 'a' of 'are' is neither written nor pronounced. The use of 'They are' or the contraction 'They're' can be done only in the Present Simple or the Present Continuous Tense. e.g.

1) They are leaving Pune tomorrow by the Jhelum Express.
1) **They're leaving Pune tomorrow by the Jhelum Express.**
2) Madhuri Dixit's proposed visit to the school has made the students excited and they are dying to meet her.
2) **Madhuri Dixit's proposed visit to the school has made the students excited and they're dying to meet her.**
3) You are looking everywhere for your keys, they are in your bag.
3) **You are looking everywhere for your keys, they're in your bag.**

All these sentences are correct for 'they're' is simply the contracted form of 'They are', with 'they' being the 3rd Person Pronoun in the plural and its corresponding verb 'are'.

LESSON 6
'There' – An Adverb meaning 'in that place'

After the word 'they're', let's look at the word 'there'. The word 'there' means 'in that place' and is the opposite of 'here' which means 'in this place'. The word 'there' shows an area, a spot or a direction that is a little away or quite distant from a person or an object. 'There' is also sometimes used to declare a fact. In such cases, the word 'there' usually begins a sentence, e.g.

    1) There is a disagreement between the two of them.
    2) There are many issues connected with this matter.
    3) There is a city known as Timbuktu.
    4) There is so much to see in this world.

When we use 'there' as an Adverb, we point toward someone or something not near us or at a slight/great distance from us e.g.

    1) "Can you see my bike? It is there!"
    2) "Take a look at the jet flying high up there behind the clouds!"
    3) "My cousin's house isn't very far, shall we walk there?"
    4) "I wonder how you'll get home." "Don't worry, I can see a taxi there!"
    5) "I was worriedly looking for my daughter and there, I found her."

Students must make it a point to remember that the word 'there' is an Adverb and can never be used as a Preposition.

LESSON 7

'Their' – A Pronoun for Belonging

Having studied 'they're' and 'there', we come to 'their'. It is very easy to remember the meaning of 'their' for it is associated with possession. When we use the Third Person Pronoun in the singular, we say 'This is his/her car', Being a Possessive Plural Pronoun in the Third Person, 'their' indicates ownership of something /s belonging to more than one person, e.g.

1) "Ram and Shyam have bought a new car, their car is lovely."
2) "Seeta and Geeta are going to get wet in the rain, they've forgotten their umbrellas."
3) "I love my parents and never go against their wishes."
4) "The children have dirtied their shoes in the mud."

As you can see, when we continuously practice after having understood the meanings and correct usage of words, English becomes easier. Simply pronouncing these words will not help. Put them correctly in sentences, read/speak these sentences correctly and loudly and then you will gain a stronger grasp over English. Always remember – 'PAP' for the three words which confuse millions of Indians.

'They're' – They+are-a=they're (Plural Pronoun)

There – To indicate the opposite of 'here' (Adverb)

Their – An object belonging to 'them'. (Plural Pronoun)

LESSON 8

| Plural Nouns – with and without 's' |

In English, most Nouns take 's' to denote their quantity to have increased from one to more than one. The moment the Noun becomes plural, it must be read/written/spoken in its plural form. A most commonly committed mistake:
"I have many friend."
'Many' definitely means more than one. 'Friend' must therefore become 'friends' to make the above sentence correct, i.e.
"I have many friends."

When we do not denote the plural, then the use of a particular Verb can be incorrect. The following sentences will show you the importance of reading/writing/speaking the plural form of the Noun.
1) *My brother has two blue shirt.*
2) My brother has two blue shirts.
3) *The postman has brought two letter.*
4) The postman has brought two letters.
5) *Ravi has three sister.*
6) Ravi has three sisters.

Remember, there are many Nouns which do not take 's' to be denoted as the plural and some don't change at all. Here are a few Nouns which do not take 's' to denote that their quantity is more than one:
One deer-many deer;
One sheep-many sheep;

One child-many children;
One man-many men;
One woman-many women;
One aircraft-many aircraft;
One thief-many thieves

One thesis-many theses;
Analysis-Analyses;
Information – a lot of information.
Equipment – a lot of equipment.

Remember, only Nouns/Pronouns are singular/plural. The Subject of a Sentence is always a Noun or Pronoun. Subject/Verb Agreement therefore is the key to good English grammar.

LESSON 9

'One of the ....'

Continuing with plural Nouns/Pronouns, when we use the phrase 'one of my _____', the Noun/Pronoun denoted must always be in the Plural. e.g. **'One of my colleagues is very good at English.'** Unfortunately, whenever this phrase is heard, the Noun in the plural is never clearly pronounced. It is rarely written correctly in the plural, and the same error can be repeatedly heard - 'One of my *colleague* is very good at English.' The Noun, pronounced in the Singular where its Plural is required, makes the language incorrect. Simple arithmetic will tell you that 'one of one' makes for no logical or mathematical

reasoning. It always has to be 'one of many'. Therefore whenever we say 'one of my ….. ,' the Noun/Pronoun that follows must be clearly written/pronounced in the plural form, e.g.
1) One of the books you returned to the library was torn.
2) One of my neighbours is a chartered accountant.
3) Bihar is one of India's poorer states.
4) One of us is a painter.
5) One of them is a very rich man.
6) One of our bikes is very old.
7) One of our students is a very good dancer.
8) One of my colleagues is very good at English.

LESSON 10

Redundant - (Unnecessary) Use of 'Colour'

My bike is red in colour.
The sentence above isn't good English. Why? It is because the words 'in colour' are redundant (not necessary). The use of *'in colour'* is incorrect. Red by itself is the name of a colour, therefore:
My bike is red.
OR
I have a red bike.
If at all the word 'colour' is to be used, then it must be before the name of the colour:
"Would you like this T-shirt in the colour yellow? "
"Do you think this wall would look attractive in the colour

orange?"

Notice, when the word 'colour' is removed, both sentences continue to make sense:

"Would you like this T-shirt in yellow?"

"Do you think this wall would look attractive in orange?"

Whenever we wish to offer the choice of a colour the words 'what' and 'in' are very important. We cannot use the word which. An object, where English is concerned, comes 'in a colour.'

"*Which colour you want this dress?*" is incorrect;

The correct question is:

"What colour do you want this dress in?"

"In what colour should we get this room painted?"

"What colour candle would your daughter like on this cake for her birthday?"

LESSON 11

'Birthday' and 'Date of Birth'

The previous lesson ended with "birthday". And who doesn't want his/her birthday to be happy? However, we invariably say: *"Today is my happy birthday!"* The association of happiness with a birthday is natural, but the use of them together is unnatural and poor English.

The correct sentence is:

"Today's my birthday."

OR

"It is my birthday today. Naturally, I am very happy."

We have become so habituated using 'birth' and 'date' together, that when we wish to know details, we ask:

"*May I know your birthdate?*"

The correct question is:

"May I know your date of birth?"

Remember, if someone does not wish to reveal this information, s/he is well within her/his rights. You cannot force a person to tell you his/her date of birth, unless required by law. You must also remember that in English, it is considered bad manners to ask a woman her age. It is also considered impolite to ask a man how much money he earns. Therefore, always remember this couplet:

"Never ask a woman her age
Never ask a man his wage."

The word 'wage' in the above-quoted couplet stands for the money earned by a gentleman.

LESSON 12

Verb, Tense and Gender

The previous lesson was on dates of birth. Likewise, many of us while speaking about our background, say "*I am born in _____.*" This is incorrect. The Verb 'born' cannot be used in the Present Tense and must always be used in the Past Tense with 'was/were' e.g.

"I was born in Ernakulum."

"S/he was born in Kolkata in 1962."

"Those two are twins and they were born in Pune on 16th July, 1997."

In English, the Noun/Pronoun is masculine/feminine but unlike many other Indian languages, the Verb is applicable both in the same basic form. Verb-change does not take place with gender-change in English. The change in Tense definitely makes the Verb change. This rule must be applied while changing from the present to the past or the future tense :

    I am - I was; We are - We were; You are – You were;
    S/he is – s/he was; They are – they were.

With the verb 'born', we also get to listen to the word 'native' on so many occasions. The word 'native' is often incorrectly applied:

    "I am going to my native place in the holidays."

This is incorrect and should be:

    "I am going to my native village/town in the holidays."

LESSON 13

'Driving' and 'Riding'

In India, two-wheelers are popular. When we speak of using them, we often use the wrong Verb such as:

    "I was driving my bike when you called"

The correct sentence is:

    "I was riding when you called."

Here the word 'riding' is associated with a two-wheeled vehicle and therefore the need to use the word 'bike' does not arise. Had you been on a horse, then the following would have been required:

"I was riding a horse when you called."
OR
"I was horse-riding when you called."

Similarly, where driving is concerned, many of us mistakenly say:

"I was driving my car and so couldn't take your call."

Here, it is important for us to understand that driving is always connected with 'car' and the use of 'car' with 'driving' and its related form is not necessary. The correct sentence is:

"I was driving and so couldn't take your call."

'Two-wheeler' - 'four-wheeler' are today obsolete and you must use 'bike' or 'car' instead. 'Bike' stands for a motorized two-wheeler, and a non-motorized two-wheeler is known as a 'bicycle'. Incidentally, 'cycle' is not a vehicle and means a 'circular or a continuous or regular chain of events'.

LESSON 14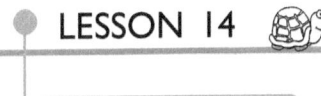

'Bear' and 'Bare'

Pronunciation is a very important aspect of a language. When a language is not your mother tongue, correct pronunciation gains the utmost importance. In English, pronunciation is very often mistaken for accent. Correct pronunciation has got to be learned by regular practice and associating the correct meanings of words. Thousands of words in English have more than one meaning. The appropriate meaning of a word has to be understood by looking at its context.

Look at the following :
bear – We all know this to be a Noun denoting a large wild animal, e.g.
    I saw a bear in the zoo.

But the same word *bear* has a different meaning as a Verb and can mean *'to carry'; 'to undergo', 'to hold'*, etc, e.g.
    I cannot bear this pain.

There is yet another word 'bare', an adjective which means 'empty' or 'without contents', e.g.
    'When she opened the cupboard, it was bare.'

Many mistakenly pronounce 'bear/bare' as 'beer'. The word 'beer' means a mildly alcoholic drink and the pronunciation of 'beer' is a combination of "be here" without the "h" sound.
You must learn correct pronunciations as well as meanings of words. Otherwise, you may convey a different meaning. Remember, "bear/bare" are pronounced to rhyme with "air".

LESSON 15

'Countable' and 'Uncountable' Common Nouns

With plural Nouns, remember that all Nouns cannot be quantified or measured. There are many Uncountable Common Nouns. When we wish to connect a question with an Uncountable Common Noun we ask 'How much?' With Countable Common Nouns, we ask 'How many?'
Nouns denoting emotions, feelings, sensations etc. are known

as Abstract Nouns and are always uncountable.

Let's look at some Nouns:

Q 1) 'How much water do you drink every day?'

A. I drink at least three liters of water every day. (Countable – liters; Water-Uncountable)

Q 2) 'Doctor, how many glasses of water should I drink every day?'

A. You must drink at least ten glasses of water every day. (Countable – 'glasses')

Q 3) 'In a world of cut-throat competition today, how much honesty is more than enough?'

A. As much as your conscience thinks is necessary. ('Honesty'–feeling-Uncountable)

Q 4) How many known planets are there in our solar system?

A. There are nine known planets in our solar system. ('planets'-Countable)

Like 'water', some Uncountable Common Nouns are 'rice', 'sugar', 'wheat', 'butter', etc. The word 'money', generally supposed to be Countable, is actually Uncountable, e.g.

"How much money do you have?"

When we indicate the use of currency, then the currency becomes Countable. e.g.

"How many rupees/pounds/dollars do you have?"

Some other Countable Nouns are 'cars', 'rooms', 'drinks', 'bottles', etc.

Some examples of Abstract Nouns are 'smartness', 'handsomeness', 'integrity', 'cruelty', 'selfishness' etc. all Uncountable.

LESSON 16:

'Brought' and 'Bought'; 'Thought' and 'Taught'

When speaking in English, we assume that, since we're using English, we're speaking correct English. Howsoever, grammatically correct-sounding sentences sometimes contain incorrectly-pronounced words. Now, let us examine:
   'I was born and bought up'.

This common mispronunciation shows misplaced confidence many of us have that nobody will notice our errors in English. 'Bought' is the past tense of 'buy' and cannot be used in combination with 'I was born and ....' The sentence then leads to a wrong meaning of purchase with the word 'bought' by not pronouncing the letter 'r'. The above expression however concerns upbringing in a particular village/town/city–
   'I was born and brought up in _____.'

Incidentally, in American English the same idea is conveyed by:
   'I was born and raised in _____.'

A somewhat similar situation occurs with 'thought' instead of 'taught' by mistake. The pronunciation as well as the meaning of 'taught' is distinctly different from 'thought'. Invariably, somebody says:
   'My teacher thought me Geometry very well,'
However, he means:
   'My teacher taught me Geometry very well.'
The past tense of *'bring'* is 'brought', *'buy* - bought', *'teach-*

taught', 'think-thought'.

Practice pronouncing words correctly, as part of sentences, so that you absorb the correct meaning as well.

LESSON 17

'Resume' and 'Résumé'

Almost all of us have applied for a job, at some time or the other. When we send an application, we also have to attach a Résumé The word Résumé is mostly mispronounced as 'resume'. The meaning of these similar-looking words is different; functionally, the first is a Noun, the second is a Verb. When used as Noun, it should be written with 'r' capital as Résumé. There should also be the small accent marks above each 'e'. Résumé has a definite connection with the process of applying for a job and the sentence informing its attachment should be:

> Please find my Résumé attached.

Résumé should be pronounced *Res-you-may* as Noun and *re-sume* (rhyming with *assume/consume*) as Verb. When we say "resume" we mean 'to begin again', or 'to *start again* after an interval' e.g.

> 'I hate to resume work on Mondays after a thoroughly enjoyable weekend.'

Initially, to remember the difference between resume and

Résumé, you must, in your sentences, correctly use 'to' in combination with 'resume', signifying it as Verb. When practicing pronouncing Résumé, the sentence showing it as part of a job-application as given above, must be used.

LESSON 18

> 'Do' - the grammar, the purpose
> 'I do exercise every day.'

The meaning of this sentence, because of the misplacement of 'do', is different from that what you are thinking it to be. The sentence is grammatically correct, but, the use of 'do' changes its meaning to be an aggressively positive answer as if you have been challenged and questioned whether you actually exercise daily or not. The best answer when asked a question about this daily activity is:

    'I exercise every day.'

We must be very careful in English when using 'do', 'be' and 'have'. Each one of these three Verbs has a complex variety of roles. When 'do', 'be' and 'have' are not clearly understood or practiced to perfection, their misplacements in sentences can lead to innumerable mistakes and can unwittingly convey a meaning other than desired, e.g.

'Do' mustn't be used with the present-tense form of another verb, which is self-explanatory, e.g.

    'I do walk/work every day.'

Although grammatically correct, this sentence conveys the denial of an accusation that you don't walk/work. A better sentence therefore is:

'I walk/work every day.'

In the sentences above, when placed before exercise/walk/work', etc. 'do' gets converted from a Verb to an Adverb. Do be careful therefore when using 'do'.

LESSON 19

The Use of 'Have'

After 'do', we must understand the correct use of 'have' - what it means and how it is to be used. We use a different form of 'have' with the Third Person Pronouns singular i.e. he/she/it. This form is 'has'. 'Have' is used with the First Person Pronoun —Singular — 'I' as well as its Plural — 'We'. It is also used with the Second Person Pronoun — Singular — 'You' as well as its Plural — 'You' or 'You all'. With the Third Person Pronoun in the Plural 'They' we continue to use 'have'. When 'have' is followed by the Participle form of the verb, the Tense of the sentence becomes the Present Perfect Tense e.g.

They have decided to relocate,
They have thrown the ball.
OR
S/he has decided to relocate.
S/he has thrown the ball.

When 'has/have' is followed by a Noun, then the Tense becomes the Present Simple Tense and 'has/have' becomes a verb of Possession e.g.

>'I/We/You/They have the right to demand immediate payment.'
>Or
>'S/he has the right to demand immediate payment.'

You must be very careful when using 'has/have' and avoid the use of 'having'. Later, we'll see mistakes related to 'having'.

LESSON 20

The Use of 'Make'

Like 'do' and 'have' we must also be extremely careful with 'make'. Remember, with certain actions only 'make' and no other verb can be considered appropriate e.g.

>*'I did a mistake.'*

A **mistake is made**, and not done. The correct sentence, therefore, is:

>'I made a mistake.'

Similarly,

>*'I have taken an appointment with my doctor.'* – Incorrect
>'I have made an appointment with my doctor.' – Correct.

With 'make', many combinations exist and its use with other words makes for interesting descriptions of a number of situations. Of so many, let's take two: (a) to make up (to patch-up after a fight or a quarrel) e.g.

>'My counsellor has asked me to apologize and make up with my wife.'

(b) to make it (to have become successful), e.g.
>After so many failures, he has finally been able to make it.
>OR
>After so many failures, he has finally made it.

When we choose and use words carefully, we get the right meaning across. Nowadays, 'make' as a Noun is also used to get information of brands. e.g.

>'I bought a new car last month.'
>'Congratulations, what make is it?'

You must therefore, ponder over what meaning you wish to convey and only then appropriately use 'make'.

LESSON 21

Contractions: 'I'll', 'He'll', 'She'll'...

Contractions in English are very important. Contractions generally consist of a combination of a Noun/Pronoun with a Verb. Combining two words into one, Contractions make use of the apostrophe. Many of us however read/speak the two words separately even when they are written/printed as one word. Do not read/speak the contraction as "I will" or "I shall", when it is clearly written/printed as "I'll". The word "I'll" is short for "I shall" and is pronounced as "isle" ('s', being silent, is not pronounced.) Practice the correct pronunciations of Contractions by speaking/reading them as single words. A Contraction is always one word.

"We'll" (Pronounced "wheel" without the 'h' sound)

"He'll/she'll" (Pronounced "heel" and "sheel" respectively)

"He's/She's" (Pronounced "heez" and "sheez" respectively)

Let's look at these Contractions in sentences:
"I'll surely fulfil my promise."
"We'll cross the bridge when we come to it."
"He's a gentleman and he'll definitely keep his word."
"She's very beautiful, and she'll definitely be Miss World some day."
Contractions are also used to show the Possessive, i.e. the Genitive Case in English grammar and we shall see this later.

LESSON 22

Contractions: 'I'm', 'I've', 'We've', 'You're'...

Continuing with Contractions, remember Contractions are single words that combine two words (Noun/Pronoun +

Verb). Contractions must always be pronounced as single words.

I'm (I + am-a) very easy to pronounce

I've (I + have) - pronounced the same as 'hive', but without the 'h' sound.

We've (We + have) – pronounced the same as 'weave'.

We're (We + are – a) - pronounced to rhyme with 'veer'.

You've (You + have) – pronounced as the first three letters of the Indian name Yuvraj

They've - (They + have) – pronounced the same as the Indian name Dev.

It's – (It + is) – very easy to pronounce. "It's/its" is the only Contraction which can also be written without an apostrophe.

Let's now look at these Contractions and practice them in sentences:

"I've always wanted a new bike, I'm glad I sold the old one."
"After so many years, we're finally going on a holiday."
"For Teacher's Day, we've decided to give our teacher a lovely gift."
"Thank you for dropping me at the airport, you've been very kind."
"After so many days of rain, the sun is shining, it's lovely, isn't it?"

LESSON 23:

Negative Contractions: Won't, Can't, Couldn't, Shan't...

Contractions denoting the negative are also extremely important in English. We must pronounce Negative Contractions clearly and correctly by stressing on the "n't" combination.

I/We/You/They -
won't/can't/couldn't/shan't/shouldn't/wouldn't/mustn't
aren't/don't/haven't

Please note that 'shall' or its negative "shan't" can be used only with the First Person Pronoun – Singular – I or the Plural - We. The other Contractions such as won't/can't/couldn't/shouldn't/wouldn't/mustn't are used with the first and second Person pronouns. The Contractions isn't/doesn't /hasn't are used with the third Person pronouns he/she/it.

At times Negative Contractions in English are used in question tags. Question tags are used to reinforce what is mentioned in the first part of the sentence by using the opposite (Negative-Positive Verb; Positive-Negative Verb) mode in the latter half.

"They can't answer these questions, can they?"
"You won't be late today, will you?"
"We mustn't criticize them so often, must we?"
"I haven't been very co-operative lately, have I?"

"You aren't the man who helped me yesterday, are you?"
"It isn't polite to keep one's elbows on the table, is it?"
"She isn't good at Math, is she?"
"He doesn't believe in working hard, does he?"
"You shouldn't take things for granted, should you?"

When not being used as above, Negative Contractions can begin questions in English.
E.g.
"Couldn't you give the correct answers?"
"Won't it be possible for you to be on time today?"
"Wouldn't it be better if we took a taxi?"

LESSON 24

'Quiet' and 'Quite'

Students often create disturbances in a classroom. On many occasions, teachers order them to 'Be quiet!' However, many students hear as well as pronounce 'quiet' as 'quite', especially when they mimic their teachers. 'Quiet' and 'quite' are distinctly different in their pronunciations. They have different meanings as well. 'Quiet' is an Adjective and 'quite' is an Adverb. 'Quiet' has everything to do with noise, volume, sound and sometimes the desire for silence, e.g.
"There's so much traffic in this street, I want a house in a quiet locality."

The word 'quiet' has two syllables and is pronounced with a 'k' sound – "kwaa-yet". The word 'quite' is monosyllabic i.e. it has only one syllable, similar to the word "kite" with a 'w' sound after the 'k'. The word 'quite' is sometimes confused to be a level/degree of intensity. However, 'quite' is also connected with the positive aspect of feelings e.g. "I thought his wife didn't know how to cook, surprisingly the dishes she had cooked were quite good."

LESSON 25

'Next Week', 'Last Night', 'Previous Evening' etc.

"I didn't want to be punished, so I did my homework late in yesterday night."

As you can see this sentence is in italics, denoting incorrect English. We most often speak of the previous night as 'yesterday night' whereas the correct description should be **'last night'**. The preposition 'in' is not required. The correct sentence therefore is: "**I didn't want to be punished, so I did my homework late last night.**" When it comes to other time frames i.e. the previous week, month and year, the preposition 'in' should not be used and the word 'last' is a must, e.g.

"Our school had a series of excursions last week."
"There were six bomb blasts in Pune last month."
"There was scanty rainfall in the south last year."

Similarly, with the future tense, we do not use 'in' e.g.

"We hope to have an abundant harvest next year."
"My parents are going abroad next month."
"I got bored at his birthday party but my party next week will be exciting."

LESSON 26

> 'This Evening', 'Tonight', 'Day before Yesterday'...

In the last Lesson, we learnt how to describe the previous and next week, month and year. Now, we will learn how to describe various activities conducted on certain days. Many of us say: *"I'm meeting him today evening."* This is improper and should be **"I'm meeting him this evening."** The word 'this' must be used instead of 'today' whether it is morning/afternoon/evening. Similarly, *"We are going to a wedding today in the night."* This is incorrect and should be, **"We are going to a wedding tonight."** Many of us mistakenly use the preposition 'on' with 'days', e.g.

"I wrote a letter to my cousin on yesterday."

The correct sentence is, **"I wrote a letter to my cousin yesterday."** Similarly, **"I am spending the day at my friend's house tomorrow."** There is no need to use 'on' with tomorrow/yesterday/the day after tomorrow/the day before yesterday e.g.

"Our neighbours weren't home the day before yesterday, and so the couriers had handed over their parcels to us."

We use 'on' with the name of the day and 'in' with the name of the month, e.g. "on Monday", "on Tuesday", etc. and "in January", "in February" etc.

LESSON 27

Wishing People: 'Good Day', 'Good Night', 'Good Evening'

Where days are concerned, wishing each other in English using the word '...Day' is also important. The first quarter of the day up to 12 noon or 1 p.m. is 'Good Morning'. Please remember **"Good Day!"** or **"A Good Day to You!"** is used as a term of farewell during the early part of day. Post-lunch, we use 'Good Afternoon' and beyond 5 or 6 p.m. we say, 'Good Evening'. It is very important for us to remember that 'Good Night' is used only when we leave the company of others or also spoken sometimes as substitute for 'Farewell!/Goodbye!', i.e. when departing from someone's company at night. When we first meet someone late in the evening or even during the early part of the night, we cannot say, "Good Night to you!" No matter how late in the night it might be, the correct form of greeting is **"Good Evening"** or if greeting someone informally, you can simply say "Hi!" or "Hello!".

LESSON 28

Plurals in Clothing: 'Jeans', 'Pants', 'Shorts' etc.

"Where are you going just now?"
"I'm going to buy a jean"

The answer to the question asked above is incorrect English. As mentioned earlier, when we speak English, the plural must be correctly pronounced and communicated; otherwise the grammar becomes full of errors. In English, when we speak of certain articles of clothing, footwear, etc. these are all in pairs. If the words 'a pair' are used, even then the plural must be clearly added. e.g.

"I'm going to buy a pair of shoes."

"I've ordered a new pair of spectacles."

The following is a list of some articles that are always spoken of in the plural - scissors, trousers, socks, shorts, pants etc. The correct way of using them in sentences is as follows:

"Your old socks are torn, you'd better buy a new pair."
"I feel relaxed whenever I wear Bermuda shorts."
OR
"I feel relaxed whenever I wear Bermudas."
"I simply cannot afford these cargo pants."

LESSON 29

Homonyms: 'Complement' and 'Compliment'

One of the reasons for confusion in English is that many words sound similar to each other but have different meanings. These are known as homonyms and their exact meaning is correctly conveyed only when we write these words with their correct spelling.

Let us take the example of 'compliment/complement'.

The meaning of 'compliment' or in its verb form 'to compliment' is to praise someone for having done something well, or to admire a person's clothing/vehicle/articles, etc. e.g.

> "I must compliment you for the lovely furniture you have."
>
> "The boss paid me a compliment the other day, admiring the methods I had used in that project."

The word 'complement' denotes something by the use of which required as well as admired completion/totality is achieved. e.g.

> "The 'dupatta' she is wearing complements her Punjabi suit very well."
>
> "His suit was fashionable and the dazzling tie complemented its elegance."

There are many such combinations that need to be closely looked at, to improve our English skills.

LESSON 30

English in Job Interviews: Conveying your expectations

In today's techno-savvy world, the use of correct English in an interview, either personal or telephonic, is a must. Practice English regularly to eliminate mistakes.

While speaking in a personal/telephonic interview, be very clear and see to it that the interviewer receives the best answers from you. Do not sound confused or unclear. If you are asked about the salary you expect, give the exact figure. Do not sound wishy-washy, e.g.

"I would like my salary to be between 25,000 and 30,000 per month."

Instead, be extremely particular and say:

"For the work I will be doing, my take-home amount should be 28,000/- per month."
OR
"For this job, I must get 55,000/- per month in hand."

An interview now a days can be conducted over the telephone from anywhere in the world. The currency therefore has not been mentioned.

So, get the confidence within yourself by continuous practice and take home that much needed salary you so **richly** deserve. All thanks to your command over English.

LESSON 31

'First Come, First Serve'

'First come, first served' - This expression is used to convey the fact that when you are the first customer or claimant, you will be given preference. Chronology therefore entitles you to precedence over goods or services. However, when this expression is used, very often the letter "d" with 'serve' is hardly ever pronounced, and, horror of horrors, sometimes not even written. A very common error! When the Past Tense or the Participle form of the verb isn't noticeably pronounced or written, the correct meaning doesn't become clear, and sometimes, as in 'First come, first serve', the opposite meaning gets conveyed. 'First come, first serve' means that when you have come before others, you should serve those behind you or you might even be ordered to serve the establishment that was going to provide you the service. Pronounce and write the Past Tense or the Participle form of a verb clearly, strongly and correctly, so that the correct meaning is clearly conveyed. Speak and write English correctly, otherwise you might 'have to serve', instead of 'being served'.

LESSON 32

Irregular Verbs: Different Past Tense and Participle Forms

In the previous Lesson, we saw the mispronunciation of 'served'. Verbs which take '....ed' to indicate a Verb's conversion into the Past Tense are known as Regular Verbs. In the case of Regular Verbs, mispronunciations can convey an incorrect meaning. However, there are many verbs in English which do not take '...ed' as their last two letters in the Past

Tense or even in the Participle form. These are known as Irregular Verbs and we must know their correct Past Tense and Participle forms. Let's take some examples: The verb 'throw' becomes 'threw' in the Past Tense and the Participle form of throw is 'thrown'. The Past Tense of 'catch' is 'caught' and the Participle form is also the same i.e. 'caught'. The Past Tense of 'eat' is 'ate' and the Participle form is 'eaten'. These are just three examples and there are a large number of Irregular Verbs in English. When we read, speak and write English regularly and correctly, then it becomes very easy for us to recognize, become familiar with, and also remember Irregular Verbs in their three different forms.

LESSON 33

Regular Verbs: Usage and Pronunciation of 'ed'

In English, the importance of correct pronunciation and lucid writing can never be over-emphasized. How many times do you get to hear the ...ed in 'missed' call? *"I got a miss call"* is heard so often with reference to mobile phones. Similarly, *"there are very few calls in my Calls Receive register"* when the person actually means "received". Again, on many occasions, *"I have joined the 'Advance' course"* when the person actually means "I have joined the 'Advanced' course." The last two letters of English verbs generally indicate the Past Tense or the Participle form of a Regular Verb and sometimes also indicate that the same word is being used as an Adjective. Take a look at the following sentences: "They defeated him in that battle" and "His face wore a defeated look." In the first sentence the word 'defeated' is a Regular Verb in the Past Tense and in the second the same word is an adjective. When you can easily frame two or more sentences correctly, with the same word being used as a different Part of Speech in each of them, it shows your command over English.

LESSON 34

Participle Form of Verbs: Use of 'has/have' and 'had'

The Participle form of the Verb for many of us is not easy to understand. Consequently, correct use of the Participle does not take place. If certain points are kept in mind and we regularly practice framing sentences using the Participle form of a Verb correctly, we can definitely learn to speak and write English correctly. The compulsory use of 'has/have' or 'had' with the Participle form of the Verb is a clear indication of time. In the Present Perfect Tense, we use 'has/have' plus the Participle form of the Verb and in the Past Perfect Tense we use 'had' plus the Participle Form. Taking the Regular Verb 'defeat' as example, let's see what 'has/have defeated' means and how it is different from 'had defeated'. "Leander Paes has defeated Mahesh Bhupathi" means that this event has just got over (relatively speaking). "Leander Paes had defeated Mahesh Bhupathi" needs elaboration and the sentence can be termed complete only when we add another time-frame in the Past, either spoken or implied, e.g.. "Leander Paes had defeated Mahesh Bhupathi in the previous tournament too." We will see these Tenses in detail later.

LESSON 35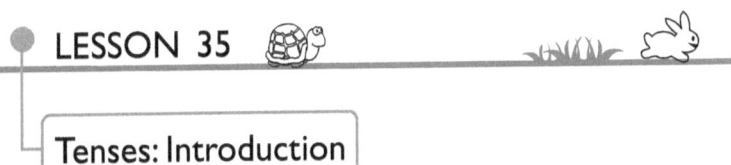

Tenses: Introduction

When learning Tenses and the change of the Verb into the correct form required, you must try to stop the process of thinking in your mother tongue / local language first and then trying to translate the same into English. This is because other Indian languages do not have the same Tense formats that English has. No matter how many mistakes are made, you must continue to learn English through English. It might appear difficult initially, but with practice and hard work Tenses in English grammar become easier to understand and implement when learnt only through English. The Present, the Past and the Future Tenses each have four segments, i.e. the Simple, the Continuous, the Perfect and the Perfect Continuous. Only when you have thoroughly understood all the segments of the Present Tense should you move on to the Past Tense and then on to the Future Tense. It is extremely important to understand the time-frame required to be described. Once understood, you must then choose the appropriate Verb Form. Then, the Verb in the correct Tense form will ensure that you need no longer remain tense.

LESSON 36

Present Simple Tense

"*I am coming from Parbhani*" is a type of answer you get to listen to when someone is questioned regarding the name of his native village or town. Look carefully at the question, "Where do you come from?" You will see that it has been framed using the Present Simple Tense. The answer should also have been given using the same Tense. Therefore, the correct reply should have been, "I come from Parbhani." When replying to a question in English, the answer should also use the same Tense format. The Present Simple Tense is used in certain areas which you will do well to remember when framing sentences in English, viz. (a) Regular Action - "I <u>go</u> to school every day." (b) Habits – "I <u>drink</u> four glasses of milk every day." (c) Natural Phenomena (Facts) – "The earth <u>revolves</u> round the sun. (d) Universal Truths (Proverbs) – "Honesty <u>is</u> the best policy." Now, keeping the above examples in mind, make your own sentences, underline the verbs, become intelligent and understand English better.

LESSON 37

Present Continuous Tense

The word 'continuous' means an action going on without interruption. The Present Continuous Tense, therefore, always describes an action which in the present, i.e. at the moment (NOW), is going on and has not been interrupted. The Present Continuous uses 'am/are/is/are plus the ....ing' form of the Verb to indicate uninterrupted movement and action. "I am reading/learning/studying" etc. is a sentence that indicates that the action being described is even now going on. The Present Continuous Tense, in contrast to the Present Simple Tense, does not indicate regularity of action, and is mainly concerned and focused on informing the reader/listener of that one action that is happening NOW. The Present Continuous Tense also shows us that the Verb in English, in its totality, need not be one word but may be a combination of two or more than two words. e.g. "They <u>are listening</u> to music."

LESSON 38

Present Tense for 'Near Future'

We have seen the Present Simple Tense and the Present Continuous Tense and their areas of function. Although both of them indicate action in the present, they can also be used to indicate action in the future. However, when used to indicate action in the Future, the indication must be only of the near Future, e.g.
"I <u>am going</u> to Mumbai tomorrow, my train <u>leaves</u> at 7.15 a.m." The first is the Present Continuous Tense indicating action in the very near future i.e. tomorrow. The second is the Present Simple Tense declaring a fact, for the same train leaves from

Pune every day at 7.15 a.m. The near Future can be limited to approximately a month. When indicating the future, the verb 'going + to + infinitive, also declares an intention. e.g. "I am sick of the local bus service, I am going to buy a bike." Here, the desire is clearly declared; the action isn't happening now, but will take place soon. Once again, choose the correct verb-form for the selected time-frame, practice making a number of sentences and then see your confidence rise.

LESSON 39

Present Perfect Tense

The use of 'has/have' plus the Participle form of the Verb constitutes the Present Perfect Tense. This Tense describes an action which began in the past but has got completed in the present, leading up to NOW. The use of 'has/have' with the Participle form of the Verb connects us with the present, irrespective of the time or period of the point of time of the origin or the beginning of the action. The concerned action may/may not continue. e.g.
"India and Pakistan have always fought over Kashmir." The conflict began long ago, exists even today and doesn't seem to have an end in the foreseeable future. Similarly, "I have done my homework" implies that you have completed this task sometime in the very recent past most probably,. today. "*I have done my homework yesterday*" is incorrect English for it implies completion of the action much earlier and should use the Past

Simple Tense e.g. "I did my homework yesterday." Additionally, you must also remember, 'has/have + Noun = The Present Simple Tense.' When has/have is followed by a Noun then the Verb is a Verb of possession and the Sentence is in the Present Simple Tense, e.g.

She has a lovely smile.

They are very rich, they have four cars.

LESSON 40

Present Perfect Continuous Tense

"India and Pakistan have been fighting over Kashmir since 1947." This sentence is in the Present Perfect Continuous Tense as it involves the use of 'has/have' + been + the '...ing' form of the Verb. It also indicates continuity of the action and the action is going on at this very moment. Once again, as in the case of the Present Perfect Tense, the point of time of the beginning of the action isn't important. What is important is that the action has been brought over to the present in a state of continuity and is on even NOW. "I have been waiting for my friend outside Screen I for half an hour." This is a common situation, and needs the use of the Present Perfect Continuous for the waiting isn't over as yet. The difference between the Present Continuous and the Present Perfect Continuous is the origin of the action with the use of the word 'been'. "I am swimming" (Present Continuous) indicates action going on right now without mentioning its beginning. "I have been swimming since 8 a.m." indicates the point of time when the action began. "I have been swimming for two hours," indicates the period of the continuity of the action.

LESSON 41

Past Simple Tense

The Past Simple Tense, to put it simply, is the description of an action that took place in the past and is complete now . The passage of time, on completion of this action, keeps increasing, making us aware of the distance between that time and now. "I slept well last night."; "I ate an ice-cream after lunch yesterday."; "I read a wonderful book last week." (pronounced 'red', written 'read'). "I bought a new car last month." "I did well last year."; "I went to college in the seventies." The Past Simple Tense, as you can see in the examples, describes the completion of an action in its totality. The Past Simple Tense also gives an indication of the conclusion of a whole time period. In the negative, the Past Simple Tense may employ 'not', e.g.

 "I did not go to college in the seventies."; "I did not do well last year."; "I did not buy a new car last month."; "I did not read a wonderful book last week."; "I did not eat an ice cream after lunch yesterday."; "I did not sleep well last night."

LESSON 42

Past Continuous Tense

The Past Continuous Tense describes an action that began in the past, continued for some time or for a very short while and then got over. The Past Continuous employs 'was/were' + the..ing form of the Verb, e.g. "He was walking in the garden, when he fell."
"I was having a bath when the phone rang."
"He was cooking dinner while she watched her favourite serial.". Imagine yourself as a witness to an accident and the police question you, "What were you doing when the accident happened?" If both the Verbs are used in the Past Continuous Tense, then the sentence loses its meaning. e.g. *"He was walking in the garden when he was falling."* The Present Simple Tense of the second Verb, either written or implied with the Past Continuous Tense, is very important to indicate completion of both actions as action within action. Interchange of both the Verbs does not change the meaning of the sentence. e.g. "He fell while he was walking in the garden."

LESSON 43

Past Perfect Tense

The Past Perfect Tense uses 'had' plus the Participle form of the Verb. In this tense, 'had' is common and it does not matter whether the Noun/Pronoun is singular or plural. The Past Perfect Tense is used to indicate that when one action had been completed, another action also took place in the past, e.g. "When I reached his office at 2 p.m., he <u>had</u> already <u>eaten</u>."; "When they entered the auditorium, the play <u>had</u> already <u>begun</u>."; "By the time his mother called, he <u>had had</u> dinner." The use of 'had' twice is correct; the second 'had' denotes the participle form of the verb, in this case 'had completed the act of eating.' Whenever 'had' is used twice in a sentence the first 'had' is the Past Perfect Tense of the verb of the longer duration and the second 'had' is the Verb of the action of a shorter duration e.g. "In the year 2012. I had had a dream that I was going to be famous one day." The second 'had' will always stand for another Verb in its participle form. This sentence can also be stated as: "In the year 2012 I <u>had seen </u>a dream that I was going to be famous one day." As in the case of the Past Continuous Tense, the Past Perfect Tense must also employ the Past Simple Tense as the second Verb to indicate completion of both actions. Again, interchanging Verbs does not lead to change in the meaning.

LESSON 44

Past Perfect Continuous Tense

The Past Perfect Continuous Tense employs 'had'+ been + the ...ing form of the Verb to indicate that an action had been going on for some time when another action took place. e.g. (A) "I <u>had</u>

been living in Mumbai for thirty-four years when I decided to move to Pune." (B) "She had been working with Wipro for eight years when she applied for a job at Infosys." (C) "I happened to see her when I had been waiting for the traffic lights to turn green."

You will notice that in all these sentences, the time duration of the action using 'had' is irrelevant. The Verb has more to do with the action rather than the period. Once again, there has to be the Present Simple Tense also to indicate completion of both the actions. Interchange of both actions is possible without changing the meaning of the sentence e.g. "I had been waiting for the traffic lights to turn green when I happened to see her."

LESSON 45

Future Simple Tense

In the Future Tense, the Verb in English does not adopt a distinct form as it does in the Present as well as in the Past Tenses. To make the Verb indicate the Future Simple Tense, you can take any Verb (Regular OR Irregular), and add 'shall/will' before it. The Verb following 'shall/will' must be in its Present Tense form only. Remember, 'shall' can be used only with the First Person Pronoun i.e. I/We. 'Shall' cannot be used with the remaining pronouns i.e. you/he/she/it/they. The Future Simple Tense indicates the imagination of an action in the future e.g.

"We shall do a great job at our college's Annual Day next year."

"I will visit China next year."; "She will be an actress by 2018";

"They will graduate two years from now.";

"This sapling will become a strong tree within a few years." However, when we speak of two imagined actions in the Future, one must be described using the Present Simple Tense, "I hope you will call on us when you are in Pune." 'Shall/will' must never be used twice in the same sentence.

LESSON 46

Future Continuous Tense

The Future Continuous Tense describes an imagined action, that will begin and continue in the future. The Verb uses the 'shall/will be' form + ...ing to indicate what we imagine will be happening sometime in the future. "When you come to my office at 2 p.m., I shall be having lunch."

"Two years from now, I shall be driving my own car."

"When we reach the party, they will be dancing."

Once again, you will notice that the Future Continuous Tense is accompanied by the Present Simple Tense, either spoken or implied. As far as the Future Tense is concerned, because the action has not taken place yet and is only imagined in the future, the Future Perfect Tense and the Future Perfect Continuous

Tense are rarely used and can definitely be studied and understood only if one wishes to pursue a course in higher English. Otherwise, these two Tenses today belong to the realm of Science Fiction.

LESSON 47

'Alphabet', 'Letters', Consonants', 'Vowels'

Many a time when we want to know the spelling of a particular word in English, especially on the phone, we ask, "Could you spell the word slowly, speaking out each *alphabet* correctly and loudly?" The word 'alphabet' used in this question is inappropriate. The correct word is 'letter'. The English language has twenty-six letters. These twenty-six letters together form the English Alphabet. Each single unit beginning with "A" to the unit "Z" is known as a 'letter'. In American English the letter 'Z' is pronounced 'Zee' Five of these twenty-six letters i.e. 'a-e-i-o-u' are known as 'Vowels' and the remaining twenty-one are known as 'Consonants'. The five Vowels are important because it is virtually impossible to spell a word in English that does not have any one of these five. Some words that do not use even one of these five vowels end with the letter 'y' e.g. by, cry, dry, fly, fry, my, sly, sky, sty, try, and last but not least, why.

LESSON 48

'Afraid of' and 'Afraid'

"I'm afraid of dogs."
"I'm afraid a room with a view isn't available."
The word 'afraid' is used to describe fear in the first instance. In the second instance, the adjective 'afraid' is simply an expression of regret that what the listener preferred or wanted could or would not be made available to him/her. When 'afraid' is followed by the preposition 'of', the word following 'of' must be a Noun/Pronoun. "I'm afraid of _____ ", is used to describe names, places, animals, things or people generating fear within someone. When a person has any kind of fear or phobia, we must use 'of' with the word 'afraid' before 'of'. e.g. "I'm afraid of heights, that is why I don't go mountaineering."
"I don't swim because I'm afraid of water." When we use "I'm afraid" without 'of', we indicate the use of an entire clause to follow including the conjunction 'that', which, if not spoken or written, is clearly implied e.g. "I'm afraid /that/ you won't be allowed to write your exam as you've reached very late."

LESSON 49

'Loose' and 'Lose'

Do you go regularly to a gym? On your way, have you noticed advertisements that say *"Loose Weight"*? The word 'loose' in this

advertisement is incorrect. "Loose" is an Adjective and 'lose' a Verb. The correct advertisement would have said "Lose weight!" The word 'loose' denotes the fastening or positioning of something that is not tight, e.g.
"My younger brother's clothes for me are tight; my elder brother's are loose."
The verb form of 'loose' is 'loosen'. When we 'lose' something it does not remain in our possession anymore. "We must tighten our purse strings so that we don't lose more money". When we do not use the correct word in a given situation, the meaning to be conveyed becomes incorrect too. It is therefore very important to first confirm the meaning of certain words before using them.

LESSON 50

'What is your good name, sir?'

"*What is your good name, sir?*" This is the most typical of all examples of transliterating other languages into English, and then assuming the sentence to be pure and unadulterated English. A name by itself cannot be termed 'good' or 'bad'. The use of the word 'good' and the old-fashioned 'sir' shows unnecessary interference. English can certainly do without this kind of interference. There will of course be arguments for and against. What matters most is that we have to think of how best to use correct English in our country that has so many languages. Each language user tries to wield influence over English. The most useful method of learning correct English is by unlearning that what was assumed to be grammatically correct English. So, the next time you want to ask somebody his/her name, be as simple as possible and correctly ask, "May I know your name?"

LESSON 51

'Cold' and 'Hard' Drinks

"It is so hot, why not have a cold drink?" The word 'cold' used to describe a drink is misplaced. 'Cold' has more to do with the temperature rather than being a description of the type of drink. We are so obsessed with ideas of conveniences, that we more often than not forget that we are tampering with the fundamentals of a language. There are two types of drinks, hard and soft. 'Hard drinks' are drinks that contain alcohol and the term 'soft drinks' covers drinks that are non-alcoholic. The best way to be courteous would be to ask

"It is so hot, why not have a chilled soft drink?"

It would also help for you to remember, except for beer hard drinks are not served chilled and are not stored under refrigeration. Many alcoholic drinks are stored at room temperature.

LESSON 52

'Sink' and 'Drown'

How many times have you seen the film 'Titanic'? Did you not feel sad with the tragedy that had struck the ship in the form of an iceberg? However, there is a difference when we wish to describe the fate of the ship and that of the passengers. A human being or an animal 'drowns' whereas a ship 'sinks'. Whenever we describe the action of an object or a non-living thing going down in water we say, "The huge vessel simply sank." Describing the same action, when applicable to human beings and other living creatures, we say, "Many passengers and animals aboard that ship drowned." The following sentence combines the two appropriating the correct verbs,
"She cries a lot whenever she watches 'Devdas', for her heart sinks when she sees the hero drown himself in alcohol." In this example, the 'heart' of the watcher becomes an object whereas the hero Devdas is conveyed as a human being, with the use of the word 'drown'.

LESSON 53

Articles: The Use of 'a'

"*We were just having a fun.*" The word 'fun' is an Abstract Noun and the article 'a' cannot be used with it. Similarly, "*We have just received a news that ......* " is incorrect. When we wish to display our joy and happiness at having enjoyed ourselves, we must say,
"**We were just having fun**" "**We had a lot of fun**" or when we wish to enjoy ourselves we must say, "**Let's have fun.**" Similarly, when we talk of some news having been received, the article 'a' cannot be used, and the correct form of the sentence would be,

"We have just received news that ...." In the case of particular news, the article 'the' is appropriate and carries enough weight e.g. "We have just received the news that ...." With 'fun' also, we can use 'the' to specify a particular incident, "I remember the fun we had that day."

LESSON 54

'Disinterested' and 'Uninterested'

"I don't want to watch that game, I'm disinterested." The word 'disinterested' has a totally different meaning from the one you are trying to associate it with, in this sentence. When we say we are 'disinterested' it actually indicates that we have decided to be impartial and committed toward justice. The correct word in the above sentence should be 'uninterested' and the correct sentence is "I don't want to watch that game, I'm uninterested." A better option would be, "I don't want to watch that game, I'm not at all interested." With the word 'disinterested', it is clear that we wish to convey a sense of fairness. It is very important that we act in a disinterested manner when hearing arguments. To sum up, "A sincere judge must be disinterested and not uninterested in a case."

LESSON 55

'A Pack', 'A Herd', 'A Flock'...

"My family are made up of five members." There are many instances in which the word 'family' is assumed to be plural, when, in actuality, it is singular. Although the word 'family' indicates more than one person, it is, in combination, a single constitution. Like the word 'family', in English we have words such as 'team', 'group', 'crowd', etc. All of these, although symbolizing the coming together of more than one person, together by themselves stand for a single unit. Similarly, when we wish to denote many objects/animals/birds etc., together as one singularly constituted unit, we have different words. e.g. 'a herd of cows', 'a pack/deck of playing cards' , 'a flock of sparrows,' 'a gaggle of geese,' 'a pride of lions,' etc. Remember, each term of this kind while symbolizing many together, by itself, is a unit in the singular. In American, English, 'My family are very understanding' is correct.

LESSON 56

' Weather' and 'Climate'

The use of correct English grammar also involves the use of general knowledge. When GK is applied to and with grammar, it leads to proficiency in English. Many of us are unaware when to use the word 'weather' and when to use the word 'climate'. What is the difference between the two? The word 'weather' stands for the conditions prevailing in the atmosphere on any one particular day or may even be indicative of the conditions for a period extending over a week, or, at the most, a fortnight. 'Climate', instead, stands for atmospheric conditions that prevail over an area or a city or a particular region lasting for a much longer period i.e. for a whole year e.g. "Pune has a generally cool climate, but the weather today is rather hot." Please note that 'weather' and 'whether' sound the same, but 'whether' has more to do with 'if/if not'.

LESSON 57

'I am *very* better...'

Q: "You were not looking well yesterday, how are you today?"
A: "*I am more better today.*" / "*I am very better today.*" Use of 'more' or 'very' with 'better' is incorrect. The word 'more' indicates comparison and any student of English grammar will tell you that 'more' is generally accompanied by the word 'than', either spoken or implied. The word 'very' is an Adverb modifying an Adjective or another Adverb but cannot be used here with 'better' for 'better' is by itself an Adverb/modifier of degree/comparison. The correct sentence therefore is, "**I am better today**" OR "**I am feeling much better today.**" The meaning which the word 'better' conveys, itself shows comparison i.e. "I am feeling better today (as compared to /than/ how I was feeling yesterday)." It would be advisable to remember that when a comparative Adjective/Adverb ending with ...'er' is being used, no other Adjective/Adverb must precede (come before) it, except 'much'.

LESSON 58

'Would': Courtesy and Possibility

Many speakers of English are unable to comprehend the meaning of 'would/could/should' and their use in sentences. As a general rule, none of these can be used by themselves, and must be accompanied by the main verb, either spoken or implied. The three, 'would/could/should', are the past tenses of 'will/can/shall' respectively, but each has an identity of its own and can be used in different ways in any of the three tenses. It would do well for you to remember that the three also generally indicate possibility in varying degrees. First, let us take 'would'.

"Would you like a cup of tea?" is a question involving courtesy and hospitality in the Present Tense.

"I would have been a rich man if I had worked hard" shows that I did not work hard in the past and so I am poor at present.

"I would be very happy if you came to my party," shows the possibility of happiness if certain conditions in the future turn out to be favourable. Think of the correct meaning and association of words and then use 'would'.

LESSON 59

'Could': Ability and a Stronger Possibility

The word 'could' has greater force and strength than 'would'. 'Could' does more than 'can'. 'Can' has more to do with ability than the possibility or immediacy of action. When dining, it is always better to say,

"Could you pass the salt please?"

This prompts the person involved to pass the salt quickly. The word 'could' is also, like 'would', used with 'have' + participle to indicate a greater sense of possibility. e.g.

"I could have been rich had I worked hard." Here, 'could' associates the attribute of prosperity with hard work in a much stronger manner than 'would'. The word 'could' is also used to put across force with requests. e.g.

"Could you please open the door?" is more of an order than a request when the listener is discourteous enough not to get up and do it for a lady. The next time you wish to borrow, it will therefore be better to ask, "Could you lend me some money please?"

LESSON 60

'Should': Advice and Suggestion

When compared with 'would' and 'could', the word 'should' has less force and is more concerned with advice and suggested actions. e.g.

"How does this black T-shirt look on me?" "You should buy a yellow one, for yellow looks good on you." The word 'should' with 'have' + participle, like the examples with 'would' and 'could', also indicates that what did not happen. e.g.

"I got a poor score in this test." "You should have worked harder." As mentioned earlier, the word 'should' may be used more in an advisory capacity, e.g. "You are going high up in the mountains, you should carry a small oxygen cylinder." The use of 'would' 'could' and 'should' always involves the use of the Verb which can be considered to be the main one, and so, these three being Modals can never be used by themselves. Even when "would/could/should" are used by themselves, the main Verb is clearly implied, e.g. "Would you like a sandwich?" "Yes, I would." (like (to eat) the sandwich). Here, it is clearly implied that the person definitely desives eating that sandwich.

LESSON 61

'It' instead of 'them/they'

In a North Indian marriage ceremony, it is generally customary for the bride's sisters, friends and relatives to steal and then hide the bridegroom's footwear while the rituals are on. The bridegroom, of course, has to shell out a hefty amount for the footwear or is later teased and forced to walk barefoot. Many a time, however, the stolen pair of footwear is spoken of as 'it' instead of as 'them' or 'they'. "Have you stolen the shoes? *Where have you hidden it?*" A common error when communicating in English! As has been pointed out earlier, it is very important to denote the plural to communicate correctly in English. *"I have two books on Math, and it is very helpful."* The correct sentence of course is, **"I have two books on Math and they/these/those are very helpful."** We use 'this' for the singular and 'these' to indicate the plural when the object/s is/are nearby. When the object is afar, the correct word to denote it in the singular is 'that'. When the objects are more, and at a distance, they should be denoted using 'those'.

LESSON 62

'Cloths' and 'Clothes'

The use of the word 'cloths' instead of 'clothes' is very common and can lead to embarrassment. Whenever we speak of a dress or attire as connected with the human body, the correct word is 'clothes'. A cloth is a small piece/article which is generally used to clean a surface. A handkerchief can be considered a cloth whereas shirts, trousers, saris etc. are articles of clothing or what we know as 'clothes'. You must have seen some people at traffic lights selling flannel 'cloths', mostly in the colour yellow. As far as the human body is concerned, we wear 'clothes' and not 'cloths' e.g. "During Diwali, we buy and wear new clothes."

"The clothes she is wearing are very smart." Looking at 'cloth', "When wiping your glasses, please ensure that you use a clean cloth."

"The shoeshine boy's clothes are old, dirty and torn but he always wipes his customer's shoes with a clean cloth."

LESSON 63

'Mediocre' and 'Average'; 'Awesome' and 'Awful'

"The performance of that famous artist was mediocre, just average." The word 'mediocre' is not synonymous with 'average'. Instead, it means 'below par, of a very poor standard'. e.g.

"We thought his paintings would be exceptionally beautiful, but, disappointingly, they were mediocre."

Due to the first three letters being the same as those of 'medium', we wrongly assume 'mediocre' to be the same as 'in the middle'. In the same way, the word 'awesome' has a different meaning as compared to 'awful'. The latter is a negative word and the former is extremely positive. e.g.

"The view from the mountain-top was awesome." Conversely, "The food at that restaurant tasted stale, it was awful." The word 'awe' in English means wonder, or a pleasant feeling which has positive overtones. When positive, 'awe' has 'e' in it. e.g. "The blind runner's winning sprint and spirit were indeed awe-inspiring."

LESSON 64

'Hard' and 'Hardly'

There are instances where an association of ideas in English takes place which unfortunately turns out to be incorrect. When using the word 'hard' to describe a difficult or tough situation, many of us utilise the suffix 'ly' to show its association, employing it as an Adverb of Manner. e.g. *"He works hardly"* is spoken many times to show that someone works very hard. Users of 'hardly' have the adverb 'slowly' in mind and presume that the suffix 'ly' can be similarly used. However, 'hardly' in this context has the opposite effect and means that this person does almost no work. The word 'hardly' is associated more with infrequency and suggests 'almost never' than being related with 'greater or more serious efforts.' The correct sentence is, **"He works very hard."** In a similar context, we must also remember not to use 'fastly'.

LESSON 65

'Abroad' and 'Foreign'

How often do you use the word 'abroad'? Do you know that it is an Adverb? If yes, then why do you use it as a Noun or Pronoun by saying *"My sister is going to abroad next month with her husband"*? The correct statement is, **"My sister is going abroad next month with her husband."** More often than not, the word 'foreign' is also used mistakenly by saying, *"All my friends and* *relatives live in foreign."* The word 'foreign' is an Adjective and when used, a Noun must follow it. e.g. "All my friends and relatives live in a foreign country." The word 'foreign' means 'not belonging to ......'. The Common Noun of 'foreign' is 'foreigner' and its Abstract Noun is 'foreignness'. In order to make it simpler for you, remember 'abroad' is a place far away and 'foreign' is a quality.

LESSON 66

Subject+Verb+Object

There are very few of us who take care to think that what we are speaking is grammatically correct when using English. Invariably, transliteration occurs and we unconsciously put across in English, what we are actually thinking in our mother tongue/local language, e.g. *"India must corruption banish."* This is an idea very much in vogue because of the overwhelming presence of scams. However, language used to convey this thought makes it nonsense in English. The construction of a sentence in English, being S+V+O i.e. Subject+Verb+Object makes it important, that we put across correctly what we wish to say. Many other Indian languages including Hindi and Marathi have S+O+V as the construction of their sentences and this leads to glaring errors when transliterating. Constant practice of correct English with proper sequencing of S+V+O will lead to fewer mistakes. The correct sentence as you by now very well know is:

"India must banish corruption."

And the quicker we Indians do it, the better for India.

LESSON 67

'I' and 'Me': Placing with Courtesy

Q: "What are you doing on your holiday tomorrow?" A: *"Me and my friend are going for a movie."* The correctly framed question has received an incorrect answer. You must be thinking that the word 'me' has been misplaced. Actually, 'me' is a misfit in such a situation. The use of "I" instead of 'me' is important here because the suggestion is about this person and his/her friend together doing something. Additionally, it is extremely important to remember, when we use "I" with somebody else, "I" must always follow. The correct sentence therefore is, **"My friend and I are going for a movie."** If more than two persons are being spoken about, even then, "I" must come last, e.g. **"Navin, Pravin, Sunil and I are going for a movie."** In each and every language, courtesy demands that you place yourself after all the others.

LESSON 68

'Understand' and 'Understanding'

"I am not understanding what you are saying." This is a common sentence used to convey incomprehension of some kind of utterance. However, it is incorrect. The word 'understanding' is a Noun but is more often than not used mistakenly as a Verb. The correct sentence is **"I do not understand what you are saying."** The following are some forms of 'understand' to be used to make your English correct and fluent: (a) "Have you understood?" (b) "Do you understand?" (c) "I hope you have understood what I wanted to say." (d) "Please try to understand me." The word 'understanding' also implies an

agreement. You must always remember that 'understanding' is a Noun and must use it accordingly, e.g. "They have reached an understanding." The word 'understanding' also means 'knowledge'. Therefore, "When you are able to understand all these lessons, I'm sure your understanding of English will improve by leaps and bounds."

LESSON 69

'Make/Made' + 'Up'

In an earlier lesson, the importance of 'do', 'have' and 'make' was pointed out. However, when using 'make', we incorrectly add 'up' to it to describe the material or method used in the construction or creation of something. When we look at a structure, or some photographs, especially of old architectural wonders, we have a tendency to ask, *"What is this building made up of?"* The preposition 'up' over here is unnecessary and incorrect and the correct question is **"What is this building made of?"** When the material used is clearly visible, the answer would be **"This building is made of stone."** There are times when the final product does not show the raw material used. Then, the preposition 'from' is correct, e.g. "Glass is made from sand." / "Steel is made from iron." Please remember when we use the combination 'make+up' we imply that there is more to it than meets the eye, i.e. the person may be telling lies e.g. "He is very good at making up excuses and stories for not doing his homework."

LESSON 70

'Knock' + 'On'

When the wolf was able to cleverly get the address from the innocent Little Red Riding Hood, he quickly ran to her grandmother's house. On reaching it, did he *knock the door* or **knock on the door?** The answer is 'on'. When we do not use 'on' with the word 'knock' the meaning changes and it also leads to incorrect grammar. When we say, *'he knocked the door'* we imply that he almost broke the door down, and the sentence is grammatically incorrect for the word 'down' is not used. When the preposition 'on' is used with the verb 'knock', it implies drawing someone's attention. Sound or noise can be produced only when we knock on a hard surface. The next time you visit someone and the bell doesn't work, don't knock the door, but 'knock on the door'. Remember, an opportunity or a golden chance sometimes knocks on your door. When we narrate an event in the past, then knock 'at' is used, e.g.

"There was a knock at the door."

LESSON 71

Regular Verbs not using 'ed'

Where the Past Tense of a Regular Verb is concerned, by now we know that the rule makes for '...ed' to be added to it. However, English grammar is full of exceptions and we must always remember that there are some Verbs which do not take '...ed' for them to be denoted in the Past Tense. "That T-shirt costs a lot but I'm going to buy it." The same sentence in the

Past Tense is used by many of us as *"That T-shirt costed a lot but I went and bought it."* The correct sentence is **"That T-shirt cost a lot but I went and bought it."** In the same way, the following are some verbs that do not take '....ed' to become the Past Tense: *cut, put, broadcast, telecast, burst, shut, grind,* etc. Here are a few sentences showing their correct use:

(1) Last month a driver on the expressway lost control as a tyre burst at high speed."

(2) "I didn't enjoy India's victory in a recorded match but loved it when the tournament was telecast live."

LESSON 72

'Live', 'Alive' and 'Living'

The previous Lesson ended with 'live'. Although spelt the same as a Verb, when used as an Adjective, 'live' is pronounced to rhyme with 'dive' or 'hive'. You will see 'live' generally in the right/left hand upper corner of your television screen when an event is being shown the same time at which it is taking place. The words 'live' and 'alive' (both adjectives) have slightly different methods of use. We use 'live' generally followed by a noun but 'alive' is more often used at the end of a sentence. e.g.

"The stray dog sleeping on the street looked dead from a distance, but nearing it, we saw it was alive."

"Never touch it when you see it exposed, it may be a live (electric) wire."

When used as a Verb, 'live' is pronounced to rhyme with 'give'. "They may actually be burglars just waiting to burgle your house, don't ever tell strangers where you live." While 'living' is a form of the Verb 'live', it is also used as a Noun to indicate your livelihood i.e. what you earn, e.g.

"What do you do for a living?"

LESSON 73

'Live' and 'Stay'

What is the difference between 'live' and 'stay'? When to use the former? When should we use the latter? "I'm going to Delhi in my Christmas holidays and I'll be staying with my aunt." A holiday is generally for a short period of time, and so the word 'staying' is used. e.g. "Mahabaleshwar is a lovely hill station, what is the name of the hotel you stayed in?" When we use 'live' or 'living' as a verb, it indicates a longer period of residence with inclination towards permanency. "I have lived in Mumbai all my life" is the correct sentence for a permanent resident of Mumbai. The word 'reside' also indicates a fairly longer period of life in a particular area/town/village/city as compared to the word 'stay'. When a person says, 'My residence is not very big', he indicates that the house he has been occupying for a very long time may be quite small. Remember 'stay' – a short period; 'live' – a longer duration.

LESSON 74

'Expire' and 'Pass Away'

In an earlier lesson, we saw the use of 'sink' as different from 'drown'. Now we will see a somewhat similar differentiation between 'expire' and 'pass away'. Whenever we speak of a person's death in English, we generally soften the harsh reality of dying by saying that that person passed away. The word 'died' is generally used in newspaper and other media reports. When speaking of the final act of a human life, we use the expression 'passed away'. e.g. "His uncle passed away last month." To say that *"his uncle expired last month"* is incorrect for the word 'expired' is used to describe the conclusion of the validity of a document. We can use 'expire' only for documents or medicines and perishables, e.g. "His Driving Licence expired last week."

"I must get my Passport renewed as soon as possible, it expired three months ago." "These pills have lost their potency for they've crossed the expiry date." Remember, whenever we speak of a human being's demise, even though s/he may have been only an acquaintance, we must say, "S/he passed away….."

LESSON 75

'If only I were…'

"If only I was the Prime Minister." Why is this sentence in italics? It appears to be correct English. Then what is wrong? When we speak of a situation that is imaginary or in supposition, then we use 'were' instead of 'was'. Why? To show supposition or condition, because of 'if only' even with the singular "I". The correct sentence therefore is, **"If only I were the Prime Minister."** Generally, the word 'were' is used to indicate the subject in the plural in the Past Tense. e.g. "We were going home when it started to rain."

"We were very happy when we all lived together."
Use of the conditional 'If only ……..' makes the use of 'were' instead of 'was' mandatory. 'Were', in this situation, clearly

indicates that what is/was not. The next time therefore you see a contestant on a TV show unable to answer a question to which you know the answer, speak the correct sentence, "If only I were in the hot seat."

LESSON 76

Do we 'drink' soup or do we 'eat' it?

Where English is concerned, a question that foxes many is: Do we *drink* soup or do we eat it? Human ingestion involves the swallowing of soup. But, after eating or drinking it? However, it is considered much better to use 'eat' where soup is concerned. The reasons are not far to seek. In the preparation of soups, solids i.e. vegetables or chunks of mutton or chicken or fish are essential ingredients and integral to the recipe. What therefore gets consumed by a human being is not only the liquid but also the cooked solid soft edible pieces. These are but naturally, eaten. Furthermore, when soup is served, it is done in a soup-bowl with a spoon for the diner. Soup is also transferred from a big soup tureen to smaller vessels with a ladle and not by using jugs. No straw is provided for the intake of soup. Therefore, soup is better eaten than drunk. The next time you are using English and say that you are drinking soup, you might find yourself in a soup.

LESSON 77

Preposition, Articles and Tenses

The proper placement of various Parts of Speech in English is very important to convey correctly what you wish to. That is why, amongst other grammatical precautions, the following are imperative for the use of correct English:

- Concentration on the positioning of Prepositions
- Correct positioning of Articles
- Putting verbs in their correct Tense forms.

You must also always remember that Articles and Tenses are NOT Parts of Speech. You must have seen quite a few of these lessons and will continue to see more wherein PAT takes precedence i.e. mistakes and cautionary steps related to Prepositions, Articles and Tenses. To take a simple example: When we call on someone, what do we do? How is it different from calling someone? When we call someone, we speak to that person on the telephone. When we call on someone, we visit that individual in person. It is definitely considered bad manners to visit someone at his/her home without prior intimation. Therefore, when you wish to visit someone, first call him/her and only then call on him/her.

LESSON 78

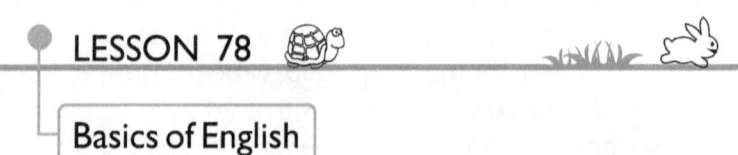

Basics of English

For us to become fluent in English, it is extremely important to know what the correct Word Order of a sentence in English is. In this endeavour, it becomes very useful if, when using English, one makes continual efforts to proficiently learn the eight Parts of Speech, i.e. Nouns, Pronouns, Verbs, Adjectives, Adverbs, Prepositions, Conjunctions, and Interjections and how, where, when and why they are used. When we are able to correctly identify the Part of Speech, which each and every word of a sentence is, then we move closer towards becoming fluent. Fluency however cannot be taken for granted, nor is confidence so easily attained. Learning to speak a language involves developing the ability to understand its nuances, to comprehend what is written, and also to effectively communicate what we wish to. All this is possible only and if only, we continue to regularly and religiously practice Reading, Writing, Listening and Speaking. Grammar and Vocabulary are the other two important skills, with the former being the base of every other language skill, more so where correct English is concerned.

LESSON 79

Parts of Speech

A good, standard (not a pocket one) dictionary is a mine of information. Nonetheless, many are unaware that in addition to the meaning of a word, a dictionary also acquaints us with its correct pronunciation and its etymological source i.e. its origin. Nowadays, a good dictionary also carries one or more sentence/s to demonstrate a chosen word's correct usage. A salient feature of every dictionary is that it carries adjacent to every word its Part of Speech. In English, Nouns, Verbs, Adjectives and Adverbs are four Parts of Speech which can be constantly changed. From each one of these four, a word can be transformed into any one or two or all of the other three. These four are therefore known as Open Parts of Speech. The other four i.e. Pronouns, Prepositions, Conjunctions and Interjections cannot be transformed and are therefore known as Closed Parts of Speech. The correct choice of any one of the four Open Parts of Speech is very important while transforming sentences. Remember when transforming a sentence, its meaning must never change.

LESSON 80

Prioritize Books

In a techno-savvy world, an online dictionary is a real boon, especially so, when you wish to learn correct pronunciation. If you spend a small part of your day referring to an online dictionary, it can give you wealth that can never be stolen. Social networking sites are definitely useful for making people aware of your opinions and provoking some with catty comments, but these can never be considered tools useful to the acquisition of knowledge. Call it being old-fashioned or outdated or whatever, nothing can substitute good books. Put your face into a book and watch it hook you if you're truly interested in learning. Haunting and hunting libraries for good books is a great pastime for serious learners. Looking up books and when required material is not found therein, then surfing the Net is a good activity. Unfortunately we do the opposite nowadays. Give books the priority they deserve. Then see your life change. Obviously, for the better!

LESSON 81

'Accept', 'Except' and 'Expect'

"If you **accept** her behaviour and **except** her misdeeds, she's going to constantly **expect** you to pamper her." The three words in bold i.e. 'accept', 'except' and 'expect' are Transitive Verbs i.e. Verbs that have objects. However, their pronunciations and meanings are vastly different from each other. 'To accept' means to take willingly or to acknowledge a fact or a situation, to tolerate, or to take the blame or to gladly receive a gift. The Noun is 'acceptance' and the pronunciation 'ack-sept' with the first three letters pronounced the same as in 'acknowledge'. The second Verb 'except' means 'to leave out', or 'to overlook' as suggested in the sentence above. The Noun is 'exception'. Whenever a word uses 'ex' almost as a prefix, it should be pronounced with a stress. The third Verb 'expect', as we all know, means 'to look forward to something' or 'to hope for'. It is also used regularly where travel is concerned e.g. 'the expected time of arrival of the train/bus/flight is ..... .' "Improvement in your English is our expectation". (Noun)

LESSON 82

'Most Happiest Day' – Use of Superlatives

We earlier saw the incorrect combination of more + better. Now we shall see another common and erroneous combination i.e. most + happiest (The Superlative). We commonly get to hear "Today is my most happiest day." The word 'most' is the uppermost degree of comparison i.e. the Superlative. The word 'happiest' too is a Superlative. Combining the two Superlatives leads to incorrect English. The correct sentence is **"Today is my happiest day."** Howsoever, it would be better to say, **"Today is the happiest day of my life."** Whenever the Superlative is used, the article 'the' must precede it, e.g. "That is the tallest building of our city." "She is the cleverest of all students in that class." Remember, degrees of comparison (Positive, Comparative or the Superlative) are always Adjectives or Adverbs. Like 'most + the Superlative', the combination of 'very + perfect' or any other Superlative is also incorrect. The word 'very', although not a Superlative, most often gets used as one. You must make a conscious effort not to use such combinations. Unlearning is the first step towards learning English well.

LESSON 83

Nouns and Verbs: Inter-conversion

At a restaurant, Mahesh finished eating and left the table. When he hadn't returned for a long time, Rajesh went looking for him. In the washroom, Rajesh saw Mahesh soaping the sink. When asked, "What are you doing?" Mahesh pointed to the sign above the sink, "Wash Basin". Mahesh had comically misconstrued 'wash' as a verb commanding him to clean the sink, whereas 'Wash' was clearly a Noun used adjectivally demonstrating that diners should, before or after a meal, use the basin to wash their hands therein. Virtually every Noun in English can be converted into a Verb and vice versa. The word 'wash' is Noun as well as Verb. Framing of a sentence to convey 'Wash' as Noun is definitely done differently as compared to the framing required to convey 'wash' as Verb. Incidentally, this joke falls flat if you consider that the article 'the' has not been used before 'basin'. More about articles later.

LESSON 84

Nouns and Verbs: Some Basic Rules

In the previous Lesson, we saw the way the same word in English can be denoted as Noun in one sentence and as Verb in another, subject to proper framing. A simple point, when kept in mind, will help you to use it as the chosen Part of Speech that you want. Verbs can never be written in capital letters. A Noun, when it is Common, gets converted into a Proper Noun for some purpose and so denoting it with the first letter capital for that particular purpose is acceptable. When we say, "My friend is a president of a club", the word 'president' need not be written with P capital (Upper Case). However, when we wish to point out this designation with reference to a particular club, then the sentence should be, "My friend is the President of the Defence Services Club." Remember, these are pointers useful to connect with the fact that Verbs can never begin with the first letter capital except at the beginning of a sentence.

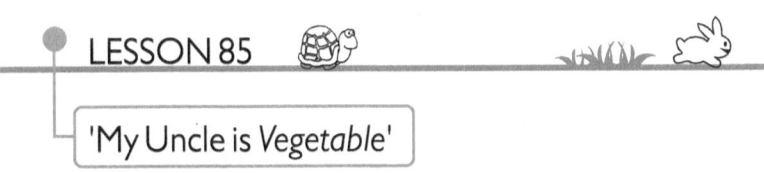

LESSON 85

'My Uncle is *Vegetable*'

"My uncle doesn't eat meat, he is vegetable." Even though the meaning of this sentence has been correctly understood because of the first half, the second half makes us laugh because of the word 'vegetable'. What the speaker actually means is 'vegetarian' but because of his/her poor knowledge of, and reluctance to practice speaking correct English, s/he is unable to use the correct word. This is a problem typical of a multitude of us. Even on coming to know the correct words, we do not make serious efforts to practice using them. As a conscientious student of English so succinctly says, "If we don't use it, we lose it." It is extremely important that the correct sentence should be practised in full when you come to know your mistake.

LESSON 86

Carnivorous, Herbivorous and Omnivorous

Where human beings are concerned and where there is an aversion to meat-eating, we describe people as 'vegetarian'. A human being who eats animal flesh or 'meat' as it is known as in English, is described as 'non-vegetarian'. When we associate eating habits with animals, they are classified as 'carnivorous', 'herbivorous' and 'omnivorous'. A 'carnivorous' animal is one which eats other animals including bird and fish, e.g. a tiger is carnivorous. A cow eats only grass or small shrubs and is therefore known to be herbivorous. An omnivorous animal is one which eats both 'meat' as well as grass (in a broad sense), e.g. Bears are omnivorous. Remember, all these words are Adjectives and their Noun forms are Carnivore, Herbivore and Omnivore respectively. We have already seen terms used to define human eating behaviour i.e. 'vegetarian' and 'non-vegetarian'. There is yet another category of human beings i.e. 'vegan'. People who are against the consumption of milk or any dairy product are known as 'vegans'. The number of vegans all over the world is increasing day by day. A vegan is naturally, a vegetarian too.

LESSON 87

The use of 'Only'

Time and again, it has been pointed out that the best way to learn correct English is only through English. Look at the placement of the word 'only' in the previous sentence. The word 'only' is Adjective as well as Adverb. As far as correct English goes, avoid 'only' at the end of a sentence. We are so accustomed to transliterating, that in order to stress the importance of a situation that has no alternative and assuming that position to be the most effective, we place 'only' at the end of a sentence e.g. *"He said that he loved her only."* What this person wished to convey was that that man did not love any other woman. The best way to have conveyed it would therefore have been, **"He said that he loved only her."** In English, we must avoid ending a sentence with 'only'. Many students, who wish to become engineers, begin their essays with *"I want to study engineering only."* The correct sentence is **"I want to study only engineering."**

LESSON 88

'Find' and 'Finding'

"I can't remember where I kept the ball - I am finding and finding it since morning." This refrain is very common when children are unable to play due to a required article missing. "Finding" or "finding and finding" is used in such situations. When learning to speak correct English, remember there are a number of verbs which do not convey the same meaning in their ...ing form, 'finding' being one of them. The word 'finding' is a noun, and means 'result' or 'observation'. This word is very often used in its plural form as 'findings', e.g. "Findings of this research have already been published in many newspapers." The word 'find' is also used to get to know your opinion, e.g. "Have you read that novel? Did you find it interesting?" In the case of the ball, looking at the word 'find-finding' - if you have found something after having searched it out, then how can it not be with you? The correct statement therefore is, **"I can't remember where I kept the ball, and I've been looking for it since this morning."**

LESSON 89

'Taking a Test'

"My daughter always gets loose motions the day she has to give a test." We are so accustomed to assuming this sentence to be correct English that we get astonished when pointed out that it is incorrect. That is why it is in italics. In English, one doesn't give, but takes a test. The word 'take' is used more with 'test' and the word 'appear' is used with 'exam'. When appearing for an exam or taking a test, one's capacity at various levels, academically, emotionally, intellectually is brought into question. Preparation made for the test/exam is also brought

into focus. The verb 'take' over here does not mean 'to accept' but 'to perform' or 'to do'. The verb 'give' cannot be used in this situation. Once again, it is very important to point out that 'give' is used as a result of thinking in one's mother tongue/local language, mentally transliterating in nanoseconds and then speaking in English. The next time you visit the RTO, say it correctly, "I failed the last time, but am determined to take my driving test successfully tomorrow."

LESSON 90

'Answering a Paper'

A huge number of guides, notes and books on how to crack important exams are available in the market. Where English is concerned, they all claim to help you *'solve'* the paper you are preparing for by compiling *'solved'* and model Test Papers. English is a language but unfortunately has been taught more as a subject in schools and colleges all over India especially after Independence. That is why we have such an approach. Questions concerning a language cannot be *'solved'* but only 'answered'. The grammars of languages go on evolving every day and the possibility of more than one answer being correct is very high. Answers based on language- skills related questions cannot be evaluated in the same way as done in Math or Physics, e.g. essays written in important language-related papers can be evaluated using multitudes of parameters. Languages have got to be learnt and their nuances imbibed, so that associated skills get developed. Where languages are concerned, memory is of secondary importance with skill being primary.

How Not to Speak English

LESSON 91

Cousin *Brothers*, Cousin *Sisters*

English is relatively poor in kinship terminology, i.e. in being able to identify the exact relationship that exists between various relatives. There are broad terms such as Uncle, Aunt, First Cousin, Second Cousin, Distant Cousin, Nephew, Niece, Brother-in-law/Sister-in-law. Please do not use *"He/she is my cousin brother/sister."* The words "brother/sister" are illogical in English with the word "cousin" because the Proper Noun (Name) or the chosen pronoun "she/he" clearly identifies the sex. The correct sentence therefore is, **"S/he is my cousin."** We are familiar with non-English Indian languages clearly-defining terms used for identifying one's paternal grandfather (father's father) and maternal grandfather (mother's father) and also one's paternal and maternal grandmother. Non-English languages, especially Indian, have words that clearly identify relationships of relatives. We also have terms which clearly denote whether a particular relative is younger or older. However, it is not so in English. If you wish to elaborate on a particular relative then you may say, *"She's my aunt, being my mother's younger sister."*

LESSON 92

Addressing People – Mr./Miss/Mrs./Ms

Where formal relationships are concerned, it is better to address people using their surnames, e.g. "How are you today, Mr. /Mrs. Kulkarni?" When speaking English, please do not use "Uncle/Aunt(y)",to address neighbours/acquaintances /strangers you meet on the street. The cultural background of English considers it extremely insulting if strangers are addressed as "Uncle/Aunt(y). This is true for British as well as American English. Although the American may become informal quickly, an Englishman might take longer. Until then, you have to use formal terms of address by using Mr. / Miss /Mrs. /Ms. + the person's surname. 'Ms.' is most preferred by women as its use accords them dignity and respect beyond being dependent on a man. 'Ms.' can be used to address single as well as married women. Remember, that the word 'madam' or its short form 'ma'am' should not be used to address women except as a salutation in a formal letter.

LESSON 93

'Teacher' and 'Sir'

In India, when using English, we assume the word "teacher" to be associated generally with a lady and "Sir" with a gentleman. We saw in the last lesson that we should not use 'madam' or 'ma'am' to address women. So also, a male teacher should not be addressed as 'Sir' but by using 'Mr.' with his surname. If he, irrespective of his age, wishes it to be so done, then you may even use his first name. This helps build student-teacher rapport. The words 'sir' or 'madam' should be used only when writing letters and not when speaking as terms of address. The word "Sir" in English is used to address a person who has been knighted for great achievements and it is therefore used to address only a chosen few. When a woman gets a similar honour, the word "Dame" is used as a term of address. "Sir" and "Dame" are used only in these contexts and cannot be used formally to address people. Generally, the only area in which we may use "Sir" and "Madam" is when we begin a letter.

Lesson 94

'Respected Sir/Madam'

"*Respected Sir /Madam*" is the opening (salutation) of many letters in which the individual addressed is of seniority in position or age as compared to the one writing the letter. Unfortunately, this form of address is incorrect. Please note that there is no salutation when writing a letter in English that begins with, "Respected". A letter, when formal, can begin only with "Dear Sir/Madam" or simply "Sir/Madam". When an informal letter is begun then you may use the relationship or the first name of the person with or without 'dear'. It is highly inconceivable that a person to be accorded respect should be addressed as "*Respected Sir/Madam*". Even when addressed as "Dear" a person gets the respect you wish to accord him/her. Respect, as we know, is more to do with feelings rather than empty words. Although email etiquette is newly developed, there are many areas where the same precautions are necessary as followed earlier with traditional mail or 'snail mail' as it is now known.

LESSON 95

'Thank you in *Advance*'

Many times when we request somebody to do something for us, we use the expression, "*Thank you in advance*" to end the letter or even when speaking. 'Thank you' is an expression used to manifest one's gratitude for a favour/help/gift or any positive action that was required to be done or for any of the aforementioned unexpectedly done. The action being done, presupposes the past tense and therefore there can be no question of thanking someone in advance. At the most, the expression, **'thanking you in anticipation'** is correct, because the writer wishes the reader to act as per his/her expectations, the keywords here, being 'in anticipation'. The change of form from 'thank you' to 'thanking you' puts forward the corollary that the action has not been completed as yet. This is conveyed by the ...ing form of the verb in its Participle form. *'Thank you in advance'* therefore has no meaning. Grammatically too it has no identity for it tries to join two timeframes, creating confusion. 'Thank you' is the shortened form of 'I thank you for what you have done/did'. Therefore, *'thank you in advance'* has neither meaning nor logic, thank you.

LESSON 96

'No, thank you', *'You're Welcome'*

"Please have some/ some more biscuits"
    "No, thank you"
    "*You're welcome*"

Now, how can somebody be welcome to something that s/he doesn't want nor has taken in whole or in part/of? The expression "You're welcome" simply means you are glad to have been of assistance or that you are happy that somebody has accepted what you offered him/her. It also indicates that you do not mind if the same person takes more of that what you had offered. It is an expression of generosity clearly conveying the association of happiness with the kind act/deed/favour/gift performed/given by you. When the offer is turned down the person politely says, "No" and then adds "Thank you" indicating that even though s/he has not accepted it, s/he wishes to thank you for offering it. Therefore, when someone says "No, thank you" it is the end of the matter. You don't have to say anything regarding it. Incidentally, many

SMSs in reply to "Thank you" carry "*Your welcome*". Remember, 'you're welcome/you are welcome' is correct and the meaning changes when you use '*your welcome.*'

LESSON 97

'Excuse Me'

"Excuse me please, I'm sorry I didn't say 'thank you'." "Please excuse me for I'm sorry I didn't say 'thank you'." The first sentence draws the listener's attention and then conveys regret. The second displays genuine regret from the third word onwards. When we say "Excuse me please....," it is to announce some kind of inconvenience or to draw attention to oneself. When we say "Please excuse me for ......," we convey regret for something done by mistake. In both these sentences, these four expressions expressing consideration, politeness, regret and gratitude have been used. These expressions are integral to English and they must be used wherever necessary, and as often as possible. Many of us think that by using these, especially 'please', we are reducing our dignity. Instead, it is the opposite. When we use these expressions regularly and with genuineness, we enhance our dignity and also make the listener/reader worthy of respect, regard and consideration. Regular use of these expressions clearly reflects social and business etiquette and proper upbringing.

LESSON 98

'Career' and 'Carrier'

'*I want to learn English to make a good carrier.*' 'Career' is one of the most misspelled English words in India. And also one of the most mispronounced. A 'carrier' is a vehicle used to transport goods. That is why on trucks/lorries etc. you see the words "Public Carrier". A 'career' is the sum total of professional work that one does over a prolonged period and generally one with which job satisfaction can be associated. Spellings of English words have foxed millions, including the people of England themselves. Correct spellings and pronunciations for non-native speakers of English can definitely be worked at to be improved upon. Knowing the correct meaning of a word also helps in being able to pronounce and spell it correctly. Do not confuse pronunciation with accent. The trick is always to divide words into their parts i.e. syllables. Words have got to be split into syllables and practiced, both for developing Speaking as well as Writing skills. When so done, errors in spelling as well as pronunciation get minimized. Seriousness, uninterrupted interaction in English and perseverance are stepping stones towards proficiency at English.

LESSON 99

English – An Indian Language

No country can beat India for the number of languages its peoples speak. The incredible number of languages is now leading to combinations with English and creating newer variations of hybrid languages. Unfortunately, in our haste and desire to make things easy for ourselves, we are making things difficult as far as correct and proper English is concerned. English today is an Indian language. All rules, acts, laws as per the Constitution of India have been written in English. As lingua franca, the adoption of English has led to tremendous growth and development. English is the language that links India where commerce, trade, science and finance is concerned. Not only within, but Indians outside India as well have benefited tremendously from English. A strong urge in students to acquire higher education abroad has led to a huge number constantly preparing for IELTS/TOEFL. Many mistakenly assume these tests to be very simple. It is imperative that a student first become conversant with English grammar, practice the language and only then take these tests.

LESSON 100

No Short Cuts to Success

A century is always special. Even those who aren't avid cricket fans are aware of Sachin Tendulkar's passion for centuries. After his retirement from ODIs, all of us were eager to see yet another century in Test cricket from the master blaster. We all know and accept that hard work and continuous practice are important ingredients in Sachin's recipe for success. Short cuts do not lead to success. Cricket was brought into India by the English over two centuries ago but nobody can today deny the mastery that a huge number of Indians crave, but very few possess, over it. Mastery over cricket comes only with grit, perseverance and practice. So also with English. Many of us crave mastery over English without working hard and practising it. The key is to never get bored, be it cricket or English.

LESSON 101

'Postpone' and 'Prepone'

In an earlier lesson, mention was made of hybrid languages being created in India by combining native languages with English. We have also seen various examples of Indianisms, the commonest being "What is your good name?" However, there have been instances where certain words made in English by Indians have become internationally acceptable. The most commonly used such word and one that is extremely popular is 'prepone'. Conveniently devised as an antonym to 'postpone' the word 'prepone' however does not exist in many English dictionaries. Those, in which it does, clearly indicate it to be of Indian origin. The meaning, evidently exploiting the suffix 'pre' indicates 'to bring forward to an earlier date'. American English however does not accept this word with the computer suggesting it be corrected as 'prep one' and also offering some other alternatives. So, when you are communicating with an American, it is best to say or write, "The date of the event has been advanced / brought forward from the 15th to the 12th."

LESSON 102

'Aks' and 'Riks'

"Can you come to play now?" "Wait, I'll just aks my mom." The word 'ask' as you are reading it in italics has been mispronounced not only in India but all over the world. While speaking English, many of us when mispronouncing it, simply assume it to be the correct pronunciation. It is extremely important that we learn correct pronunciations, practice them regularly and understand the meaning and use of words. It does not matter if the word is small or ordinary or does not seem to have great significance. If you find it difficult to pronounce 'a-s-k' as 'ask' the best way to do it is to first say the word 'task' loudly many times and then, removing the 't', go on saying 'ask'. A similar situation exists with the word 'risk' with a number of Indians dabbling in risky business ventures, some of them at the Stock Exchange continuously saying, *"I am taking / not taking that riks."* So as to get the word 'risk' pronounced correctly, first say 'brisk' many times, and then, removing 'b' pronounce 'risk' correctly.

LESSON 103

'Day-dreams' and 'Nightmares'

When we are fully awake and conscious, we are able to participate in our day-to-day activities in a concentrated manner. However, many of us dream even when we are awake. This phenomenon in English is known as 'day-dreaming'. Dreaming while sleeping is considered a natural phenomenon. It is not possible for us to remember what we dreamt of when sleeping, but when the dreams are pleasant and positive, on remembering them we feel good. Dreams that are negative and horribly frightening and which, when awake, alarm our consciousness are known in English as 'nightmares'. The memory of a nightmare may make not just one day but a long period of one's life disturbed. The human mind is the most complex of mechanisms and with the forces of the world, both conscious and subconscious acting upon it, there is no way in which one can safely and surely predict peoples' reactions. Day-dreaming, therefore, sometimes becomes necessary for us to think of possibilities never thought of before. When Gandhiji first spoke of non-violence as a method of trying to obtain freedom, his ideas were dismissed as day-dreams.

LESSON 104

A '*Soft*' Skill

Great damage to English has been done in India by terming it a 'soft' skill. People all over the world find the learning of English to be quite difficult. The main reason for this difficulty is that they do not work hard. It is erroneously thought that being a language, English can be easily learnt in the shortest of periods. All over India, a proliferation of institutes promises the student proficiency in English within a month and some, even within a week. Promotions, social status, and peer pressure are some reasons why a huge number of Indians now wish to learn English. Sadly, all this means that there is a desire to learn English because people **have** to learn it and are being consciously or subconsciously forced into learning it. We are so obsessed by the relationship of high incomes with science, technology and commerce that any learning outside the purview of these gets no importance whatsoever. If you wish to be able to learn English well and do well at it, you must **want** to do it and not be forced to do it.

LESSON 105

'Leave', 'Drop' and 'Pick'

"I met the Team Leader today and I'm so happy I have more than fifteen leaves remaining." The word 'leaves' in this context is incorrect. The correct sentence is: **"I met the Team Leader today and I'm so happy I have more than fifteen days' leave I can avail of."** A constant defence being put forward to the use of incorrect grammar is that when we are communicating information there is no need for us to take care of our grammar. Nothing could be further from the truth. The word 'leaves' is either a Noun - the plural of 'leaf' or a Verb with negative overtones. *"My father leaves me at the college every day,"* is incorrect and the correct sentence is, **"My father drops me to college every day."** If a man says to his wife that he would be leaving her at the railway station, it could be clearly implied that he would be separating from her. The correct sentence showing the opposite action is "My mother picks me up from college every day."

LESSON 106

'Infant', 'Child', 'Youth', 'Adult'...

We Indians generally associate the word 'baby' with the female sex. When a male infant catches one's attention, the remark made is, "What a cute *baba*!" The word "baba" is hopelessly incorrect. The correct term is 'baby boy' or 'baby girl', e.g. "My cousin is unhappy as she has no nanny to look after her baby girl / baby boy." Similarly, the word 'child' is of common gender, applicable both to boys as well as girls. With the word 'baby' the word boy/girl is used after it, e.g. baby-boy, baby-girl. With the word 'child', the word 'boy/girl' is used before it, e.g. boy-child, girl-child. With growth, the word 'youth' replaces the word 'child'. 'Youth' is applicable more to boys and a girl is described as a "young girl". Adulthood formally and legally begins at eighteen, but socially and physiologically, a sixteen year old can also be termed 'adult'. Between youth and adulthood, there is 'adolescence'. The word 'teenager' is applied to youngsters between thirteen and nineteen, because of 'teen' being a part of these numbers. Overlapping of terms is possible as increase in age has no breaks. A general sequencing in ascending order of age therefore is: new-born, infant, baby, child, youth-young girl, adolescent- teenager, and finally, adult.

LESSON 107

The 'Alleged' Crimes

"Mr. XYZ, a resident of Delhi, had allegedly misbehaved with the complainant, a young woman." This is part of a common news item even though it may not be headlines. Many readers do not understand the word 'allegedly' and the implications that it has. When a crime has been committed, a court of law has to try the accused, and with evidence presented, decide whether the accused is innocent or guilty. Occasionally the accused is declared 'not guilty' and therefore acquitted. The word 'allegedly' is an adverb and clearly adds to the situation in which the crime was committed giving the accused benefit of doubt. It can also be used as an Adjective, e.g. "Mr. XYZ was alleged to have stolen the money." That is because, at the time of going to press, the guilt of the accused has not been proven. The word 'allegedly' also protects newspapers from defamation cases. When the word 'allegedly' is inserted, it clearly indicates to the reader that "Mr. XYZ has been accused of this evil act, but his guilt has not been established yet."

LESSON 108

> **'Advice' and 'Advise'; 'Device' and 'Devise'**

Making mistakes, we are in constant need of guidance. Advice can be professional, personal, or given by a counselor in an educative manner. The word 'advice' is on many occasions used in the plural as '*advices/advises*' which is incorrect, e.g. *"She was given many advises against it, even then she married him."* An example of 'advises' as Verb (Present Simple Tense) is: "My elder brother advises me on financial matters." When the Verb 'advise' is converted to a Noun, then it becomes 'advice' and the pronunciation also changes accordingly. Being an Abstract Noun, 'advice' cannot be used in the plural, and therefore the correct sentence is, **"She was given advice by many against it, even then she married him."** A similar situation exists with the Verb 'devise'. The Noun of 'devise' is 'device' and 'device' being a Common Noun, can be used in the plural as 'devices'. A device is a useful gadget and "to devise" is to plan a course of action or a strategy.

LESSON 109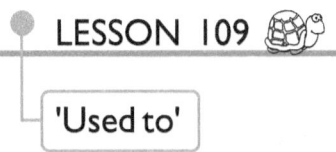

> **'Used to'**

With Regular Verbs, the addition of 'ed' as we have seen, converts the action into the Past Tense. Some Verbs which end with 'e' in the Present, however, do not use 'd' after 'e' in the Past and this can lead to confusion. A common example is 'use' and 'used'. When we use something, we put it to a purpose. When the purpose has been fulfilled we express completion by adding 'd', e.g. Q: "How did you come here?" A: "I used my car." OR "I use the school bus to go to school every day." There are instances however, when the word 'use' does not carry the

required meaning. Specific note must be made of the combination of 'used' with 'to'. When the word 'used' is put before 'to', we convey action/s which is/are not being done anymore by us, e.g. "I used to pretend to have a stomach-ache to avoid going to school." This sentence means that now you do not put forward this false excuse. Remember, use/d+Noun (machine/object/system) = purpose whereas used+to+Verb (Present Tense Form) = action/s in the past, and without exception, no more being done in the present.

LESSON 110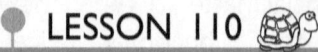

'Suppose', 'Supposed' and 'Supposedly'

The word 'supposed' at times makes for a lot of confusion. What does it mean? How is it to be used? "You were supposed to be here at 5 p.m., why are you so late?" This is common where students are concerned. The word 'supposed' brings upon a person expectations that are grounded in formality and which were to govern that person's actions. For the student, it was important to have ensured that s/he reach the institution at 5 p.m. Even without the word 'supposed', which is an adjective, the sentence conveys a meaning. e.g. "You were to be here at 5 p.m., why are you so late?" But when the word 'supposed' is used, it fortifies the sentence conveying that the action was to have been committed in accordance with expectations. "Its December, I suppose it would be snowing heavily in Simla". When it is winter, the association of ideas gets stronger with the word 'suppose'. The Adverb is 'supposedly' and can be used as "Many of the protestors are in hospital as a riot supposedly broke out between the two communities." Here the word 'supposedly' indicates that the riot began as a small fight.

LESSON 111

'Preconceived Notions'

You must have often come across the term 'preconceived notions'. What do these words mean? First, let us take the meaning of the word 'notion'. A notion is an idea or an opinion which exists in one's mind regarding certain issues or subjects. The word 'conceive' means to 'bring into existence that which did not earlier exist.' By adding the prefix 'pre' we confirm that the notion was already in existence. 'Preconceived notions' is a term that stands for thoughts that make us believe that a particular situation is already in place for some period of time. We therefore adopt a definite and particular behaviour or attitude. Many Indians assume that in the West every one speaks English. The fact is that there are many people in the developed world who do not speak English at all. Asawari Joshi, a teacher of English, who recently got her Cambridge Certificate in Teaching English to Speakers of Other Languages (CELTA) in Germany, had classmates from Argentina, Brazil, Portugal, Russia, Spain, etc. Their English was not as good as hers. To imagine or assume that every citizen in the West knows English well and also likes to communicate using it, is to have preconceived notions.

LESSON 112

'Boy' and 'Buoy'

The word 'boy' is pronounced by a number of Indians, especially from the North, as 'buoy'. However, the meaning of the latter is quite different from the former. The word 'buoy' means an object that floats on water and can also be used in life-saving exercises. A buoy also acts as a marker showing the level of the tide to a swimmer as well as a sailor. The Verb 'to buoy' indicates 'to lift up or take to a higher level', e.g. 'He was depressed but her call buoyed his spirits.' When speaking English, correct pronunciation is extremely important. Otherwise we may be communicating something else to the listener. The word 'boy' should be pronounced to rhyme with 'toy' or 'joy' and the word 'girl' to rhyme with 'pearl' or 'curl'. Sometimes the word 'lad' is used to denote a boy and 'lass' to denote a young girl. However, both, considered to be old English, are no more in favour.

LESSON 113

Why is English so popular?

A huge number of Indians attribute the popularity of English to almost four centuries of British rule. Contrary to preconceived notions, English is in great demand today even in countries where the British never set foot. An important reason for the popularity of English is the ease with which non-English words become English words. Many words today are part of the English vocabulary in their original language forms. From India, there are thousands, and a few examples are: avatar, bungalow, chapatti, Mahatma, pucca, and pundit. A few years ago, a student of Chinese origin could not win the International Spelling Bee in the US because his opponent, a student of Indian origin, spelt "satyagraha" correctly. Similarly, there are today in English words from almost every language on this earth in its original language form. Once a word gets mentioned in an English-English dictionary, it becomes an English word, notwithstanding the language of its origin. That is why, English today has the most extensive vocabulary in the world. Of course, to improve your Vocabulary skills, you have to first develop the ability to grasp English Grammar.

LESSON 114

'Indeed' and 'In Deed'

"A friend in need is a friend indeed." How many of us have actually understood this proverb? Most of us incorrectly divide the word 'indeed' into two, i.e. *'in deed'*. When we look at the use of 'indeed' as *'in deed'*, this proverb becomes meaningless and does not convey the correct meaning that 'indeed' does. 'Indeed' is an adverbial expression, confirming the truth about a fact or situation, e.g. "That is a very tall building indeed," OR "Indeed, CAT is one of the most difficult tests in the world." The use of 'indeed' goes a long way into corroborating, i.e. confirming, what has been said before it or that which follows. Consequently, when used at the end of this proverb, 'indeed' simply means that a friend who has got into a difficult or a dangerous situation or troubled times, does not lose the right to be considered a friend, and truly, in spite of that, continues to remain a friend. The word 'deed' by itself in English means 'an act' or 'a legal document' and its combination with 'in' is therefore meaningless. Indeed!

LESSON 115

Anybody, Nobody, Somebody, Everybody...

A popular T-shirt slogan: *"Nobody is perfect, I am nobody."* Omission of the article 'a' between 'am' and 'nobody' makes nonsense of the grammar as well as humour. The words 'anybody', 'nobody', 'somebody', 'everybody' are all singular. They have to be used in a form that would, therefore, connect and convey an action involving an individual, e.g. (a) "Anybody can say what s/he wants." (b) "Everybody must take care of his/her bag." (c) "Nobody is responsible for your actions." (d)

"Look, somebody has broken that window." The clue lies in the use of the word 'body' which is clearly singular. Similarly, where the use of 'anyone', 'everyone', 'someone', and 'no one' is concerned, the clue lies in the use of 'one'. All these words must be used in the singular only. The word 'all' however is plural, and indicates collective denotation e.g. "All students must report in time for the picnic." Similarly, when 'some' is used without 'one' or 'body', it becomes plural with the Noun/Pronoun following being spoken or implied, e.g. "Some of our guests are going to leave early." "Some of them have already gone."

LESSON 116

A/AN, THE

Where Articles are concerned, you must always remember that the word 'an' is NOT the third Article. There are ONLY TWO Articles in English - 'a' and 'the'. The letter/word 'a' gets converted into 'an' when the word following it begins with a vowel sound. It is therefore 'a' OR 'an', e.g. "My friend's uncle is a doctor" but "My friend's aunt is an engineer." When the word following the supposed placement of 'a' begins with a vowel sound, the indefinite Article 'a' gets converted into 'an', e.g. "He is an honest boy." "She is an exceptionally talented woman." The Vowel Sound and not the Vowel, is key to the correct use of articles. e.g. "She has an M.A. in English " The Article 'a/an' is Indefinite because it indicates the Noun to be one of many. *"My father is farmer"* is incorrect and the correct sentence is **"My father is a farmer."** When 'a' is inserted, it clearly communicates that there are innumerable farmers in the world and the speaker/writer's father is also one. Articles are inextricably linked with Nouns and have no connection with any other Part of Speech. Articles are words that are known as 'determiners' because these words determine the word following them to be a Noun.

LESSON 117

'The' and Common/Countable Nouns

"I go to park every day." The speaker wishes to describe the activity of visiting a recreational area every day. However, non-use of the Article 'the' conveys the activity of parking a vehicle every day. That is because 'go to park' is a composite Verb using the Infinitive. The Infinitive, "to park" means "to place a vehicle in a stationary and safe position". The correct sentence describing a daily recreational activity is, "I go to the park every day." Now, because of the Article 'the', the word 'park' gets denoted as Noun. When Articles are not used, the Noun, provided it is Common and Countable, can be misconstrued to be a Verb and can convey a different and sometimes opposite meaning of the sentence e.g. "I go to market every day," means that you sell something every day whereas you want to say that you visit the market every day to buy something. To convey the latter meaning, the correct sentence is, "I go to the market every day."

LESSON 118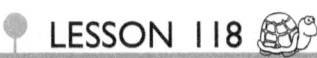

'A', 'An' and Vowel Sounds

Let's come back to the indefinite article 'a'. When followed by a word beginning with a vowel sound, 'a' gets converted to 'an'. Please note that it is not the vowel, but the vowel sound of the first letter that is the deciding factor. e.g. *"He is an European"* is incorrect and the correct sentence is, **"He is a European"**. This is because the sound is actually that of the consonant 'y' as 'yoropean'. Similarly, the word 'University' does not have a vowel sound although its first letter is a vowel. With the article 'the', there is no difference in pronunciation although earlier grammar experts insisted on 'the' being pronounced as 'thee' when the word following had the first letter beginning with a vowel sound. The article 'a/an' is always used for the Singular but the article 'the' can be used with the Singular as well as the Plural Noun.

LESSON 119

'The' Definite Article

The article 'the', being definite, also denotes the plural as part of a whole. 'The' is not needed when each and every unit of that particular Noun gets mentioned, e.g. "Cows eat grass" means that each and every cow on this earth eats grass, but "The cows I saw this morning were eating grass," clearly speaks of a particular group of cows and therefore needs the article 'the'. When a species is to be outlined as part of the genus, the article 'the' is a must, e.g. "The whale is a mammal." Switching from the indefinite article 'a/an' to the definite article 'the' is done when the subject is mentioned in the beginning and then specifically described so as to draw the reader/listener's attention. e.g. "There was a king named Midas. The king possessed that special ability of turning everything he touched into gold." The Articles 'a/an' and 'the' are also part of the group of words known as 'determiners' in English. However, Articles should never be confused to be Parts of Speech.

LESSON 120

'The' and Proper Nouns

Whenever we use Proper Nouns, Articles are unnecessary. Many say, *"I came to Pune yesterday from the Kolkata."* The correct sentence is, "I came to Pune from Kolkata yesterday." However, there are exceptions e.g. "I visited Germany last year and this year I'm visiting the UK." *'The'* before UK is necessary because *"U"* stands for the adjective 'united' and as part of the name of this country gets considered to be a Proper Noun. Before 'England' and 'America' however, 'the' is unnecessary. Similarly, it is the Punjab, because 'Punjab' stands for 'a combination of five rivers'. Another instance of exceptions where Proper Nouns are concerned, involves the use of 'the' with famous personalities when comparisons are unavoidable, e.g. "She is so proud of her singing she thinks she's the Lata Mangeshkar of India." We have earlier seen that the Superlative also necessitates 'the' preceding an Adjective/Adverb e.g. "He is the biggest liar." "I am the best, believe me I am."

LESSON 121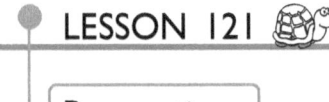

Pre-postions

Prepositions have no equivalents in many non-English Indian languages and in these languages we have 'Postpositions'. It is therefore, once again important to understand that transliterating can lead to innumerable problems especially where English is concerned. A Preposition is a word that shows the relationship i.e. the position of one Noun/Pronoun in connection with another Noun/Pronoun. It can also indicate the direction/situation/location of a Noun/Pronoun in connection with another. The Noun/Pronoun can be interchanged e.g. "The sun went behind the clouds," can become "It went behind the clouds," OR "The sun went behind them," OR "It went behind them." In all these sentences you will notice the preposition 'behind' in the middle of the sentence. The prefix 'Pre' followed by 'position' places the Preposition before a Noun/Pronoun. For many, it is a challenge to keep in mind what Preposition suits a particular context. Some regularly used Prepositions in English are: 'about'; 'in'; 'out'; 'of'; 'on'; 'up'; 'down'; 'above'; 'below'; 'from'; 'to'; 'between'; 'with'; 'without'; against'; 'by'; 'through'; 'into'; 'upon'. In the next four Lessons we shall see more of them as well as general guidelines regarding Prepositions.

LESSON 122

'On', 'At', 'With'

"My girlfriend is angry on me, for I made a mistake when speaking English." - A common mistake involving the preposition 'on'. When the adjective 'angry' is used, the most suitable preposition is 'with'. One can be angry 'with' (not 'on') a person, however one can be angry 'at' a situation, e.g. "People are angry at these developments resulting because of government inaction." It is important to practice the most suitable preposition with the appropriate situation for more than one preposition is acceptable in English. We can say, 'at the corner' as well as 'in the corner'. The former is done when connected with an open area and the latter with an enclosed area, e.g. "I'll be outside my office building, meet me at the corner." "Ravi was punished by his teacher and made to stand in the corner (of the classroom)." Both are correct, for the suitable Preposition has been used keeping the appropriate context and area in mind.

LESSON 123

'On', 'In', 'About'

Continuing with errors regarding 'on', many of us, while moving towards a destination, answer the phone, *"I am on the road."* Now, why is the use of 'on' incorrect in this context? The answer is very simple. The expression 'on the road' is an idiomatic one, conveying that the speaker has gone bankrupt, and is in a most difficult situation, financially speaking. The correct preposition therefore is 'in the road'. Now, considering that we are so used to using 'on', it becomes virtually impossible to begin using 'in the road / in the street.' However, if you keep the idiom in mind and practice 'in', you won't take long in using the correct Preposition, e.g. "I am in M. G. Road." Similarly, there are many Verbs in English which do not take Prepositions e.g. *'Let's discuss about our marriage plans.'* The verb 'discuss' itself means 'to talk about'. The correct sentence therefore is, 'Let's discuss our marriage plans.' 'Discuss' needs no preposition. It is however better to use the noun 'discussion' with the preposition 'on', e.g. "In our discussion on pollution, we found many causes for it."

LESSON 124

'Into', 'Between', 'Among'

"Please enter into the room." The Verb 'enter' means 'to come/go into'. It therefore needs no Preposition. The correct sentence is "Please enter the room". Similarly, the word 'comprise' is very often mistakenly used with 'of', e.g. *"Water comprises of hydrogen and oxygen."* This is incorrect, and the correct sentence is **'Water comprises hydrogen and oxygen.'** These examples should be noted, practiced and then

perfected. Now, let us look at 'between'. The word 'between' is very often combined with 'in' i.e. *'in between'*. The expression 'in between' is incorrect and when 'between' is used, it must be done to show the position of the Noun/Pronoun as related to two, and not more than two objects/persons etc. "Dheeraj is standing between Suhas and Brijesh" is correct whereas *"Dheeraj is standing between Suhas, Brijesh and Rishab"* is incorrect. When more than two are defined, then the correct Preposition to be used is 'among'. In a similar context, please note that 'off' is mostly used as an Adverb and 'of' is always a Preposition. We shall soon see the difference between these two.

● LESSON 125

'On', 'Off' and 'Of'

"Please turn the fan on/off." The use of on/off in relation to the fan is being done adverbially. In both cases, the action indicates the blades of the fan either revolving or stationary. In both cases, you will note that 'on/off' to be ideally used at the end of the sentence. While 'on' is a Preposition being used adverbially in this sentence, 'off' is generally an Adverb. The word 'on' as a Preposition is used to indicate a surface or a connection, e.g. "I recently read a book on waterborne diseases." The word 'off' indicates a direction and also implies the end of a sentence on many occasions, e.g. 'He was riding and fell off.' The word 'of' implies belonging/possession and is therefore a Preposition whereas 'off' is used to indicate 'away from' and is therefore mostly an Adverb, e.g. "The wheel-cap of the front right wheel fell off." Similarly, 'here'; 'there'; 'far'; 'near'; 'nearby' and some other words which appearing to be Prepositions are actually Adverbs.

LESSON 126

Conjunctions-1

Pursuant to our Lessons on Prepositions, we now shift focus onto Conjunctions. As we have studied at school, Conjunctions are words joining two sentences, and combining them into one Unit. It is important however, to remember that parts of the same sentence are known as Clauses. Please note that a Clause may be a Sentence by itself. There are three main kinds of Conjunctions and they are (a) and; (b) but; and (c) because. The first two are known as Coordinating Conjunctions and the third is a Subordinating Conjunction. In addition to these, there are more Coordinating as well as Subordinating Conjunctions. What is most important to remember is that one should never begin a sentence with a Conjunction. So as to remember this most significant aspect, look at the following sentence containing the word 'because' used consecutively three times: "We cannot begin a sentence with because, because because is a Conjunction." The words 'and' and 'but' are used twice e.g. "We cannot begin a sentence with 'and/but' because 'and/but' is a Conjunction."

LESSON 127

Conjunctions-2

Many new learners of English are unable to distinguish between 'and' and 'but'. It is important to understand the difference between the two so that when we use each of them we know exactly what we wish to convey. Look at the following sentences: (A) He reached home and found the door locked. (B) He reached home but found the door locked. What is the difference between (A) and (B)? In sentence (A) the person's two actions of reaching home and finding the door locked are almost simultaneous. However, in (B) there is an element of surprise as the person was not expecting the door to be locked. When 'and' is used, it leads to joining and combining whereas 'but' divides and separates actions, emotions etc. The following two examples should clarify the utilization of 'and' and 'but' further: (A) "It is raining heavily and I am expecting a holiday tomorrow." (B) "It rained heavily last night but no holiday was declared by my school."

LESSON 128

Conjunctions-3

Let us now look at 'because' and a few other Subordinating Conjunctions. The word 'because' is a short form of 'by being the cause of'. The word 'because' is used when a reason, excuse or explanation has to be put forward. The use of 'because' is done to clearly join two sentences (clauses) and to clarify. The word 'because' is considered the most basic of Subordinating Conjunctions for it divides a Sentence into a Main Clause and a Dependent Clause. Let us look at the following Sentence: "He went away because he found the door locked." "He went away" is the Main (Principal) Clause and "because he found the door locked" is the Subordinating (Dependent) Adverb Clause of Reason modifying the Verb 'went'. There are a number of Subordinating Conjunctions, similar to 'because'. Some of them are 'although'; 'though'; 'even though'; 'in spite of'; 'despite'; 'whereas'. Where Subordinating Conjunctions are concerned, they make one Clause dependent on another. With Coordinating Conjunctions, the Clauses remain equal to each other.

LESSON 129

Compound / Complex Sentences

A sentence consisting of two or more Coordinating Clauses is known as a Compound Sentence and a Sentence consisting of two or more Subordinating Clauses is a Complex Sentence. While this information may not be of as much use to the layman as to a school/college student studying formal English grammar, it is always beneficial for the general public to keep certain points in mind. Now, let us look at certain Subordinating Conjunctions: "Although it was raining, but he didn't take an umbrella." The use of 'but' with 'although' is incorrect. The correct sentence is, "Although it was raining he didn't take an umbrella." The word 'although' can also be placed elsewhere as: "He didn't take an umbrella although it was raining." "Despite of the rain, he didn't take an umbrella." The word 'despite' does not take 'of' and the correct sentence is, "Despite the rain, he didn't take an umbrella." We must however add 'of' with 'in spite' e.g. "In spite of the rain, he didn't take an umbrella."

LESSON 130

Subordinating/Conjuctions

You must have noticed from the earlier Lessons that when we use Subordinating Conjunctions, with the exception of 'because' we may begin sentences with them although it is inadvisable. Some more Subordinating Conjunctions are: 'since', 'whereas', 'while', 'when', 'as soon as', 'no sooner than'. The word 'that', which is a Demonstrative Adjective is also a Conjunction, e.g. "He said that that car was his." The first 'that' is a Conjunction with the second being a Demonstrative Adjective. When we use the Coordinating Conjunctions 'either...or' and 'neither.....nor' we must keep certain points in mind, e.g. "You can either take a train or walk uphill to Matheran. It is advisable not to go by car." Where 'neither.....nor' is concerned a sentence has the greatest effect when it begins with "Neither ..." with the helping verb following immediately e.g. "Neither can you buy forgiveness from God nor can you escape punishment for your sins." Always remember that "either...or" means choosing one of the given two and "neither....nor" means no choice at all i.e. none of/from the two given actions/objects/situations etc. In short, either....or = 1; neither....nor = 0.

LESSON 131

Have a Heart

The human heart is a vital organ. We know what happens when it stops beating. The word 'heart' in English, is used to describe emotions, and these carry weight. Let's see a few. Where sympathy is concerned, 'heartfelt' is appropriate, e.g. "Please accept my heartfelt sympathies on your uncle's sudden demise." Do not use 'heartiest' in messages of condolences and likewise, do not use 'heartfelt' for joyous events. 'Heartiest' is used for positive and happy happenings and occasions, e.g. "Heartiest congratulations on having been appointed Managing Director." "Have a heart" means to request someone to have pity or mercy while 'have the heart' means to ask someone to have courage. The following examples clearly illustrate both: "Have a heart and stop translating every sentence from/into English." "Have the heart to accept you don't know English as well as you claim to." "To lose heart" is to become discouraged and to 'lose one's heart' is to fall in love. So, 'do not lose heart if you've lost in love, you'll soon get a chance to lose your heart again.'

Lesson 132

Re-redundant

The letters 're' begin words which show an opposite direction or action to be undertaken. However, many of us do not realize it when we use words beginning with 're' and add 'again' or 'back' or some other unnecessary word after it, e.g. *"My teacher couldn't read my handwriting, and has asked me to rewrite my essay again."* The word 'rewrite' itself means 'to write again' and so doesn't need the Adverb 'again'. The correct sentence therefore is, 'My teacher couldn't read my handwriting and has asked me to rewrite my essay.' In classrooms, when the teacher reads out words and sentences in Dictation exercises and tests, students always shout out *"Miss, please repeat again."* The correct sentence is, "Miss, could you please repeat the word/sentence?" The following are similar sentences with the unnecessary word in brackets: (A) Please reverse the car (back/behind). (B) Please revert (back) to us. (C) Please reconsider your decision (again). (D) Please return (back) the goods by tomorrow. (E) After necessary corrections have been made, kindly resend the file (back) (to us).

LESSON 133

Carton - Cartoons

"The two cartoons have come." We generally dismiss the mispronunciation of 'cartons' as 'cartoons' as a mistake by those who didn't study English well at school or college. However, you would be astonished to note that 'cartons' is mispronounced as 'cartoons' by many of us who have studied English in formal environments. A carton is a box made of pasteboard or cardboard whereas a cartoon is a comical or

satirical drawing making us laugh. Nowadays, cartoons are animated drawings seen on television and cinema. Some television channels show only cartoons. The best way to remember the correct pronunciation of 'carton' is to associate the word with the weight 'ton' which was earlier spelt 'tonne' but is now acceptable as 'ton'. A ton is equal to a thousand kilograms. A 'carton' however can be small enough to carry two or three kilograms. As for a 'cartoon' it helps to lift the weight of sadness from our minds. So, smile and get it right.

LESSON 134

Corpse-Copse-Corps

Moving on from 'cartoons', we need to look into the pronunciation of some more words beginning with 'C'. The word 'Corps' is very often mispronounced as 'corpse'. What is the difference? First, let us see the meaning of "Corps". "Corps" stands for a unit or division of the army or is a unit of armed personnel. It is pronounced as Kor, with both 'p' and 's' being silent. You can make it easier by pronouncing Corps as 'Kaur' a surname or middle name denoting a Sikh woman. Do not mispronounce 'Corps' as 'corpse'. The word 'corpse' stands for a dead body of a human being. The word 'copse' stands for a small wooded area, or a dense growth of trees within a specific area and its pronunciation again begins with a 'k' sound. The dead body of an animal is known as 'carcass' once again pronounced with the 'k' sound. Very few words beginning with 'C' are pronounced with the 'C' sound. Certainly!

LESSON 135

Amateur Expert Novice Professional

In our daily interactions with work-related activities we often come across the words 'amateur', 'professional', 'novice', 'expert'. What do these words mean? An 'amateur' is one who indulges in an activity for the sake of pleasure and doesn't use this activity to earn money, e.g. "She is very good at singing but chose to remain an amateur singer." A 'professional' gets paid for whatever activity he is supposed to be good at, and therefore his money-making activity becomes his 'profession' e.g. "Nowadays many parents in India want their children to become professional sportspersons." A 'novice' is a person who has very recently entered an area of work, e.g. "He's a novice, having joined this company only a month ago." Finally, an expert is a professional who has vast knowledge and experience in his area of work, and is considered by many in the same field to be far above them e.g. "Dr. XYZ is the expert whom doctors also consult when they themselves are patients. He's really the doctor's doctor."

LESSON 136

Abuse

Generally, people who don't know English are well-versed in using bad-words in English. Not only do they use them with style and regularity, but also feel extremely proud when doing so. A foul or bad word in English is known as 'abuse'. It is Noun as well as Verb (Regular) e.g. "I don't know why the taxi-driver abused the passenger." "The old lady was shocked at the abuse directed at her when she gently picked up the stray dog."

Words that should never be used in daily interactions involving English are also known as 'foul words'; 'four-letter words'; 'expletives'; 'invective'; 'vituperation'; 'imprecations'. In written English, anger, disgust, fear, jealousy etc being manifested through foul language is done by omitting bad words and using signs such as *#*#*! It is considered to be extremely bad manners and poor upbringing to use such language when ladies are present. Sometimes the word 'unparliamentary' is used to describe such language. However, many a time it has been seen many Members of Parliament speak in a manner that is most unparliamentary.

LESSON 137

Positive Interjections

Moving on from the negative to the positive, there are a number of words in English which stress on the positive side of human nature. When we wish to show wonder and appreciation, we use expressions such as "Great!" "Wow!" "Superb!" It is always a sign of maturity to use positive sentences especially when dealing with difficult situations, e.g. "You can't do anything right!" Instead of being so negative, it is better to say, "Come on! You can do better and will definitely succeed the next time." Words and expressions used to denote encouragement, as well as sadness, are known as Interjections in English. Of the eight Parts of Speech, they are the last and easiest to identify. Interjections are sometimes also called 'Exclamations' because the exclamation mark (!) is always used with this Part of Speech. In American English, it is put at the end of the sentence whereas in British English, it is placed immediately after the first word (the Interjection) e.g. American English: 'Hooray, no bugs here!' – British English: "Oh no! He speaks English, but broken."

LESSON 138

Chore-Errand

Men work outside the home while women are supposed to be generally busy doing household chores. What do we mean by 'chore'? A 'chore' is a word used to describe some kind of activity within one's household e.g. sweeping the floor, vacuuming the house etc. It is definitely not a welcome assignment but necessary to be done. When done every day, chores become an inescapable part of a home-maker's (housewife's) duties. Liberated men also do them without embarrassment. Those who are rich, hire servants to do their chores. But then, managing and supervising these servants also becomes a chore. An 'errand', conversely, is an act performed for buying things for the day-to-day running of a household. One 'does' a chore while one 'runs' an errand e.g. 'My dad runs the errand of getting milk every day from the market.' The word 'chore' is pronounced the same as the Hindi word denoting a thief. The word 'errand' consists of two syllables with 'err' being stressed and then 'and' pronounced with 'a' almost silent Remember, both 'chores' and 'errands' can also be perfprmed in non-domestic areas.

LESSON 139

Work / Job

After having seen the difference between 'chore' and 'errand', let's see the difference between 'work' and 'job'. The word 'work' is both Noun and Verb. Look at (A) and (B). (A) I couldn't come yesterday for I had a lot of work. (B) I work hard every day. In (A) 'work' is obviously a Noun, but in (B) the word 'work' becomes a Verb. However, as Noun, 'work' can't and shouldn't be used in the Plural e.g. *"I have many works today"* is incorrect, with "I have a lot of work today" being the correct sentence. The word 'job' on the other hand, can be used in the plural e.g. "Due to automation, many manual jobs have become history." The word 'job' is also associated with (A) an assignment, (B) a post, or (C) a responsibility e.g. (A) "They have given me the job of looking after their child when they're away." (B) - "I'm looking for a job as Senior Manager." (C) - "It is your job to ensure the fifty clocks in the office building always show correct time."

LESSON 140

Soft not Silent Music

A problem encountered very often with English is the correct terminology to be used when we wish to describe something. A lot of people when asked what their favourite hobby is, say, "I love listening to music." When asked what kind of music is their favourite, they invariably say, *"I love listening to silent music."* If the music they are listening to is silent, then what are they listening to? When you listen to silence, in reality you are not listening to anything. "Silent music" therefore, is clearly a term being used while attempting to conveniently transliterate another language into English. What this person actually means is, "I love listening to soft music." In a similar vein, whenever people name a season they use the word season which is redundant and understood e.g. *"In winter season we feel very cold."* The correct sentence is, "In winter we feel very cold." Whenever we talk of summer, winter, autumn, spring or the monsoon the word 'season' should not be used.

LESSON 141

Apprise / Appraise

"I'm eagerly awaiting this year's Appraisal. I'm sure the Team Leader will be happy with my work." So many of us, while using 'appraisal', are aware of what it involves, but don't know how to explain it. An 'appraisal' is the act of a senior, ably and correctly analysing the performance of a junior employee over a particular period of time, and then informing the management. Information thus handed over helps management decide as to how much investment can be made in the annual salary of the concerned employee by way of increment. To "apprise" is to inform someone of some happening. It is used with 'of' e.g. "The employees were apprised of the Managing Director's foreign trip." To 'evaluate' is to determine a value, e.g. "An expert was called to evaluate the exact market price of the disputed property." To 'assess' is to fix the value of a product, a service or even a performance e.g. "This year students are going to be assessed using stricter parameters." Remember, evaluating is not assessing. Taxes are levied on incomes, products and services after these are assessed.

LESSON 142

Quotation / Estimate

What is a 'quotation'? How is it different from an 'estimate'? A quotation is the price to be paid by a prospective customer to a seller in the relatively near future, for goods or services. An estimate is the worth of goods or services that is asked for by the seller from the prospective customer to pay for goods or services. A Bill is a document showing the sale of goods or services containing the amount and taxes to be paid by the buyer or hirer. Many establishments do not bill you legally because they just write the items' names on a plain piece of paper which does not contain a tax registration number and threaten that you will have to pay tax in case you want a bill. An Invoice is not a bill, in a technical sense. It is a list of goods or services with the amounts mentioned, including taxes and the mode of supply or delivery. A Proforma Invoice is like a quotation, putting forward details of payments to be made after the goods are dispatched/supplied. A Proforma Invoice is also used when applying to banks for loans for specific purposes.

LESSON 143

Cards Debit / Credit

When goods are sold and money handed over immediately it is known as a 'Cash' transaction. When payment is not immediately made and promised later it is known as a sale on 'Credit'. The word 'credit' ('c' being pronounced as 'k') has more than one meaning. Where trade is concerned, with payment not being made immediately, it means, 'sale on trust'. The seller trusts the buyer well enough to hand over the goods and expects payment for the same within a promised period. One has to be extremely careful in extending credit to unknown persons when selling goods and/or services. A Credit Card is one in which money is electronically transferred by a bank or an organization on behalf of the card-holder to a seller's account and then the bank/organization, using certain interest mechanisms, timeframes and methods, collects it from the card-holder.. A Debit Card immediately pays the seller by electronically transferring the money from the debit card-holder's account to the seller's account. Debit therefore means money deducted or subtracted for a specific purpose from the amount already existing in the Debit Card-holder's account.

LESSON 144

Schedule

Should it be pronounced 'shed-yool' or 'skej-yool'? The former is the British pronunciation and the latter American. However, it is also important to know the correct meaning of 'schedule'. This word is used as Noun as well as Verb. It is nowadays generally used to mean a timetable so that one can arrange one's activities according to it. It is also used as an Adjective in India to describe what were earlier known as the Untouchables in the Hindu religion i.e. the Scheduled Castes. A Schedule can also be a document, an appendix to a bill or even an Act of Parliament. Most of us use the word 'schedule' when we are about to embark upon a journey or when we talk of the scheduled time of arrival or departure of a bus/train/plane/ship etc. A schedule can also be a set program of events held through a particular period of time so that the event proceeds smoothly, e.g. "Your speech is scheduled immediately after the one-act play." The expression 'stick to a schedule' means that you have to complete assigned tasks within the period of time already fixed and desired.

LESSON 145

The Tough get goin

"When the going gets tough, the tough get going." From this saying, one can understand better the way Nouns, Verbs and Adjectives get changed into each other without a single letter being removed or added to a word. When we say 'the going' it does not mean a physical journey but the circumstances or situations which one is facing and in the first part the words 'gets tough' with 'tough' being Adjective, stands for the extent of difficulties or hard to manage situations. In the second part, 'the tough' stands for those people who are mentally and emotionally strong enough to withstand pressures due to the extent of those difficulties. The last part 'get going' as Verb clearly indicates that because of the toughness of these mentally strong individuals, they are able to overcome extensive and damaging difficulties. Carefully note that the use of the Article 'the' clearly denotes 'going' in the beginning and later 'tough' as Nouns. When using proverbs or idioms in English do not add or delete words, especially Articles, for when we do so, we weaken these wonderful sayings and expressions or convey a different or incorrect meaning.

LESSON 146

Indianism

Many of us, who work in the IT sector, are faced with the peculiar problem of many American, British, as well as citizens of some European countries unable to understand the English spoken by us Indians. The reason is very simple, for we create what are known as "Indianisms". While Indianisms can be understood by Indian speakers of English, these cannot be followed by native and other international users and speakers of English. At times, these Indianisms do get accepted (as in the case of 'prepone') but on a number of occasions, Indianisms lead to English becoming adulterated or impure. Let us take some examples: *"Can I do something from my side?"* This question has no meaning and the correct question is: "Is it possible for me to do anything?" So many times in order to appear to be extremely cooperative, we end up saying, *"I'll go ahead and help you."* This statement is also incorrect, and the correct form of expressing willingness to cooperate is, "I would be happy to help." We will see more Indianisms in the following lessons.

LESSON 147

Indianism 2

Continuing with Indianisms, we generally assume them to be correct English, because the language we are using at that time happens to be English. Many of us are happy on being granted leave and display our pleasure to our colleagues by saying, *"I am going on leave next-to-next week."* Obviously, this display is incorrect and the correct sentence is, "I'm going on leave two weeks from now." Similarly, while giving the reason or excuse for not having done something, we say, *"I went on leave last to last week."* Once again this is incorrect, and the correct sentence is, "I was on leave two weeks ago." While using the day, we must put it at the end of the sentence. The Adverb of Time, when placed at the end of a sentence, renders the best meaning as well as eliminates chances of errors, e.g. *"Tomorrow I will get back to you,"* is incorrect and the correct sentence is "I shall get back to you tomorrow."

LESSON 148

Pardon

On a number of occasions, especially on the telephone we are unable to hear correctly what the speaker on the other side wishes to convey to us. When we wish the speaker to repeat himself, we put across, *"What?"* However, it is important to be polite to the speaker and the best way to request that speaker to repeat himself/herself is by saying, "I beg your pardon." The word 'pardon' in English has many meanings, and in the expression mentioned above, it means a request to the speaker to repeat himself/herself. The word 'pardon' means apology, forgiveness, excuse etc. When it is used in the form of a plea to God, then it has a deeper meaning, of wanting to be forgiven for some kind of a crime, e.g. "I hope God will pardon me for my sins." The word 'pardon' is a word that has the best form of a request, and grants the speaker earnestness and politeness. The word 'pardon' has more force and strength as compared to 'sorry', 'excuse' and 'apology'.

LESSON 149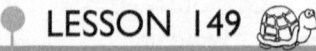

Very detailed

Assuming a number of points, we have a tendency to put in more words than necessary when we use English. *"The store/firm/company/office shuts down at 8 p.m."* is a clear example of unnecessary words being added. The correct sentence is, "The store/firm/company/office shuts at 8 p.m." – Similarly, *"the book is very much detailed"* is incorrect and the correct sentence is "The book is very detailed" OR "the book has a lot of details." The word 'detail' itself has a meaning of 'to relate minutely' and many times we erroneously say, *"Can we have more details?"* the correct question is, "Could we please have details?" The use of 'very' and 'much' with 'detailed' is unnecessary and we can speak good English when we do not use them with 'details". Similarly, when we use the word 'information' we must always remember that there is no plural and the same word cannot be said as, *"I have got many informations."* The correct sentence is, "I have been able to get a lot of information."

LESSON 150

Grammar & Vocabulary

"Could you help me with your name?" "I will explain you this plan" "Is Mumbai your native place?" "Not a problem, I will help you with that." As you can see, most of us have been speaking English utilizing such sentences and questions. These are standard forms of Indianisms. There is a great deal of argument that even though Indianisms seem to adulterate English, they help in facilitating communication. Be that as it may, it is important for us to understand that when we use English at an international level, then the constant utilization of Indianisms may just about backfire. The correct sentences and questions, acceptable at an international level are: "May I have/know your name please?" "I will explain this plan to you." "Are you originally from Mumbai?" "Certainly, I will help you with that." Please understand that when correct English is used, practiced and communicated, it leads to greater fulfillment. Practising correct English in all four segments of Reading, Writing, Listening and Speaking can lead to great satisfaction. Before improving on these skills however, it is most important to improve on your Grammar and Vocabulary.

LESSON 151

Idioms and Proverbs

We have seen in earlier lessons the need to stick to the original number of words while quoting and using Proverbs. Similarly, when using Idioms in English, we must never forget the exact expression, including the correct number of words. Let us first however, understand the difference between Idioms and Proverbs. A Proverb is a universal truth related to human beings. When applied to life or put into practice it can lead us to wisdom, success or even riches. An Idiom is a figurative expression and when used, lends expressive weight to a sentence. A Proverb is a whole sentence whereas an Idiom is part of a sentence "Look before you leap" is a Proverb while 'His business progressed/grew by leaps and bounds' contains an Idiom showing the quantum of progress to be much more than normal. To progress, by 'leaps and bounds' is comparative, using the movement of a kangaroo, which, when taking a step, generally takes a big one. Idioms begin with the infinitive form of the Verb 'to'. The Idiom is 'to move by leaps and bounds'

LESSON 152

Negative Idioms

Idioms can be used on a number of occasions depicting negative emotions. Idioms are used to effectively convey an idea. "To be down in the dumps", "to be a spoilsport" "to put a spoke in the wheel" "to suffer from sour grapes" - these are some negative idioms which convey emotions effectively. The use of an idiom is figurative i.e. it does not have to be taken in a literal sense. Let us see the use of idioms in sentences: "On being refused permission to go out, the young girl was down in the dumps." "It was a bright sunny day for a cricket match, but then the rain played spoilsport."

"Sheila's outburst was a spoke in the wheel when her daughter Leila wanted to go for a movie."

"Meena suffered from sour grapes for Leena had got the role that Meena so badly wanted."

When you look closely at the Idioms, you will realize that these sentences could have been completed without the use of these Idioms. Without Idioms, the sentences would not have been able to carry emotional weight.

LESSON 153

Positive Idioms

As we have negative emotions conveyed expressively through Idioms so also positive emotions can be. Look at the following: 'to be on top of the world' 'to be on cloud nine' 'to jump for joy' 'to walk on air'. Let's now look at these idioms in sentences:

"He felt on top of the world when she said 'yes' to his proposal of marriage." "She was on cloud nine on being declared winner of the jackpot."

"He jumped for joy when he discovered the cause of the snag." "She's been walking on air ever since some critics praised her as a fashion diva."

Whenever you come across an Idiom that strikes your fancy, you must use it in a sentence of your own as quickly as possible. Then, you must get it checked by an expert and ascertain that it has been correctly used. It cannot be overemphasized to say that only when we begin to put into use what we have learnt that we actually begin to practise a language. Otherwise, all that you have acquired in the classroom would remain memory, without ever becoming knowledge.

LESSON 154

Idioms – For every emotion

Idioms, as we have seen by now, can be used to express positive as well as negative emotions. Additionally, they can also be used to describe situations with pungency and flavour. When idiomatic phrases are used, then there is no need to elaborate and the expression by itself becomes clear. Over here, students will do well to remember that a phrase is a group of words that does not possess a finite verb. That is the reason why these idiomatic phrases begin with the infinitive form of the verb. Let us see a few examples: 'to be in dire straits' 'to clutch at straws' 'to face the music' 'to come up against a brick wall' 'to draw a blank' 'to spread yourself too thin' 'to be left holding the baby' 'to put one's foot in one's mouth'. Idiomatic phrases in English are countless and there exists one for almost every situation and emotion. It is only by constant reading that one can get a grasp over these and also be able to use these correctly in one's spoken and written attempts. Last, but not least, one should not add or subtract any word from Idioms, especially Articles.

LESSON 155

Some Famous Idioms

"To be in dire straits" means to be in an extremely precarious financial situation, e.g.: "Having lost millions in speculations on the Stock Exchange, he is now in dire straits."

"To clutch at straws" is self-explanatory and means that when you are drowning, anything that appears to be of use to save yourself will be grabbed.

"To face the music" is an idiomatic phrase that indicates definite punishment for an indiscretion, an illegal act or even a crime, e.g. "The college student stole that car for a joyride and now must face the music."

"To come up against a brick wall" is to suddenly be faced with stiff opposition, e.g. "Marshall ran through the Indian batsmen but suddenly came up against a brick wall named Gavaskar."

"To draw a blank" is to fail in getting results when one is making serious enquiries, e.g. "The police were unable to get information from witnesses, each time drawing a blank." We shall continue with Idioms in the next few lessons and then take a close look at some famous English Proverbs.

LESSON 156

The 'eye' of the beholder

In a recent awards show on a TV channel, a famous senior Hindi film actress made the remark, *"Beauty lies in the eyes of the beholder"*. She had obviously not given the Proverb much thought, taking it to mean what she thought it did. However, the moment 'eyes' is used instead of 'eye' the meaning of this Proverb changes. When we say that beauty lies in the eyes of the beholder, then it clearly implies that the eyes of the person who is looking at something, are beautiful, instead of implying that the object being looked at, is being perceived as being beautiful. In English, when we speak of thinking as associated with the singular 'eye', it clearly expresses that what exists in our mind. It is also known as 'the mind's eye' or 'the eye of the mind'. The original Proverb is, "Beauty is in the eye of the beholder." Here, it is important to understand that by 'eye' is not meant the physical faculty of seeing, but the deeper psychological and mental act of 'perceiving' i.e. forming an opinion about an object/person/scene etc. that one is looking at.

LESSON 157

Proverbs – Similar and Opposite

Like other languages, English too has its fair share of Proverbs. Many English Proverbs have equivalents in other languages and in them too, mean the same as they do in English. As time passes, newer Proverbs are added, and thanks to the Internet, many Proverbs are being translated into English and easily become English Proverbs. Sometimes, two Proverbs in English show opposite meanings and one needs to be extremely careful in choosing the one that is most appropriate and relevant to that point of time and situation. "Great minds think alike" is comforting for people who think of themselves to be great, but, at the same time, "Fools seldom differ". In a similar vein, "Take care of the pennies and the pounds shall take care of themselves" is a striking contrast to "Penny wise, pound foolish." There are other Proverbs however that are supportive of each other, e.g. "An idle mind is the devil's workshop" and "Think of the devil and the devil appears." Being idle is actually inviting the devil. You must therefore, always be occupied, for 'Actions speak louder than words.'

LESSON 158

'Well' – Adverb, Adjective and Noun

"Well begun is half done." "All's well that ends well." In the first Proverb, the word 'well' is an Adverb. "Well" in this Proverb signifies that when an activity has been competently and confidently started, the manner of its start would definitely lead to its development almost half-way. In the second Proverb, the first 'well' after 'all's', clearly demarcates it as an Adjective and the rest of the Proverb indicates that if the ending of an event or action is good then everything about that event or action should be acceptable. What kind of course the middle of the action took, doesn't matter. The word 'well' is Adjective, Adverb and also a Noun. As an Adjective, it indicates positive developments and also suggests something better than just 'good'. We use it also as a form of encouragement, e.g. "Do well in your exams!" and in other expressions. As a Noun, 'well' means a natural or man-made resource generally providing water. As the famous joke goes, Q: "What did Little Johney say as soon as he reached the well?" A: Little Johney said, "Well, well, well!"

LESSON 159

Proverbs and Literature

"Every dark cloud has a silver lining." In times of depression and stress, this Proverb has been a beacon of hope that all is not lost. It has given great cheer to those who had imagined destruction round the corner. Similarly, Proverbs provide warning, e.g. "Do not count your chickens before they are hatched." This Proverb means we shouldn't assume that things will always go as per our expectations and we must patiently wait for certain events. A number of Proverbs in English were originally statements in works of great Literature e.g. "It's better to have loved and lost than never to have loved at all" is taken from Tennyson's poem "In Memoriam". "The law is an ass" was originally part of Charles Dickens's "Oliver Twist". "Power corrupts, absolute power corrupts absolutely" is today a well-known Proverb, and was part of Lord Acton's famous speech. The most popular and, by now, proverbial definition of democracy, as "government of the people, by the people, for the people" is actually the last line of the famous Gettysburg address by Abraham Lincoln on November 19, 1863.

LESSON 160

Proverbs – the moral side

As we have seen, many Proverbs are self-explanatory, although a few need explanations. Let us see a few more Proverbs that help us lead better lives. "If you fail to plan, you plan to fail." We all know and realize the value of this Proverb. Many Proverbs in English describe the importance of relationships but the most poignant one regarding the relationship one has with one's mother is, "The hand that rocks the cradle rules the world."

This Proverb forms the basis of many essays in school and college exams. A few other pertinent Proverbs that rule over human existence are also important. The most important one is, "Money is the root of all evil." Proverbs also help us realize that human beings are but human and liable to make mistakes and therefore it is important for us to forgive people when they make mistakes. When we do that, we show how much above humanity a human being can rise, and therefore, we stand true to the Proverb: "To err is human, to forgive, divine," again, a statement first made by Shakespeare.

● LESSON 161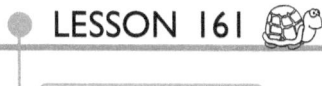

How are you?

Q: "How are you?"
A: *"I'm good."* This answer although accepted in spoken English, carries with it illogicality. The statement *"I am good"* implies incompletion. When we hear *"I am good"*, the question that immediately rises in our mind is: *"at what?"* If a person were to say, "I am good at History" then the statement would be deemed complete and acceptable. As an answer to 'How are you?', "I am good" shows an attitude of trying to ape without giving reason a second thought. The correct answer to "How are you?" is **"I'm fine" OR, any other equivalent.** Immediately after saying, "I'm fine", it is deemed polite and correct to reciprocate, "and you?" Language cannot be divorced from culture, and reciprocity involving courtesy and politeness is an integral aspect of spoken English. Many a time, deviant linguistic tendencies are sought to be excused by claiming overwhelming American influence. Although American English does have variations, extensive and damaging deviations cannot always become acceptable by default of being American. So

the next time you are asked in English, "How are you?" please reply correctly, "I'm fine, and you?"

LESSON 162

How do you do?

"How do you do?" as a form of greeting is decidedly more formal than "How are you?" However, the response to "How do you do?", believe it or not, is "How do you do?" There is confusion as to how the question and answer can be the same i.e. "How do you do?" Here, it is important for us to understand that when we ask "How do you do?" we are actually not waiting for an answer. "How do you do?" is only an expression used when introductions are made in a formal environment. This expression does not warrant a reply nor does it connect to the present circumstances of that person's life at whom this question is directed. Remember, the question/expression "How do you do?" is generally succeeded by the appendage Mr./Miss/Mrs./Ms. followed by the surname of the person being introduced. When friends, relatives, acquaintances, guests are introduced at parties, social gatherings etc., "How do you do?" isn't used. So, the next time you are being introduced in a formal setting, and asked, "How do you do?" do not commit the cardinal sin of replying *"I'm fine, thank you!"*

LESSON 163

Rain Cheque

"It isn't possible for me to come for the movie today, could I take a rain cheque?" What is a 'rain cheque'? How is it different from a cheque presented in a bank? A 'rain cheque' is a request communicating unavailability in the present. The expression 'rain cheque' may/may not involve postponement. It simply indicates your unavailability and/or request for repeating that particular event with the same person at a later point of time. It is also an expression used more in spoken rather than written English. While the history of this expression is lost in mystery, it is regularly used. We cannot keep commitments on a number of occasions. We therefore use this expression orally to communicate to the listener our earnest desire to fulfil a commitment later on a mutually convenient date. Incidentally, the American spelling of cheque as 'check' is now acceptable. However, 'check' should be used to denote this word as Verb. As Noun denoting a financial transaction, it is advisable to continue with the use of 'cheque'. The word 'check' also stands for a bill especially when eating out, e.g. "Waiter, could I have the check please?"

LESSON 164

'Back' and 'Ago'

"When I met her three months back, she was so chirpy; I wonder what has made her so sad." The word 'back', indicating passage of time, is terribly inappropriate. It has been so commonly used to denote movement of time that it becomes extremely difficult to convince someone habituated to its usage, that it is incorrect English. Let us see why. The word 'back' is used to indicate direction or the hind part of a human or an animal. It is also used as a Verb to indicate movement in reverse, e.g. "Don't back the car until you can clearly see what lies behind." As direction, it is clear that when we use it, we indicate movement towards the same position. e.g. "You're leaving home early today, when're you going to get back?" The correct word to indicate movement and passage of time irrespective of its length is 'ago'. "I don't know where the manager is right now, he was here a few minutes ago." "Hundreds of years ago, the dodo, a large bird was found in Mauritius."

LESSON 165

The use of 'yet'

"Our teacher hasn't come yet."
"I have explained to you this method so many times, yet you haven't understood it correctly."
 What is the difference in the meanings of the two sentences utilizing the same word 'yet'? In the first sentence, the word 'yet' is clearly an Adverb. In the second sentence the word 'yet' is a Conjunction, denoting 'even then' or 'in spite of that'. The placement of the word 'yet' if done at the end of a sentence clearly indicates it as an Adverb of time implying 'up to now'. Whenever we wish to show incompletion of an action or situation we place 'yet' at the end. When we use 'yet' in the middle of a sentence we indicate to the reader/listener that what was mentioned earlier did not happen in spite of certain actions having taken place. It clearly indicates that the result was not as expected, even though efforts to the contrary had been made. The word 'yet' at the end of a sentence indicates time i.e. up to now.

LESSON 166

'...to sell my land...along with my wife'

Although the following example is one showing a glaring error in written English, it is also spoken in a similar manner. An employee seeking leave wrote the following and also spoke it aloud to his boss: *"Since I have to go to my village to sell my land along with my wife, please sanction me one-week leave."* The placement of the phrase "along with my wife" being done incorrectly leads to laughter insinuating that he was going to sell his wife along with his land. It is obvious that whosoever this employee was, like millions of us, never gave serious thought to the correct framing of a sentence in English, written or spoken. Had the adverbial phrase 'along with my wife' been placed immediately after 'go', it would have communicated the correct meaning **"Since I have to go along with my wife to my village to sell my land, please sanction me a week's leave."** Once again, it becomes extremely important that we gauge and judge the correct meaning we wish to convey before we frame a sentence in English, spoken or written.

LESSON 167

'I want to shave my son's head...'

Looking at the following example, it becomes apparent that many of us don't understand how the participle form of the Verb in English is to be used. Now, imagine the following sentence to be spoken as well as written: *"As I want to shave my son's head, please leave me for two days."* This is obviously an application asking for leave to complete a Hindu religious ceremony of getting a male child's head tonsured. Here, the subject "I" gets confused with the action and conveys that it is "I" wishing to perform the said action. The grammar however, leads to a lot of humour and this kind of framing always brings about miscommunication. The correct sentence is, **"As I want to get my son's head shaved, please grant me two days' leave."** Examples of this kind lead us to clearly understand that many of us have to make great efforts to get the Subject and the Verb to agree correctly. Subject-Verb agreement in English is more important than a legal document. When the two happen to be in disagreement, humour is generated or the sentence becomes complete nonsense.

LESSON 168

'Having' a headache

"*As my headache is paining, please grant me leave for the day.*" The '...ing' form of the Verb, when used in the Present Continuous Tense in a proper manner, is able to convey the correct meaning.. Many a time however, we get to hear the incorrect use of the '.......ing' form of the Verb with 'having', e.g. "*Sheila, I won't be coming to work today, I'm having headache you know.*" The Verb 'having' in the Present Continuous Tense can only be used for eating, e.g. "Do not disturb us, we are having lunch." It is also possible to use 'having' in combination with a participle. Having said that, in the 'headache-paining' example, the person concerned does not know that 'headache' means 'a pain in the head' and consequently doesn't need elaboration. It is imperative that we know the correct meaning and are proficient enough to frame a sentence correctly before we speak or write. The two examples in their correct form, therefore, are:

'As I have a headache, please grant me a day's leave.'

'Sheila, I won't be coming to work today, I have a terrible headache.'

LESSON 169

'Male or Female...I am both...'

A candidate's job application: *"This has reference to your advertisement calling for a Typist and an Accountant – Male or Female ... As I am both for the past several years and I can handle both with good experience, I am applying for the post."* Once again, humour is generated by associating improper Nouns with the Verbs. The Subject of a sentence is a Noun or Pronoun. No other Part of Speech can become the Subject. The Subject-Verb Agreement herein is conveying something else. What is this person communicating through his statement in the letter? That he is both male and female or that he is both, a typist and accountant? It is obvious that he is referring to the combination in the second half, but the way the sentence has been framed it is referring to the first combination of male and female as its meaning. The corrected part of the sentence therefore should read:

"As I am both Typist and Accountant with the required experience of several years, I am applying for the post."

LESSON 170

'Declare' and 'Suffer'

The word 'declare' in the sentence *"I am suffering from fever, please declare one day holiday"* is more of an order than request, in spite of the word 'please' before it. In this request/order, it is apparent that the applicant wishes to take only a day's leave. The correct Verb here is 'grant' instead of 'declare' followed by 'a day's leave'. A declaration in English denotes an announcement or a grand gesture. It is only when an event on a huge scale takes place that it is declared or a declaration is made. It can also be an important written document such as "The American Declaration of Independence". Moving from 'declare' to 'suffering', it is important to understand that one doesn't 'suffer' from fever. A person may get/have/feel/develop fever but 'suffers' from a sickness or disease. It is a well known fact, medically speaking, that the fever a person may 'develop', is a symptom of a disease that may already be present in that person. Therefore the correct sentence requesting leave for a day is:

"I feel feverish, kindly grant me a day's leave."

LESSON 171

'I would be highly obliged...'

Many formal letters end with "I would be highly obliged if you ...." At times, we also get to hear sentences that use the word 'obliged', e.g. "My car has broken down, I would be highly obliged if you could lend me yours for the day." What does the word 'obliged' mean? "Obliged" denotes and involves gratitude. The use of 'obliged' indicates a request for the completion of an act of some kind. It also contains an implied promise that if the favour is extended, it will definitely be returned. Whenever we use 'obliged', it creates a kind of binding, making us responsible to ensure that the favour granted will, in the future, be reciprocated. In formal situations however, when this word is used, especially to draw attention to an act that was supposed to be performed by a government official but was not, then the binding is projected on to the official. e.g. "I would be highly obliged if prompt action in this matter is taken."

LESSON 172

'...like anything'

"*I love her like anything.*" What is this 'anything'? How does it convey the degree to which this man may be in love with this woman? Using the word 'anything' is a comparison that makes for neither logic nor sense. In addition to the example cited above, it is also used with many other activities, and two of them are: "*I was so hungry, I ate like anything*";

"*He was so good at dancing, he danced like anything.*" Whenever a person uses 'anything' comparatively, you can be rest assured that his knowledge of English is definitely poor and that he is only trying to pass off half-knowledge as wisdom. The words 'anything' 'something' and 'everything' are singular and have no connections with comparisons of any kind. Whenever you wish to compare objects or describe a rule, an act or a law or any other phenomenon, please do not use the word 'thing' by itself or in any of the three forms mentioned. Remember that when we use the word 'thing' comparatively, we are conveying to the reader/listener our lack of skills, especially Vocabulary.

LESSON 173

What's a 'Milch Cow'?

We have heard and read of cows giving milk. But, what is a 'milch cow'? The word 'milch' is erroneously pronounced as 'milk' by many of us. The letters 'ch' after 'mil' must be pronounced the same way as 'c' in 'Charlie'. What does 'milch cow' mean? First of all, the word 'milch' is an Adjective and simply put, means "a mammal's capacity to produce milk for human consumption." At times, it also indicates that the capacity of one particular animal yielding milk is much higher than others in its group. When taken together, the words 'milch + cow' form a phrase or an expression 'milch cow'. A milch cow is a cow that gives us much more milk than an ordinary cow does. The words 'milch' and 'cow' are also used together to indicate, colloquially speaking, an easy source of income for someone not used to working hard for money, e.g. "Interest from his wife's fixed deposits was his milch cow." It is used more as a negative rather than positive expression. Please note that the word 'milch' does not exist in American English.

● LESSON 174:

"D for Delhi', "B for Belly"

The previous Lesson saw the pronunciation of 'c' as 'Charlie' to correctly communicate the phonetic value of 'c'. When we want to spell the letters of a particular word on the telephone, it generally results in making use of incorrect phonetic symbols. Many a time we say, "D for Delhi" whereas the person on the other end might actually be hearing "B for belly". NATO Call-signs have been designed and developed so that there is no confusion whatsoever regarding the identity of the letter being spelt. Generally used telephonically, if we remember them otherwise too, we can definitely improve our knowledge of phonetics, i.e. the science of speech sounds. You must commit this internationally accepted code to memory for pronunciation of English words to improve. All the twenty-six letters of the English Alphabet are listed here for easy reference. You must use only that assigned specific word that represents a letter, as per the Code, when speaking English, especially on the phone: A-Alpha; B-Bravo; C-Charlie; D-Delta; E-Echo; F-Foxtrot; G-Golf; H-Hotel; I-India; J-Juliet; K-

Kilo; L-Lima; M-Mike; N-November; O-Oscar; P-Papa; Q-Quebec; R-Romeo; S-Sierra; T-Tango; U-Uniform; V-Victor; W-Whiskey; X-X-ray; Y-Yankee; Z-Zulu. Nowadays, with all words being available on computers and sophisticated mobile phones, correct spellings are at our fingertips. It is helpful to learn phonetic values through NATO call signs so that there are no mistakes when we speak English.

LESSON 175

Intonation and Stress

When a sentence, written with correct punctuation marks is proficiently read, it leads to the best meaning being conveyed to the reader. However, when spoken, it is Intonation with correct stress that conveys to the listener the speaker's intention. We cannot always speak complete sentences at a stretch and so, we pause at required points indicating that what we wish to convey. Look at the following sentences: (1) The headmaster says, "John is a fool." (2) "The headmaster", says John, "is a fool." Sentences (1) and (2) contain exactly the same number of words, but when the punctuation marks are differently positioned, the second sentence conveys exactly the opposite meaning. Since the sentences are written using correct punctuations, as aware readers we easily understand the Intonation of each. We also pause correctly at the commas. When spoken, these sentences, with correct pauses appropriately placed, convey the exact meaning we wish to convey, whether John or the headmaster is a fool. Speak these sentences without looking at them. Once you begin to practice speaking the two sentences with their opposite meanings using correct stress and Intonation patterns, your English becomes better.

LESSON 176

'Wonder' and 'Wander'

"I wander'd lonely as a cloud." This is the very first line of "Daffodils", a famous poem by Wordsworth. The word 'wander' indicates a sense of movement at random, without a specific purpose. When we wander we move aimlessly about or undertake to travel without a fixed or chosen destination in mind. Many new students of English are unable to distinguish between 'wander' and 'wonder'. Remember, 'wander' is a Verb whereas 'wonder' can be used both as Noun as well as Verb. 'Wonder' indicates puzzlement or even surprise as Noun, e.g. "He looked at the dog's action in wonder." As Verb, 'wonder' is also used to indicate politeness in requests, e.g. "I wonder/was wondering if I could use your desktop today as my laptop has broken down." The word 'wonder' also means 'to guess or speculate', e.g. "I wonder if India can beat Australia in the fourth Test too." To pronounce 'wander' correctly, think of a magic 'wand' and add 'er'. To correctly pronounce 'wonder' think of the past tense of 'win' i.e. 'won' and add 'der' The word 'wonder' rhymes with 'thunder'.

LESSON 177

'Too' and 'Very'

"That movie is too good." "That cake was too delicious". Both of these and many other descriptions involving 'too', are regularly and incorrectly used by us. In both the examples cited above, 'too' is a poor substitute to 'very'. We have heard of the expression, 'It is too good to be true'. The use of 'too' in the middle of a sentence invariably indicates something (generally negative) to follow. 'That hill is too high.' In this sentence the use of 'too' indicates that the hill's great height is going to make it difficult to be climbed. The sentence can be reframed as 'That hill is so high that I cannot climb it.' OR "That hill is too high for me to climb." Whenever you wish to praise, use 'very', because 'very' can be safely used as a positive as well as negative Adverb, but 'too' is only a negative Adverb. Always remember, the use of 'too' involves further explanation. "Too" is also used to describe some kind of addition at the end, e.g. "Are you going home early?" "Yes."

"I'm going early too."

"I love you" "I love you too!" Now, isn't s/he lucky?

LESSON 178

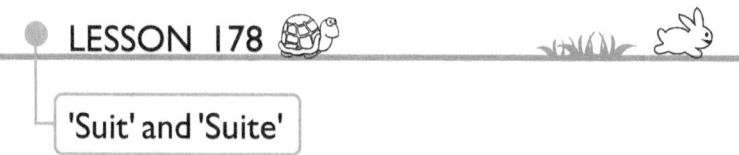

'Suit' and 'Suite'

When 'e' is added to the word 'suit' it becomes 'suite'. The pronunciation also changes. However, many people incorrectly pronounce 'suite' as '*suit*'. First, let us see the difference in their meaning. The word 'suit' is both Noun as well as Verb. As Noun, 'suit' means a set of clothes, especially the trousers, the shirt, and the blazer/coat that a man wears. A matching tie is the complement in suits for men. In India, women also wear a set of clothes known together as a 'Punjabi suit'. As Verb, 'suit' also stands for something that is appropriate/matching, e.g. "The lady's purse did not suit her personality."

"I think these seat-covers will suit my car's interiors." When 'suit' becomes 'suite', it can only be used as Noun and must be pronounced like 'sweet' is pronounced. 'Suite' stands for a special room with a view or a set of special rooms or a whole floor mostly at the top, generally of a hotel. It is also that hotel's most expensive accommodation. The next time you wish to indulge in luxury and wish to splurge, do book a suite but please pronounce it correctly as 'sweet'.

LESSON 179

Where do we eat?

Q: "Where did you eat last night when you went out to dine?

A: *We went to Hotel XYZ for dinner.*"

The word 'hotel' is mistakenly used for eating out by many of us in India. A hotel is a place where we stay, generally for a day or more. Although many hotels have restaurants attached and quite a few provide their guests with room service, when we eat out, we do not eat at a hotel. Even if we eat at/in a restaurant that is attached to a hotel, it is the restaurant and not the hotel that becomes the venue where we eat. The correct word to be used to describe a place generally where we eat a complete meal is 'restaurant'. Although the word 'restaurant' has been in vogue for a fairly long time, there are a number of names which can be used to describe a place where we eat. These names have their own importance in various areas and those connected with regular eating habits therein immediately associate themselves with that place. The following are a few names of such places: bistro, café, cafeteria, canteen, mess, kiosk, stall, eatery, etc.

LESSON 180

Rather...

"Would you like to read the book?" "No, I'd rather go for the movie." Over here, the word 'rather' is implying that the speaker is of the opinion that the movie of the same title will definitely be more appealing than the book was. The word 'rather' suggests opting for an alternative. It is also a word that immediately denotes comparison. The use of 'rather' is possible both in positive as well as negative situations. The correct Adverb showing only positivity is 'fairly', e.g.

"I thought he wasn't a bright child, but he has done his homework fairly well."

"The party was expected to be boring, but we found it fairly exciting."

The word 'rather' can be used with 'too' but 'fairly' cannot be used with 'too', e.g. 'The unlimited dinner advertised by the restaurant was rather too limited." The use of 'rather' can also indicate that the reader/speaker wishes to describe something that happened as 'more truly', e.g. "He never has problems with money for his father is rich or rather his father-in-law is richer."

LESSON 181

'Brake' and 'Break'

On the back of many cars/buses/trucks is written *"Power-Break"*. The owner never bothers to spell it correctly as "Power-Brake". Both 'brake' and 'break' are pronounced the same but definitely differ in meaning. 'Brake' is generally used as Noun to describe a contraption/device that slows/stops a moving vehicle. A set of clamps/pads moves out and grips the rotating wheel to slow/stop it. These clamps/pads with the brake-pedal/handle and a connecting system together, form the 'brake/s' of a vehicle. 'Break' generally is used as Verb to denote the division of an object into two or more pieces. It can also, as Noun, mean an interruption, e.g. "She has returned to her office after a long break." The word 'break' is also used in combination with 'down' to indicate fault/damage in/to a vehicle, e.g. "On the way, our car suffered a breakdown." 'Power-brake' indicates that this vehicle is fitted with very powerful brakes and the driver of the vehicle behind must ensure his/her safety by maintaining double the required distance in case of a sudden slowing down/stoppage.

LESSON 182

'Wind', 'Rewind'...'Rewinded'?

Some years ago, video cassette recorders were in vogue. Subscribers of video cassette libraries were usually asked whether they had 'rewinded' the cassette being returned after having watched the movie. The word 'rewinded' does not exist. To 'rewind' means 'to wind again or in the opposite direction' and indicates the present/future tense only. To 'wind' means to roll a thread or any kind of material over a round surface. 'Wind' used as Verb is pronounced to rhyme with 'find/kind'. The past tense of 'rewind' is 'rewound'. As Verb, 'wound' is pronounced to rhyme with 'found/round'. 'The word 'wound', as Verb, is differently and distinctly pronounced from 'wound' as Noun and, as Noun, 'wound' indicates injury, e.g. "The wound was bleeding badly." In English, when we need to describe air in motion we use the word 'wind'. As noun, 'wind' is pronounced with a short 'i' sound. It is used in many ways and also in expressions carrying different meanings, e.g. 'gone with the wind'; 'going against the wind' etc. Whenever 'wind' is used as Noun, a preposition or an article precedes it, e.g. the famous lyrics by Bob Dylan - "And the answer is blowing in the wind."

LESSON 183

Something fishy...

Did you know the plural of 'fish' is 'fish'? The word 'fish' has an important place in English. When something doesn't appear to be in order or there are grounds of suspicion, we say, "There is something fishy going on here" i.e. an unacceptable/illegal/anti-social activity is going on. When we wish to describe a phenomenon, person or activity not fitting into a stereotyped image, we say, 'a different kettle of fish', e.g. "XYZ, although a college student, doesn't use social networking sites, he's a different kettle of fish."
"To fish in troubled waters" means to invite trouble or take a great risk while trying to gain something or trying to secure an advantage. How many times have you been in a situation wherein you find someone trying to attract attention to a piece of clothing, watch, car, etc? When somebody tries to attract praise in this manner, we say, "S/he is fishing for compliments."

LESSON 184

'Bath' and 'Bathe'

A question asked in many classrooms where English is taught, is, "Which one of the two is correct, 'I have a bath every day' or 'I take a bath every day?'" Although both are acceptable, 'take a bath' is sometimes also used as an idiom to suggest some kind of cheating. e.g. "The customers of that bank are taking a bath for the directors have fled with their money." Other than 'have' or 'take' with the act of 'bathing', many new students of English have little idea of the Verb form of the noun 'bath'. The Verb form of the word 'bath' is 'bathe' – and it should be pronounced to rhyme with 'lathe' as in a lathe machine. When we use 'bathe' in the following sentence, it clearly indicates regular action using the verb in the Present Simple Tense, e.g. "I always bathe before praying." The Past Tense form is 'bathed', e.g. "The sunset was bewitching as I watched the sun being bathed by the sea." The word 'bath' is a Noun and cannot be used as Verb.

LESSON 185

Lakhs, Crores and Millions

On crossing 99,999 i.e. ninety-nine thousand nine hundred and ninety-nine in ascending order, we Indians call 1,00,000 a 'lakh'. Those who use English internationally know that this amount is written in figures as 100,000 and spoken and read as 'one hundred thousand'. For Indians, 'one hundred lakhs' is spoken/written as 'one crore'. The numerical equivalent of 1,00,00,000 i.e. one crore is 'ten million' in English and it is written in figures as 10,000,000. 'One million' is generally assumed by Indians to be equivalent to one crore or more but actually stands for what we know as 'ten lakhs' i.e. 10,00,000. In English one million is written in figures as 1000,000. Remember, there are six zeroes in one million and seven zeroes in what we Indians call one crore. Millions of Indians today have more than one million rupees each and a good number have more than ten million each too. However, for each and every Indian to have a hundred thousand in his/her account is going to take a long time. For crores of Indians, to have a bank balance of one crore is a pipedream even today. Remember, 'lakh' and 'crore' are not original English words and do not figure in any English-English dictionary.

LESSON 186

'Mutual' and 'Unanimous'

In a popular Hindi comedy TV serial's recent episode, the lady judge made a remark that 'it is unanimous between us.' The word 'unanimous' being misplaced, should have correctly been, 'mutual' for there were only two judges. The word 'mutual' indicates that generally two persons share the same opinions, likings, interests etc. The use of 'unanimous' immediately and definitely indicates the involvement of more than two persons in an act/thinking/decision-making process etc. and that too, without opposition of any kind. 'Mutual' and 'unanimous' indicate commonality of interest in activities mentioned, but where 'mutual' is concerned, sharing of interest is limited to two individuals. "Unanimous" has more to do with selection/election processes favouring someone whereas 'mutual' should be used more to describe interests etc. Many people say, *"You and I have a mutual friend."* A friend, being a person, cannot be mutual. Only an opinion, thinking, liking, interest, choice, etc. can be. The correct adjective therefore describing the third friend would be, 'common', . e.g. "He is a common friend of ours" or "You and I have a common friend."

LESSON 187

'Reality' and 'Realty'

On many occasions, you must have come across the word 'realty' and then thought that it was an incorrect spelling of 'reality'. Had you looked closely enough, you would have seen that 'realty' was a word connected in some way with property or as is also called 'real estate'. A property dealer, whether buying or selling property, or, when operating as a commission agent, is involved with 'realty'. S/he may also be described as a 'realtor'. When it comes to actual situations and circumstances, then we use the word, 'reality'. The opposite of 'real' is 'fake' or 'unreal'. 'False' is the opposite of 'true'. The opposite of 'truth' is 'lie'. There could however be situations when you find overlapping of fake, false, lie, untruth, falsehood etc. On reading good fiction, we perceive certain characters, their actions and situations to be real. We feel as if they actually exist or existed. This treatment of characters and situations in literature is known as 'realism'. Realism in fiction indicates the story and the characters are closer to reality.

LESSON 188

'Hawker' and 'Vendor'

"Many hawkers promised permanent stalls by the Municipality." - A news item common all over India - local authorities promising permanence to 'hawkers'. The moment a hawker sells from only one particular place he ceases to be a 'hawker'. 'To hawk' earlier meant selling goods using a vehicle or going on foot from house to house.. A 'hawker' found it extremely convenient to stock and display goods on a vehicle viz. a handcart. Mobility made it easy for the hawker to go to the customer. The word 'hawker', when used to describe a trader, diminishes the trader's status. Nowadays, 'vendor' is used. A 'hawker' may also be described as a 'street-vendor'. The word 'vendor' in today's techno-savvy world, has more than one meaning. 'Vendor' denotes a person who sells from any kind of premises - kiosk, stall, handcart, shop, factory, manufacturing unit, etc. When factories, manufacturers etc. need supplies as raw material, they then shortlist and buy from particular 'vendors'. We also have 'vending-machines' that vend goods/items such as tea/coffee/soft drinks etc. when the required amount, especially in coins, is inserted into them.

LESSON 189

'Buy' and 'Purchase'

When do we 'buy' and when do we 'purchase'? There is very little difference between the two as Verbs. Both involve the handing over of money so as to acquire ownership over some kinds of goods or getting services rendered. The word 'buy' is generally used to denote transactions which grant you ownership on handing over money, when the items/goods/services are not of a very high value. The word 'purchase' is generally used when the transaction involves substantial amounts of money. We generally 'purchase' cars, land, flats, jewellery, etc and 'buy' vegetables, daily provisions, stationery, etc. Interchange of the two Verbs however is possible. The word 'buy' cannot be used as Noun whereas 'purchase' can be, e.g. a 'Purchase Manager' is a person hired to buy goods/services etc. for his company/concern at the most reasonable price in the shortest period possible. The word 'purchase', as Noun, is sometimes also used to describe the act of getting a grip. e.g. "He saw the mountain goat get purchase in the smallest of crevices on the crags of the most dangerous of slopes at that stupendous height."

LESSON 190

'Still' – as five Parts of Speech

(1) "Still waters run deep." (2) "Are you still there?" (3) "Due to the irritating noise when rotating, I had to still the fan's blades." (4) "We knew it wasn't easy, still we persisted." (5) "The water-still in our laboratory isn't working." In sentence (1), 'still' means 'not moving' and is an Adjective. This is also a famous proverb. Sentence (2) uses 'still' as Adverb indicating time. 'Still' in (3) is a Verb whereas sentence (4) denotes 'still' as Conjunction. Sentence (5) shows 'still' as Noun denoting a distillation apparatus in a laboratory. Of the eight Parts of Speech, the word 'still' can be used as five. As you can see, the denoting of 'still' as one Part of Speech in one sentence, changes as per the role and function it is supposed to perform in another. It is important for us to first decide what we want to say and then accordingly, frame sentences. When we are able to appropriately put our thoughts across, then our grasp over English improves. Otherwise we continue to speak broken English.

LESSON 191

Short(s)

"On Sundays he lounges around the house, in Bermuda short and T-shirt." The error is in the word 'short'. The word 'short' is used to describe a situation in which, the object required, e.g. a rope/thread/wire etc., does not have the required length. It can also be used to describe the height of a person, "He isn't as short as his brother, he's tall/er." It can also be used to describe lack of any kind of phenomenon e.g. "Governments always grumble of being short of funds." "He ran short of breath" is used when we describe the after-effects of running or any other strenuous physical activity. As you can see with these two examples, in such situations, 'short' is followed by 'of' and 'of' is followed by a Noun. "I could see the dog pant with his tongue hanging out." Remember, 'pant' is a verb and cannot be used to describe an article of clothing. "On coming back home after a jog he pants like a dog." In this sentence, 'pants' is clearly and correctly used as Verb. The word 'pant' cannot be used as Noun and the correct form is 'a pair of pants' OR 'His pants were too tight.' To remember these articles of clothing keep in mind, "Half-pants are also called shorts and Bermuda shorts reach just above the knee."

LESSON 192

Sentences ending with a verb – Indirect Speech

Direct Speech: He said to me, "Where is the airport?" Indirect (Reported) Speech: *"He asked me where is the airport."* - A typical error - misplacing the Verb in the second half of the sentence when converting Direct into Indirect Speech. A Complex sentence using the Indirect Speech contains two finite Verbs, with the first part consisting of a Verb describing the speaker's speech's action. No sooner does the first Verb get placed, than the speaker/writer must remember/practice to put the Verb denoting the second action at the end of the sentence. E.g. **"He asked me where the airport is."** Here, the second Verb doesn't change into the Past Tense for the airport continues to be at/in the same location. By writing, serious students/new learners can easily avoid mistakes. Make your own sentences and write them. If in doubt, get them corrected. Read them out loud. Then speak them without looking at them. By doing this, you will be on your way to becoming an able speaker of good (correct) English. Trying to learn to speak

English well without making/writing your own sentences is a blunder.

LESSON 193

Sentences ending with a verb – Direct Speech

It is not only in the Indirect Speech that we put the second Verb at the end of the sentence. This can also happen with Direct Speech. News Channels feature ministers and other political figures debating in English. Most of them speak incorrect English, e.g. *"I don't know what is eyewash."* These are actually two sentences and both have been incorrectly combined. These sentences are: (1) "I don't know" and (2) "What is eyewash?" Combination of (1) & (2) should be, **"I don't know what eyewash is."** Flexibility in English makes it extremely convenient to go on creating variations. We then assume these variations to be correct English. Incidentally, the minister's claim of not knowing the meaning of eyewash, is eyewash. In questions, the Verb must begin the (Interrogative) sentence: "Are you coming tomorrow?" However, what you get to hear on innumerable occasions is only a transliteration: *"You are coming tomorrow?"* When you get a 'Wh' question, then the 'Wh', without exception, begins the (Interrogative) Sentence. These are: What, When, Where, Which, Why, Who. Whose. The word 'how' does not begin with 'w' nonetheless it is considered a 'wh' question.

LESSON 194

> Sentences beginning with a verb – only when Imperative

"Flourish your business with us." "Grow your business with our schemes." "Glitter the world with our jewellery." What is wrong with these advertisement slogans/ sentences? These sentences begin with the Verb. Consequently, they communicate confusion. A business cannot flourish as an entity by itself but a business can be made to flourish. A human being can flourish. Similarly, a business cannot grow as or by itself. Where jewellery is concerned, it can make the world glitter. With the third example, you must have understood this error better. When we need to describe the Subject, the Verb needs a definite form, e.g. "Make your business flourish with our help."

"Make your business grow with the help of our schemes" and finally,

"Make your world glitter with jewelry from us."

We should begin a sentence with its Verb only when it is Imperative i.e. when it is a command. If it is done in any other case, it can be confusing. The safest method of framing a sentence correctly is to place the Noun/Pronoun (Subject) in the beginning and then make the Verb follow, e.g. "You can make your business flourish with our help."

This will help in always adhering to the rule of the Subject being a Noun/Pronoun, further making the Subject and the Verb agree.

LESSON 195

'Having' – the Indian version

The rampant misuse of 'having' by us Indians must be brought to your notice once more. Incorrect use of 'having' jars on one's nerves, especially, when those who claim to know English repeatedly use it. *"You must be having our teacher's number"* is a cardinal sin and should be **"I think you have our teacher's number."** 'Having' is the Continuous Tense form of the Verb 'have' and cannot be used to denote possession. 'Having' is generally used to communicate a single action going on now in the Present Continuous (Progressive) Tense - e.g. "Let's not disturb her, she is having lunch" - and can also be used in the Past Continuous Tense form, e.g. "We had to wait a long time for they were having dinner." When 'having' is followed by the Participle form of a Verb, it becomes the Present Perfect Tense e.g. "Having said that, I would like to conclude…." We regularly also get to hear sentences such as *"I'm having a stomachache"* Now, you cannot eat a stomachache, can you? Instead, your stomach aches because of something you have eaten. So, "I have a stomachache."

LESSON 196

'Determine' – (Mis)Pronunciation

Due to its spelling, the word 'determine' is incorrectly pronounced 'de-ter-m(y)ne' by many of us. As the word 'mine' happens to be the third syllable, we wrongly assume the pronunciation of the third syllable to rhyme with 'fine'. The word 'determine' has the syllable 'mine' (with 'e' silent) pronounced to rhyme with 'pin'. The word 'determine' is a Verb and it means 'to make/take a firm decision. It also means to observe carefully or to find out, e.g. "We must determine how people in The Middle Ages calculated time as they had neither watches nor calendars." The Noun form of 'determine' is 'determination', e.g. "I was happy to note the weak student's determination to work harder for the next examination." As Adjective, the word 'determined' communicates someone/something possessing a strong will or resolute desire, e.g. "The determined look on his face made it clear that he was going to succeed." Remember, in 'determine', the last syllable 'mine' is pronounced 'min' i.e. the same as the pronunciation of the first three letters in 'minimum'.

LESSON 197

The multi-faceted 'Ego'

"Her ego was hurt when you hinted that her essay had been written by someone else."
We hear of somebody's 'ego' almost every day. Does it mean 'pride' or is it something else? 'Ego', as we know it, was first brought to our notice and later exploited successfully by the psychoanalyst Sigmund Freud. While 'ego' gets connected to the "I", it does not necessarily mean pride but has a stronger connection with 'self-worth'. What you think of yourself is your 'ego'. However, due to our actions and words, it gets erroneously assumed to be 'pride'. When 'ego' expands, a person becomes either an 'egoist' or 'egotist'. 'Ego' is an Abstract Noun while the other two are Common Nouns. There is however a difference in the meaning of 'egoist' as compared to 'egotist'. While both involve arrogance, an 'egotist' is a person who is only boastful. S/he may not be selfish or perpetually self-centered. An egoist however is a person whose world revolves round his/her 'self', with no room for consideration of any kind towards others.

LESSON 198

'Stationary' and 'Stationery'

In so many Lessons, we have seen that the addition or removal of a single letter can change the meaning of a word. It can also lead to difference in pronunciation. With its colossal Vocabulary, English has a tendency to be contextual i.e. the word has to be looked at in relation to the context in which it is being used rather than its dictionary meaning. Apart from the context, it is also the semantic value that is important i.e. what is the meaning that the writer/speaker wishes to convey and what is the meaning that the reader/listener is gathering? Let us take stationary/stationery as examples. 'Stationary' is an Adjective and means 'not moving/at a standstill'. The word 'stationery' is Noun meaning 'item/s referring to writing material/s, e.g. pens, pencils, erasers, etc.' When spoken, both words are pronounced the same, but when we write them, we must ensure the correct spelling to convey what we want. e.g. "The bus was stationary for more than an hour."
"Our office spent a huge amount of money buying new stationery last month."

LESSON 199

'Insure', 'Ensure', 'Assure' and 'Reassure'

Every day, on your phone (mobile or landline) you are inundated (flooded) with calls especially from Insurance companies. Looking at the word 'insure', do you know what it means? The word 'insure' means 'to make an arrangement to guarantee payment of a sum of money in the event of loss or injury'. So as to make sure that you get payment in such a situation, you have to first make a payment of a premium. The lumpsum guaranteed by the company will depend on the premium that you regularly pay. The word 'insure' is a Verb and its Noun is 'insurance.' The word 'ensure' is a Verb and has no Noun. To 'ensure' is 'to make sure'. To 'assure' is also 'to make sure' but 'assure' has an added advantage of bolstering confidence, e.g. "His friend, a regular latecomer, assured he would be on time for the excursion." To 'reassure' is to 'assure again' but with double the amount of certainty and confidence, e.g. "The doctor reassured her that her son had no serious injury." The word 'ensure' does not exist in American English.

LESSON 200

Mother Tongue Influence – Just an Excuse

Dr. S. Radhakrishnan, the second President of India, was officially touring in England. His impeccable command over English was so impressive that a British dignitary asked, "How is it you, being Indian, speak English so well?" Dr. Radhakrishnan replied, "That is so because it is not my mother tongue, and I have to work twice as hard as you to be able to speak it." Dr. Radhakrishnan had got it right. He had known from his student days that unnecessary transliteration from his mother tongue into English will weaken his grasp over English. The study of MTI (Mother Tongue Influence) over English is sheer waste of time and energy. Students who learn French, German, Japanese, Spanish, etc. never use MTI as an excuse. *MTI over English* is generally used as a cover-up and justification for ineptitude and the inability to grasp English grammar. Learning English isn't enough. Regular practice is a must. One must be prepared to face, accept, study and continuously practice rules and their exceptions in English grammar. English isn't easy. Without perseverance, computers and language laboratories won't lead to proficiency. The only equipment essential to learning English well is sustained passion and unwavering diligence.

LESSON 201

'Husband' – the noun, the Verb

Do you know that the word **'husband'** is also a Verb? We know what **'husband'** as Noun stands for, but what does it mean when used as Verb? When one **husbands** one's resources, one is actually gathering one's strength and all that is available towards a specific purpose leading to the man becoming a good provider. The word **'husband'** comes from the noun **'husbandry'**. The word **'husbandry'** means an occupation connected with farming or agriculture. Until the Industrial Revolution, farming was the main occupation all over the world. In a similar vein, the word **'wife'** can also be used as Verb but its use as Verb is archaic (very old-fashioned and no more in use.) The word **'housewife'** came into existence when **'wife'** got connected to the word **'house'** to indicate a married woman's occupation **within a household.** Nowadays, **'home-maker'** is used instead of 'housewife' to give respect to married women working at home. We know that for a woman to work efficiently at her household chores is not an easy task, don't we? A wag, when asked to define 'wife' said, "Worries Invited For Ever".

LESSON 202

Utterances – 'Say'

Many of us are confused as to the difference between **'say'** and **'speak'**; **'tell'** and **'talk'**. We will take a look at the meaning of each and then their finer differences. All these words are related to utterances of some kind. However, there is a difference in the way they are to be used. Let us take the word 'say'. The word **'say'**, or **'said'** in its Past Tense form, cannot be used without the preposition **'to'**, e.g. "I said to him that he was welcome." The word 'say' can also be used as a Noun, e.g. "He has no **say** in important family matters." Here, the word **'say'** clearly indicates that this person has lost the status or was never considered worthy of it in his family or friends' circle. "You **can say** that again" is an idiomatic expression which means that what you have said is absolutely correct and fits the situation in a most appropriate manner. "What do you **have to say** regarding this?" is a question demanding an explanation for some kind of behaviour that wasn't proper or acceptable.

LESSON 203

Utterances – 'Speak'

When we **speak** something, how is it different from **'saying'** it? Both are correct when we describe some kind of vocal interaction. However, with **'speak'** it is important to note that when we use it in the Past Tense i.e. **'spoke'** or in the Participle form **'spoken'**, the preposition **'with'** and not **'to'** must be used, e.g. "Did you **speak with** her for a long time on the phone?"

"I have **spoken with** your teacher regarding your sickness".

The preposition **'to'** should be used with **'speak'** in the Present Tense form only. e.g. "I wish to **speak to** the Director regarding an urgent matter."

As we have understood by now, rules in English grammar are full of exceptions and we get carried away by our own variations. However, once we get acquainted with a certain format, we should try to follow that format so as to avoid making mistakes. The word **'speech'** is the Noun form of **'speak'** and as we know, **'speak'** is a more formal word than **'say'**.

Whenever formal social interaction in English takes place, **'speak'** is a better word to use than **'say'**.

● LESSON 204

Utterances – 'Tell/Told'

The word **'tell'** or its Past Tense form 'told' does not need any preposition and can be directly followed by the Noun/Pronoun, e.g. "I must **tell** you a secret." "She **told** him she was very angry on being followed." The use of the word **'tell'** generally implies some kind of narration - "Grandfather, please **tell** us the story of the hare and the tortoise." In this context, the words **'say'** or **'speak'** cannot be used. Remember that when asked to state what happened, or narrate what took place, you have to reply to the statement: "**Tell** me/us what happened." In legal situations too, the word **tell** is always used, e.g. "Please **tell** the police/court exactly what happened." Please note many of us use **'telling'** as Verb which renders a sentence incorrect. The word **'telling'** is an Adjective. e.g. "The rains had a **telling effect** on the crops." Many students when asked to speak on an issue begin with "*I am telling about higher education.*" This is incorrect and should be
"I am going to speak on higher education."

● LESSON 205

Utterances – 'Talk'

Of the four, **'talk'** is the one that is the most commonly and correctly used as Noun. Where the word **'talk'** is concerned, it has more of an informal air about it, e.g. "The Manager will soon give **a talk** on Punctuality." Over here, it is evident that it is not going to be a formal speech but a small or informal exchange of ideas regarding punctuality. "Do you have time? I wish **to talk with** you." With the Verb **'talk'** in an informal situation, we use the preposition **'with'** and when involved in a formal situation, we use the preposition 'to'. e.g. "I wanted **to talk to** the Deputy Director regarding my promotion." When on the telephone, and asking for someone formally, it is better to use **'talk to'**. e.g. "Could I please **'talk to'** the Assistant Manager?" When **'talk'** is used with **'to'**, it indicates a very short conversation. The word **'talk'** is also used idiomatically to convey different expressions, e.g. "I hate it when people **talk shop** at parties." This means that there are people who don't stop talking about their work even at parties where they're supposed to enjoy themselves.

● **LESSON 206**

'Drawing' the Curtains

Whenever we enter a room with more sunlight than necessary or when privacy is required, or for any other reason, we generally say, "*Close the curtains!*" With **curtains**, however, when they are open, the correct expression is, "**Could you please draw the curtains?**" When the curtains are in an open position, then we use the verb **'draw'** to request for them to be closed. However, when the curtains are drawn and we need more light, ventilation, or for any other reason, we can say, "**Please open the curtains!**" It is has been seen that we rarely have a situation in which only one curtain is used, and the word 'curtain' is more often than not, used in the plural as **'curtains'**. The word **'curtain'** in its singular form is used to describe a stage performance when a **curtain** is generally raised or lowered. The same word is also used idiomatically for effect, e.g."**You cannot hide the truth anymore, the curtain has been raised.**" Here, it is obvious that the liar has been caught. **"Poor man, now its curtains for him!"** Here, it is clear that the end for this individual is near, either death or imprisonment.

LESSON 207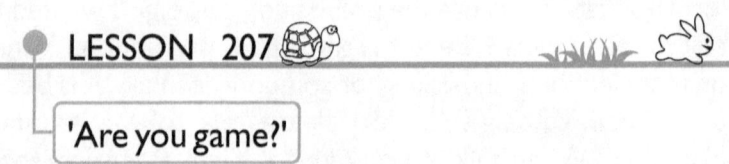

'Are you game?'

"I **was game** to change **the game.**" A famous Hindi film actress, describing the steps she took so as to become successful, made this statement recently on a TV channel, and it conveys the correct meaning. Play on the word **'game'** in this sentence is interesting. When used for the first time, the word 'game' is used adjectivally and as the last word in the sentence, it becomes a Noun. We know what **'game'** as Noun means, but what does it mean when used as adjective? **'To be game'** means that one is willing to play out the given set of circumstances arising due to changes in one's life. It can also mean that with the changes, one has adopted an adaptive approach and is willing to accept consequences. The word **'gaming'** as Verb has also now become popular with the huge amount of computer games. Nonetheless, if entertainment is the be-all and end-all of your existence, it's time to **change the game.** From our present lackadaisical approach to English, we have to become definitely earnest and serious. **Now, are you game?**

How Not to Speak English

LESSON 208

'Improve' and 'Improvise'

At times, you must have heard the word 'improvise' and misunderstood it as 'improve'. What is the difference? There is a vast difference in the two. Let us first take the Verb 'improve'. When we 'improve', then we make an existing situation, thing, phenomenon etc better than what it was.. We can also **improve 'upon'** something i.e. add a feature or any other factor that would lead to its betterment. When we 'improvise', we are generally concerned with a performance and 'improvising' means the act of speaking out or singing lines that were not part of a rehearsed speech or lyrics or script. This is also known as doing something **extempore**. The word 'extempore' is pronounced **ex-te('m' silent)-p-ree**. The Noun form of 'improve' is 'improvement' and the Noun form of 'improvise' is 'improvisation'. As far as 'extempore' is concerned, there is no Noun form of this Adjective. The word 'extempore' is used only as an adjective, e.g. '**The extempore performance was much better than the rehearsed one.**' Keep all these points in mind and go on **improving** as well as improving upon your English. Whenever improvement is undertaken, it is 'upon' something that is considered to be of not a high standard as required. With 'improve', other prepositions such as 'in', and 'at' are also acceptable, but 'upon' is ideal.

LESSON 209

To answer *your all questions...*

"I can answer your all questions." On a number of occasions, you will hear people speaking English like this. What is the mistake here? It is in the incorrect arrangement of the determiners before the Noun. The correct sentence is, **"I can answer all your questions."** The **Possessive Pronoun must come before the Noun.** This error is most often committed when 'all' 'some' 'many' 'few' 'a few' etc. are to be used with particular Nouns. In our hurry to complete the sentence, there is a tendency to interchange these words. *"Have you understood these all theorems?"* Once again, over here, the determiners have been misplaced and the question should be **"Have you understood all these theorems?"** In another typical error, many students say, especially during exam time, *"My all doubts have been cleared."* Here, once again, the correct sentence should be: "All my doubts have been cleared." Remember: **Quantity must come before the Possessive Pronoun/Demonstrative Adjective, e.g.**

"He loved her so much that he couldn't see any of her faults." The term 'determiner' is used for a word that determines the word following it to be a Noun.

LESSON 210

'Overlooking' and 'overseeing'

"The government is *overlooking* this issue." While this sentence is grammatically correct, its context must be understood or it can convey a meaning exactly the opposite of what it was supposed to convey. Recently, a government official on a television channel was conveying exactly the opposite meaning of what she wanted this sentence to mean. She had wanted to support the government but because of her poor knowledge of English, ended up criticizing it. She had mistakenly used **'overlooking'** instead of saying **'overseeing'**. When we are in the process of supervising an activity to ensure it being correctly done, then we 'oversee' it. However, when something escapes our attention or when we deliberately wish to ignore or neglect certain wrongdoings, then we **'overlook'** something. The use of 'look' instead of **'see'** with the prefix **'over'** changes the meaning from one of close scrutiny to one of neglect and deliberate ignorance. The Verb **'look'** in English has a different meaning from the Verb **'see'**. Whenever we are involved in any kind of activity using sight or vision, we must be careful and choose the Verb correctly, whether we wish to use **'look'** or **'see'**. There is a difference between **'looking at'** and **'seeing'** something. We shall understand more differences between **'look'** and **'see'** in our next Lesson.

LESSON 211

'Look at', 'look into', 'look down upon', 'look up to', 'look up'

The previous Lesson ended with 'look at' and 'see'. The Verb 'look' cannot be used singly unless it is a command. Even as command, 'look' implies the use of a preposition with it, e.g. "Look! The cat is chasing a mouse." Here, the speaker wants the listener to look at the action. With different prepositions, 'look' takes on different meanings. "To look into" – means to investigate or find out, e.g. "There was a robbery in the neighbourhood last night and the police are looking into it." "To look down upon" means to be scornful of someone you think is below your economic/social level, e.g.
"In the ancient era, Brahmins looked down upon the Shudras."
"To look up to" means to hold someone in high esteem/regard, e.g. "The workers of every political party look up to their leader." When we wish to find out the meaning of a word, we look it up in a dictionary, e.g.
"Look up the dictionary if you don't know the meaning of this word."

LESSON 212

You see...

The Verb **'see'** does not need a preposition and is used directly with the **Noun/Pronoun**, e.g. "I saw the sunset turn the sky from blue to orange-red."

"I **saw** him going into the bank." The verb **'see'** is also used in many situations to convey an observation, e.g. "I **see** your score has improved this year." As Participle, **'see'** becomes **'seen'** because it is an **Irregular Verb** and must be used as **'seen'** with **'has/have'** (Present Participle) or **'had'** (Past Participle)'. e.g. "It **has been seen** that men also take as long a coffee break as women do."

"When he left the office, he **had seen** her hard at work at her desk."

A famous saying goes, "Justice must not only be done but also **be seen** to have been done." The Verb **'see'**, in its various forms, is generally used with the physical act of using one's eyes whereas **'look'** has more to it than just the simple action of utilizing one's visual faculty. The Noun form of **'see'** is **'sight'** and very often we say, "His/her **eyesight** isn't very good, s/he needs glasses."

LESSON 213

Sixth Sense

Sight, smell, hearing, taste and touch – These are the five senses that we possess. There is however what is also known as the **'sixth sense'**. What is this **sixth sense**? The **sixth sense**, in simple words, is non-physiological. When we imagine that an

How Not to Speak English

event is about to occur and it occurs as how we had imagined it would happen, it is known as '**premonition**'. Sometimes it can also be described as '**hunch**'. The word '**guess**' is very ordinary and cannot be synonymous with '**hunch**' or '**premonition**'. Women are supposed to have a very strong **sixth sense** as compared to men. When events occur as people had imagined they would, we get to hear people saying, "I sold the shares of this company for I had a **hunch** their price would fall." "She had a **premonition** and her aunt luckily did not travel on the bus that met with an accident."

The **sixth sense** is psychological but cannot be related to **superstition**. Acts involving **superstitions** are regular, but a '**hunch**' or '**premonition**' involves acts that occur once in a while.

LESSON 214

'Superstitions', 'Omens' and 'Amulets'

Superstitions can be described as beliefs or feelings that are connected with fears, ideas and customs. These get associated with events when they occur or do not as per our beliefs. **Superstitious** beliefs need not necessarily be negative. Many a **superstitious** belief is connected with positive aspects of life. An act leading to a belief is known as an **omen**. The adjective form of '**omen**' is '**ominous**'. The word 'ominous' is generally used to signify a negative event, e.g. "The crushing of the black doll on the footpath proved to be **ominous**."

'**Omen**' is generally used to signify any kind of a phenomenon, e.g.

"The dog's return after so many days was a good **omen** as its owner began to prosper after that."

Many persons wear a charm round their arm/neck to ward off the evil eye. This kind of charm is known as '**amulet**'. Sometimes, we use a specific object, supposedly containing magical powers, and wear it round our neck. This is known as a 'talisman'. Many people wear a talisman round the upper right arm just below shoulder level.

LESSON 215

The power of a rational mind

The most sophisticated Supercomputer cannot match the complexity of the human mind. When **obsessed** with an idea or a thought, the human mind can take one to the pinnacle of success or towards destruction. When a **superstition** gets a foothold in our mind, it becomes an obsession. An **obsession** can lead to a **phobia** i.e. an **irrational fear** that something dreadful or undesirable is going to happen. One must develop the ability **to reason** or **rationalize**. One day, Emperor Akbar ordered a beggar-woman to be hanged. The reason given by Akbar was that, on seeing her, his entire day had been ruined. "If that is the case" said Birbal, "you should also be hanged, for **on seeing you, she is being sent to the gallows.**" Having understood the **logic** in Birbal's **line of reasoning**, Akbar set the woman free. Like Birbal, who had so brilliantly convinced Akbar, we must also **keep on making** efforts to get rid of **superstitions**. Numbers, colours, animals, inhuman practices, rites and rituals etc. are associated with superstitions and have been in and on our mind for centuries. It is high time we begin to try to get rid of them.

How Not to Speak English

LESSON 216

'Watch' it

We have earlier seen the differences between '**see**' and '**look**'. We now look at another similar word i.e. '**watch**'. Whenever we use '**watch**' related to the act of using our faculty of sight, we attach the added action of paying close attention to that act. The word '**watch**' is akin to the word '**see**' in the sense that '**watch**' also does not need a preposition. It can be used directly with the noun/pronoun, e.g. "That man is known to be a thief, I want you **to watch** him as soon as he enters our shop." The word '**watch**' when used with the preposition '**on**' makes '**watch**' a Noun, e.g. "You must keep a watch on him." Here, '**watch**' is being used more in the abstract. As common Noun, '**watch**' is part of a '**wristwatch**', a device gentlemen are supposed to wear on their left wrists and ladies on their right wrists, to be able to note and tell the time. With the word '**watch**', the act of viewing an action, e.g. a play, a movie, a skit, a program on television, etc. gets the attribute of concentration.

LESSON 217

Watch on the Wall

"By 5.30 in the evening I'm very tired and keep looking at the *watch* on the wall." Here, the sentence has been correctly framed but the mistake lies in the use of the word '**watch**'. A device for telling time fixed on a wall is known as '**clock**' and not '**watch**'. A '**watch**' or in its full form '**wristwatch**', is worn on the wrist. Similarly, a device used to tell time and kept on a table or any other surface is also known as '**clock**' or if it has the provision of an alarm as '**alarm-clock**'. Sometimes it is also called '**timepiece**'. Much before electronic systems came onto the scene, we had watches that needed winding because of the spring mechanism used to run them. These were known as '**analog**' watches. Then came '**quartz**' watches followed by '**digital**' ones. We now have highly accurate **time-telling options** including calendars integrated through sophisticated systems within mobile phones. You will rarely see people looking at mobile phones to note the time of the day. Sale of wristwatches, in spite of mobile phones, has increased, and not dwindled.

LESSON 218

'Complete' and 'Finish'

The opposite of '**finished**' is '**unfinished**' but the opposite of '**complete**' is '**incomplete**'. Using '**un**' as prefix to denote the opposite of a word is common. However, as with '**incomplete**', the use of '**in**' as prefix to indicate the opposite is also possible. When we use '**finish**' as Verb, we imply that the work or task at hand has been successfully brought to a conclusion e.g. 'I work from 6 p.m. to 9 p.m. and **finish** my homework.' When '**complete**' is used as Verb, it indicates **totality** of work/task done, e.g. 'I **complete** all my household chores by 12 noon, well in time for lunch.' Please note that there is a very thin line of difference between '**finish**' and '**complete**'. Both, '**finish**' and '**complete**' can be used as different Parts of Speech, e.g. "I **must finish** this Project by next month." (Verb) "This veneer has a matt **finish**." (Noun) "This is my **complete** assignment." (Adjective) "I have **to complete** that form." (Verb)... When asked to describe the difference between the two, a smart student retorted, 'Before marriage a man is **incomplete**, and after marriage he is **finished**.'

LESSON 219

Flammable-Inflammable, Different-Indifferent

On the backs of trucks/lorries/tankers carrying highly dangerous chemicals/explosives/gases/liquids etc., one sees '**Highly Inflammable**' written. Nowadays, one also gets to see '**Highly Flammable**'. Whether '**flammable**' or '**inflammable**', the writing is meant to serve as a warning to the occupants of the vehicle behind to maintain safe distance, so that, in the eventuality of a fire, their lives do not get endangered. In this situation, the prefix 'in' does not grant the word '**flammable**' the opposite meaning. However there is a slight difference in the meaning. By '**flammable**' is meant the presence of the quality of something to easily catch fire. By '**inflammable**', we mean something that is **capable of catching fire**. Here, '**flammable/inflammable**' are closely connected. Like '**flammable/inflammable**', there are words in English that do not necessarily convey the opposite when used with the prefix 'in', e.g. '**indifferent**'. The word '**indifferent**' means 'one who is totally unconcerned and unaffected by what he sees in his surroundings.' The closest and strongest synonym of the Adjective '**indifferent**' is '**apathetic**'. In its Noun form, '**indifference**' is synonymous with '**apathy**'. Have you therefore understood how **indifferent** is not the opposite of and is **different** from '**different**'?

LESSON 220

Suffixes – Typicality and Associations

As with prefixes, so also with suffixes in English, certain rules, if followed, can give us a better grasp over the language. When a word ends with the suffixes '**ment**'; '**tion**'; '**ance**'; '**ence**'; '**ity**', then it is generally a **Noun**. e.g. **enjoyment; presentation; penance; absence; eternity.** When a word ends with the suffixes 'al', 'ul', 'ous', 'ive', it is generally an **Adjective**. e.g. **casual; beautiful; jealous; creative.** When a word ends with 'ly', it is generally an **Adverb**, e.g. **carefully, furiously, slowly.** When a word ends with the suffix **'te', or 'ize'**, it is generally a **Verb**, e.g. **create; revolutionize.** In American English, the Verb's ending is characterized by using **ze** whereas British English uses **se**. For students to keep these rules in mind is always useful because it helps answer the **Transformation of Sentences** question or the **Do** as Directed. For students who wish to appear for **CAT, GMAT, GRE** and other competitive exams, these rules are extremely helpful. Remember, however, that **these rules are general** and there are a number of exceptions to each one of them.

LESSON 221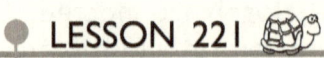

'Breaking the Ice'

During hot summer months, we crave drinks with lots of ice in them. Nowadays, many refrigerators dispense ice cubes and we don't need to undergo the bother of breaking up large ice chunks. But have you heard of **'breaking the ice'**? What does this idiom mean? When invited to a party or a get-together where you do not know anyone, you feel odd standing alone. Here, it is up to the host/hostess to introduce you to other guests so that your awkwardness or embarrassment does not continue. When your host/hostess does so, s/he is **'breaking the ice'**. At a formal gathering where nobody has the boldness to begin speaking and suddenly someone does, it brings about great relief, e.g. "When my colleague began to speak, it broke the ice." Additionally, when we use **'cuts no ice with me'**, it means that although people, in general, may assume it to be otherwise, a stated fact has had no influence on you, e.g. "His being the chairman **cuts no ice** with me." This idiom means that you have not become unduly impressed by someone's position or wealth.

LESSON 222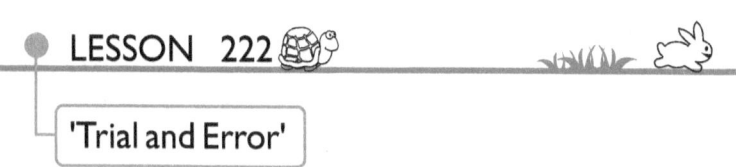

'Trial and Error'

How many times have you heard of the **'trial and error'** method? What does it imply? What is the use of this expression and what does it lead to? As you can see, the word **'trial'** is the Noun of the Verb **'try'**. In **'trial and error'**, we describe a series of events that took place, one following another, because the previous attempt wasn't successful. The use of **'and error'** clearly puts across to the reader/listener, the failure of repeated attempts. A number of great discoveries and inventions have taken place because the person concerned did not give up although he was confronted with failure when trying to succeed. Of so many idiomatic as well as non-idiomatic expressions in English, **'trial and error'** is commonly used. Many diseases as yet are unknown to have cures. Some doctors, therefore, without informing patients, use the **trial and error** method. Proceedings in court over a number of days to ascertain innocence or guilt are also known as a **'trial'**. When we wish to try on new clothes at a tailor's, we also go in for a **'trial'**.

LESSON 223

'Tying the knot'

A lot of people, when single, decide to get married. When a person wishes to make a relationship official by getting married, it is said that he/she **'wishes to tie the knot'**. A knot is generally a way to securely tie a thread or a rope or a string around any object so as to ensure the object around which it is tied, does not become loose. When the word **'married'** is used, another error commonly made in India is to use the preposition **'with'**. Remember that the preposition **'with' is never used with the verb 'married'**, e.g. "Sunita is marrying Ravindran." When speaking of a situation in the past, then the preposition 'to' is added, e.g. "Sunita was married to Ravindran." Similarly, with the Verb 'divorce' no preposition is used, e.g. 'Ravindran divorced Sunita.' OR 'Ravindran and Sunita are now divorced.' Here, it is clearly implied that they are divorced **'from each other'**. Many a time you will see the headline regarding famous personalities as "XYZ **to tie the knot**." You will therefore find it easy to connect **'tying the knot'** with getting married.

LESSON 224

'From the horse's mouth...'

Horses are wonderful animals and figure in a number of idioms in English. The most important one is **'to hear it from the horse's mouth'** or sometimes spoken as **'to hear it straight from the horse's mouth'**. This idiom means that you have obtained some kind of information from an extremely trustworthy source, e.g. "I have heard it from **the horse's mouth** that XYZ has been chosen to play the lead role in this film." When one is cautioned to control one's impulses and warned not to be impatient, one can be asked '**to hold one's horses**'. This is generally used in spoken English. "This matter has been clearly and conclusively decided, **do not flog a dead horse** by raising this issue again." When we wish that a matter should not be spoken of again we use the idiom '**do not flog a dead horse**.' 'You **backed the wrong horse**', can easily be understood contextually for it indicates that you might have voted for the candidate who lost or your judgment erred having made an incorrect choice.

LESSON 225

'Running neck to neck'

Continuing with idioms related to horses, have you heard of 'running neck to neck'? This idiom means that in a competition/campaign/race etc., the two contenders are leading the rest and are equally placed. In a horse-race, when the two leading horses are striving to go ahead of each other, the effort shows clearly in the stretching of the neck. It is only when they reach the finishing line that, with a burst of energy, one of them crosses over first. When you see headlines describing election results as 'the two candidates are running neck to neck', you then know what it means. "Wild horses can't keep me away" is an idiomatic expression that conveys to the reader/listener that no matter what happens, the writer/speaker shall make it to the event s/he has been invited to. With the use of this idiom, the utterance makes the host/hostess happy that his/her potential guest will definitely make it to the event. Animals and birds form an important segment and figure in a number of English expressions, idioms, proverbs and sayings.

LESSON 226

'No news is good news'

'No news is good news.' What does this saying mean? How do we relate to it? Let's see in detail. When there is **no news**, obviously it means that everything is hunky-dory and the possibility of anything wrong or bad having happened can be easily ruled out. In effect, this implies that **absence of any kind of news is as good as having received news that is good.** Grammatically speaking, this sentence is in the **Positive** degree and can be changed to the **Comparative** thus: "Not receiving **news** is **better than** having received **news**". Once again, this implies through the second half of the sentence that had **news** been received, it might have carried the possibility of it having been bad or unwelcome. The word '**news**' is an acronym comprising the first letters of the four directions i.e. **n**orth, **e**ast, **w**est and **s**outh. There is no plural form of the word '**news**'. The article 'a' must never be used with the **Noun** '**news**', e.g. "Have you heard **the news** that man having landed on the moon, is now trying to land on Mars?"

LESSON 227

'Not my cup of tea'

The outgoing CAG - Comptroller (pronounced 'Controller') and Auditor-General of India in 2014 on a TV channel, when asked if he would join politics after retirement, replied: "Politics **is not my cup of tea.**" Now, what does a cup of tea have to do with the activity mentioned? When somebody claims that a particular activity is not his/her cup of tea, it means that this person has no inclination towards that activity nor a liking for it. The association of tea-drinking as done regularly or as habit, is clearly manifested in this expression. In this sentence, **not being somebody's cup of tea** implies that there is absolutely no desire to take it up seriously or professionally or even to have any kind of inclination towards it. Note that this expression is to be used in the Negative only i.e. **an activity that is NOT a person's cup of tea.** The Positive cannot be used to express the contrary. So one cannot say, "*Politics is my cup of tea.*" It can never be overemphasised that an expression/saying/idiom/proverb in English must be thoroughly studied and understood fully in its original form and only then be applied, so that it is correctly and most appropriately communicated.

LESSON 228

'Economic' and 'Economical'

On a number of occasions, you must have come across the words **economic, economical, economics** and **economy**. What do these words mean, how are they different from each other and to what kind of situation does the application of each become the most appropriate? Let us take the first one – economic. The word '**economic**' is closely connected with and relevant to the **monetary situation** of an individual or entity viz. a state or a country, e.g. "**The economic situation of Rwanda in Africa is a cause of great concern.**" Being an Adjective, '**economic**' must relate to the Noun, either immediately after or by implication. The word '**economical**' is also an Adjective and involves the saving of money, e.g. "**He could afford travelling by taxi everyday; however, using public transport wasn't just being economical but sensible too.**" When we say that someone is 'being **economical** with the truth', it clearly implies that the person being referred to is telling a lie. Be economical in your actions so as to have and save money, **but do not ever be economical with the truth.**

LESSON 229

'Economics' and 'Economy'

"He doesn't have a head for Math, however he's very good at **Economics**." When we speak of '**Economics**', we mean the subject that deals with anything that has to do with money and material matters concerning mankind. **Economics** today, as an academic subject and as a field of study, is very important and there are a number of academic institutions all over the world, some of them very prestigious that teach **Economics**. They award degrees to students who pursue graduation as well as post-graduation courses in the subject. When the holder of a formal degree in Economics takes up research or works in related areas, s/he is called an '**economist**'. The word '**economy**' refers to the organized systems or methods involved in the generation of money or commercial transactions of a particular area. It can also be the description of a system in its organic whole, with all its regulations and demarcating parameters devoted to the creation of wealth, e.g. "India's **economy** today, with its variety of IT and automotive success stories besides some others, is vastly different from its ancient over dependence on agriculture."

LESSON 230

'Finance' and 'Fiscal'

Connected with economics, there are words such as '**finance**' and '**fiscal**'. What does the word '**finance**' exactly mean? The word 'finance', although connected with money, does not mean money. Let us first take it as Verb i.e. '**to finance**'. When we ask a question such as, "Who is going **to finance** the project?", the answer associates the query with who is going to put up and provide the money that will be needed for the project. As Noun, the word 'finance' means the entire system of the management of money that comes in as revenue from any kind of commercial activity, e.g. "The **finances** of banks are closely monitored and governed by guidelines set by The Reserve Bank of India." The word 'finance' is generally used with regard to matters **affecting many people** i.e. the public, and may include activities such as banking, investments etc. The word '**fiscal**' is also used to mean any such activity that involves public disbursement and attainment of huge funds. It cannot be used loosely in terms of private enterprises or in matters limited to a limited number of individuals' monetary interests.

● LESSON 231

'He came by walk'

"He has a car but prefers to come by walk." Whenever the mode of approach is described, especially when related to the absence of a vehicle, "by walk" is incorrectly used. Many a time, "S/he came walking" is also utilized. The correct sentence is, "**S/he came on foot.**" The word '**walk**' is Verb as well as Noun, e.g.

"He loves **to walk** after a heavy meal." (Verb).

"He loves to take **a walk** after a heavy meal." (Noun).

When describing a vehicle, then the word 'by' as agent should be used to convey the type of vehicle, e.g.

"He comes **by car** every day." Note that the preposition 'in' is also acceptable but then the sentence would change to 'He comes **in his car** every day.' The Preposition 'in', instead of 'by', can be used only with the Possessive Pronoun being utilized, e.g. "He came **in the company's car** today." We are so accustomed to communicating in English by using our own variations, that when correct English is demonstrated or explained, many a time it leads not only to astonishment but puzzlement too.

LESSON 232

What is a 'franchisee'?

While travelling within a city or moving from one to another, you must have often come across a signboard above a shop saying "**franchisee**". What does this word mean? A '**franchisee**' is simply a company or an individual given special rights to market the products or services of a very well-known company or firm whose goods/services have brand-value. When a company gives a **franchise**, it enables the **franchisee** to use the company's brand name, logo, and/or insignia and thereby market its products or services. The word '**franchise**' can also be termed as the granting of a license to an establishment to sell/market its products and services through the **franchisee**. However, the marketing rights are to be used only in territories as decided upon by the parent company and the signatory of the agreement to the **franchise**. When one **exercises one's franchise**, then one is simply utilizing one's **right to vote**. In earlier days, in democratic countries, people were selected to be given the right of **franchise**. Later on, the right to vote became universal and now, in many democratic countries, '**franchise**' also means the right and duty of citizens to vote. India being a democratic country, we have universal adult franchise i.e. every citizen above the age of eighteen has the right to vote.

LESSON 233

Like a chameleon...

In an armed combat, especially in difficult terrain, the ability of a combatant to '**camouflage**' himself/herself is necessary for survival. That is why you find military vehicles deliberately painted to blend with and appear to be part of the area through which they might be moving. There is a predominance of particular shades used cunningly for this purpose. In movies and television serials depicting military forces, you must have noticed that military uniforms also rely heavily on these colours. The art of concealing oneself cleverly so that one appears to be part of one's surroundings is known as '**camouflaging**'. The **chameleon** is famously known for possessing the quality of **camouflaging** when it changes the colour of its skin to disguise itself to become part of its surroundings. The chameleon is a lizard with the ability to protect itself by constantly changing the colour of its skin. We can describe a **fickle minded** person as a **chameleon**. At times, the word '**camouflage**' is also used to describe how one is trying to put across something else e.g. "Your smile and laughter cannot **camouflage** the pain in your heart."

LESSON 234

'Springing a Surprise'

"Let's **spring** a surprise **on** them" When '**spring**' is used instead of '**give**', then the intensity of the surprise is greater. When we '**spring**' a surprise, it is '**on**' somebody. When we '**give**' a surprise, it is '**to**' somebody. One can never forget the delight one felt as a child first hiding behind the door and then **springing**

a surprise on one's mother. Mothers were of course, always smart to pretend that they didn't know the child was hiding behind the door. The word '**spring**' has many meanings. It can be used both as Noun as well as Verb. As Noun, a **coiled-spring** is an object used in the fabrication of a sofa set or a seat etc. A **leaf-spring** is used to make the underside of a bus or a truck chassis. **Spring** is also the name of a season when leaves turn lush green and flowers bloom. The Past Tense of the Verb '**spring**' is '**sprang**' and '**sprung**' being its Participle form (used with 'has/have' or 'had'). Sometimes the word '**sprang**' means to have formed a crack, e.g. 'the bucket **sprang** a leak'.

LESSON 235

'Alias'

When you question a person as to why he uses more than one name, you never receive an honest answer. You will also find that people, who wish to conceal their identity for illegal activities, generally use a false name. When a second name is used by an individual, the word '**alias**' (pronounced **ay-lee-yus**) is used, e.g. "Ravi **alias** Ramakant". Generally, the Christian name i.e. the first name is changed, but in many cases even the surname becomes different, e.g. "Desai **alias** Desarda". The word 'alias' is Noun and has to be used thus: "After many years we found from our records that Prabhudas was **an alias** for Parimal." The need to change a name arises only when somebody wishes to do something socially or legally unacceptable. The use of **an alias** is predominant in Hindi films with 'Don' being very common. Of course, it is quite popular with other **aliases** in a highly pluralistic society as India where the hero may announce himself to be Amar Singh **alias** Akbar Mohammed **alias** Anthony DeSouza.

LESSON 236

'Someone's in the lobby'

"Mr. X will be down in fifteen minutes. He has asked you to please wait in the **lobby**." A **lobby** is an open area, fairly large, with comfortable seating arrangements. It may also have a table with some magazines or books to kill waiting-time. We generally find a **lobby** on the ground floor of buildings of five-star hotels, large corporate offices, banks or any agency/establishment/firm run either by a government or privately. Sometimes, the lobby is on a higher floor and leads on to other areas of the establishment. The word '**lobby**' is also used as Verb. '**To lobby**' means to forcefully influence a person in power to get something done in the **lobbyist's** favour e.g.

"Affected industrialists **are lobbying** very hard to make the government reduce corporate taxes."

The Verb '**to lobby**' is stronger than the Verb '**to persuade**' and has greater intensity where effort is concerned. To describe a waiting area, in American English, the word '**foyer**' is used. Sometimes, the words '**waiting-room**' '**antechamber**' or '**parlour**' are also used to describe waiting areas.

LESSON 237

'Destruction' and 'Devastation'

Horrific events in Kathmandu recently, have definitely not been a pleasant sight to see, with so much **destruction** having been caused by nature. The Noun '**destruction**' is derived from the Verb '**destroy**'. '**To destroy**' means '**to pull down, to ruin** or **to**

bring down an existing structure.' Not only do we use 'destroy' to describe physical acts but also feelings, emotions, thoughts etc, e.g. "His failure in meeting the deadline destroyed the faith they had reposed in him." At times, the word 'destroyed' gets mistakenly assumed to be synonymous with 'devastated'. There is a difference between the two. When we use 'to devastate' we mean 'to lay waste' or even 'to loot or plunder'. The word 'devastation' is generally used to describe the effects of violence. A feeling of emptiness is associated more with 'devastation' e.g. "When she heard he was going to marry someone else, she was simply devastated."
"Losing one's mother in childhood is devastating for human beings."
Both, 'destruction' and 'devastation' are closely linked with other events such as calamities, catastrophes, and also the apocalypse.

LESSON 238

'Calamity', 'Catastrophe', and 'Apocalypse'

We ended the last lesson with the words 'calamity', 'catastrophe', and 'apocalypse'. A 'calamity' is a disaster of gigantic proportions. It can be natural or man-made. There is debate going on whether the calamity some months ago in Uttarakhand was natural or man-made. To label it a 'catastrophe' would be making an error, for a 'catastrophe' is a 'sudden calamity'. Events leading to the huge amount of destruction by nature were not sudden. Heavy rains with flooding had been forecast in Uttarakhand three days before. For those who lost family members and for those who saw their homes and livelihood being washed away it was virtually the apocalypse. An act of destruction that takes place on a massive scale, involving an entire state, country or even the whole world, is known as 'apocalypse'. Many religious texts talk of the apocalypse before human beings get to meet their Maker. A nuclear explosion is feared everywhere in the world today, because no matter where on earth it takes place, it will most certainly lead to an **apocalypse**. Great effort, with means and methods to save human lives and salvage property after such destructive events, is known as '**Disaster Management**'. The science of disaster management is also important to be proficiently learnt and implemented to prevent man-made disasters.

LESSON 239

Disaster Management

Disaster management is not something we Indians can be proud of. For a variety of reasons, delay in remedial action leads to increase in loss of human lives and property. **Management** is the art of effective administration, superintendence and control over a set of events and circumstances. Unfortunately, **management** in India is considered to be more, of, first, academic interest and later, relative only to corporate matters. **Disaster Management** is that cluster of mechanisms that is used to effectively deploy systems geared towards minimizing loss of human lives and property. **Disaster Management** is also responsible for making people aware of risks and dangers imminent in natural and man-made situations. Good management leads to preparedness more than the development of competence in tasks necessary after the event. We are aware that '**prevention is better than cure**'. **Disaster Management** also involves the propagation of harmful long-term effects of deforestation on human beings. Earth does not belong to human beings alone. The harmonious existence of animals, birds etc. and the undisturbed natural movement of rivers and seas is vital for the well-being of mankind.

LESSON 240

'Damage' – the noun

We have, in earlier lessons, looked at 'destruction' and other descriptive words connected with negative actions. However, the first word to be looked at should have been '**damage**'. The word '**damage**' is Noun and means injury or harm to a human being or property or even feelings and emotions. Considering indiscipline rampant on Indian roads, streets, alleys and gullies, one rarely comes across a vehicle that has no **damage** on its body. A dent, scratch or bump on vehicles is common. Traffic indiscipline is the rule and not the exception in India. Once damage is done, value gets reduced. That is why the word '**damages**' in the plural is used to indicate cost/s, e.g. "You say the engine needs overhauling, could you tell me the **damages** for it?" "The Managing Committee has decided to sanction the proposal to arrange a picnic as well as buffet-dinner on the same day. Damages will be Rs. 1500/- per member." "**Damage**" can also be used to describe harm in the abstract e.g. "Always be fair in your professional dealings so that no damage is caused to your reputation."

LESSON 241

'Down' – improper associations

The use of '**down**' is very often fallacious. The word '**down**' gets attached to the Verb, unnecessarily burdening it, many a time leading to incorrect grammar. '**Down**' is very often used to indicate the direction of a fall. However, it is redundant (unnecessary), e.g. "He **fell down** from his bicycle." Can anyone fall **up**? Obviously that is not possible. So, the best sentence would be: "He **fell** from his bicycle." You will hear many people saying, "That shop **closes down** at 8 p.m." To say **closes down** is to convey that the shop is going to stop doing business for ever. The same is the case with "**shuts down**". The correct sentence therefore is: "**That shop closes/shuts at 8 p.m.**" When '**shut**' and '**down**' combine to form '**shutdown**', it indicates a **strike** or a **lock-out**, e.g. "That factory is now facing labour problems, there is a complete shutdown." The words '**close**' and '**shut**', although appearing synonymous, do have differences in meaning. What is important is, not to associate '**down**' with either of them.

LESSON 242

At 'leisure'

The following sentences, heard so often, clearly indicate some kinds of variations or transliteration - "Please come when you are *having leisure*" OR "Come when you *have free time*". The word '**leisure**' itself means 'spare or free time' and the correct sentence is, "**Come when you're free,**" OR "**Please come at leisure.**" A whole system of social etiquette and situations gets involved when we speak of people who have **leisure**. We are so much under pressure of work, that when we hear of somebody enjoying himself/herself because of **leisure** at his/her disposal, we look at that person with envy or scorn. The word '**leisure**' pronounced '**lee-zher**', an Abstract Noun, being unquantifiable, is uncountable. When someone is **at leisure**, it implies that there is very little or absolutely no pressure on that person whatsoever. S/he is therefore free to do whatever interests him/her. Earlier, whenever people were **at leisure**, they would read. Nowadays, when **at leisure**, very few read and instead watch television. Some also play games on the computer or on their mobile phones. No matter what you choose to do when **at leisure**, you must **enjoy yourself** thoroughly.

LESSON 243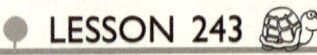

'Left-handed' and 'Ambidextrous'

Whenever we undertake physical activities using our hands, we generally use the right hand more than the left. Those who use their **left** hand to eat, write, clasp or catch etc. are known as **left-handed**. Being **left-handed** is no illness or disease but only an inclination or tendency. It may or may not be hereditary. A left-handed person in American English is also called a '**southpaw**' (slang) or '**left-handed**'. Sometimes the nickname '**lefty**' is used to indicate that the person being referred to uses his left hand more than the right. This term is generally used by school children to describe a particular classmate's inclination to use the left hand. While the predominant use of **either the right or the left** hand is common, **only a handful can use both** with equal power, strength and skill. Those who can use both hands with equal power, strength and skill, are known to be **ambidextrous**. Dexterity means 'great skill'. '**Dexterous**' means being highly skilled or possessing ability to do things that people in general cannot. That is why '**ambidextrous**' is used.

LESSON 244

'Assassination', 'Homicide', 'Suicide'

On reading newspaper headlines, sometimes you are confronted with "ABC, President of XYZ country, **assassinated**". How is the word '**assassinated**' different from the word '**killed**'? The word '**assassinated**' involves the act of being killed suddenly, secretively and with great cleverness. An '**assassination**' is generally an act involving a high official or the leader of a government or a country. It can also be the killing of an important person who is a threat to somebody in power. An **assassination** leads to the death of an important person. **Assassinations** are committed to make the victim's country go into political instability or turmoil. Generally, when a murder of a common citizen is planned and executed, the act is known as **homicide**. The act of **killing oneself** due to any reason is known as **suicide**. Even though the person who kills himself is not alive after this horrible event, it is considered a crime, and when a person survives after trying to kill himself/herself, it is known as '**attempted suicide**'. It must be borne in mind that when crimes are committed, certain terms are used as per legal language and for the common man who has to have an understanding of English, these terms are general.

LESSON 245

'Lifts' and 'Elevators'

With the growth of high-rise buildings and other structures all over the world, it is becoming necessary for mechanisms to be used to transport people to great heights in a smooth, swift and safe manner. Many such structures have '**lifts**' in them. In

American English, these are known as **'elevators'**. Both, **'lift'** and **'elevator'** are Nouns. While the Verb form of **'lift'** is **'lift'**, the Verb form of **'elevator'** is **'elevate'** e.g. "The Deputy Manager has now been elevated to the position of Manager." The word **'elevated'** works better than 'promoted' for the simple reason that it communicates the move up to a higher position, both by status as well as salary. When we need somebody's help and kindness to take us along with them, then we ask them to give us a **'lift'** in the vehicle being used by them.. The action for requesting a lift is also known as **'thumbing a ride'** because the thumb is used to indicate the direction in which one would like to take a lift to.

LESSON 246

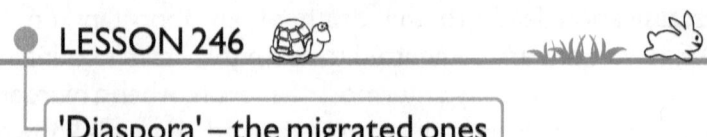

'Diaspora' – the migrated ones

Did you know that Bhojpuri has become a common language, in, of all nations, Mauritius? A small island-state in the Indian Ocean where French is the main language, Mauritius today is home to a number of Indians, especially from Bihar, M.P., U.P. and Rajasthan. When citizens from one nation **migrate** to another in large numbers, or disperse across the world, they are collectively known as the **'Diaspora'**. The word **'Diaspora'** is a Biblical term that was applied earlier to the dispersion of Jews who had to flee Babylon, their homeland, because of religious persecution. Today, this term applies to any race or nationality that voluntarily or involuntarily chooses to adopt another nation in which to seek livelihood and a secure future. The word **'Diaspora'** is Noun and written with **'D' capital**. It is mostly used in the Plural to denote the spread of a particular people across many countries. The number of **NRIs (Non-resident Indians)** settled all over the world, makes the application of **'Diaspora'** appropriate. Due to the economic success achieved by Indians, working and living in and for foreign (to us) nations, many Indians are naturally inspired to emigrate. Once a year the Government of India organizes a seminar to which such people are invited in huge numbers. On such occasions, you will definitely see such headlines in newspapers, "Indian Diaspora pleased to invest huge amounts in new Indian projects."

LESSON 247

'To emigrate', 'Work Visa' and 'Tourist Visa'

"**To emigrate**" is to leave one's homeland, i.e. where one was born and brought up, to work and live in another country. This step is taken generally in early adulthood or can be enforced upon an individual due to circumstances prevailing at a particular point of time. When an Indian resident wishes to settle in Australia, Canada, New Zealand, the UK, or the USA etc., he wishes **to emigrate**. When he fulfils conditions and begins to live in a foreign country, he is known as an '**immigrant**'. When one wishes to work in any country other than one's own, one has to apply first for a '**Work Visa**' or a '**Work Permit**'. Many countries grant a **Visa** to visit them, but getting permission to live and work in these countries is not easy. One has to fulfil a number of conditions before permission to work in that foreign country is granted by its authorities. When one visits a foreign country for the purpose of sightseeing, one is granted what is known as a '**Tourist Visa**'.

LESSON 248

'Accelerate' and 'Escalate'

As with 'lift' and 'elevator', there is a difference between 'accelerate' and 'escalate'. The Verb 'to accelerate' is used to indicate increase in the speed of a moving object, a plan or mode of action. The accelerator pedal in a car is purposefully longer and narrower than the flatter and broader brake and clutch pedals. Better speed control is ensured because of the shape of the accelerator pedal. The Verb 'to escalate' implies an upward trend in intensity or momentum, e.g. "The exchange value of the Rupee per dollar has escalated to sixty-plus, from fifty-five over the last three months." An escalator is an electrically operated moving staircase on which one stands, to be mechanically and gradually transported upward, and at an incline, to a higher level. Escalators are commonly seen in malls, at railway stations, banks etc. Some premises are also fitted with escalators that move downwards. The Noun forms of 'accelerate' and 'escalate' are 'acceleration' and 'escalation', respectively. In some sale agreements, there is, what is known as an 'escalation clause', making it compulsory for the buyer to pay the difference, as, if, and when, the price escalates.

LESSON 249

'Doing a fight'

Climactic changes in Uttarakhand due to the deluge brought to the surface bickering by political parties. On a TV News-channel, spokespersons of political parties were seen hurling accusations at each other, so much so that one said the other was '*doing a fight*'. A fight cannot **be done**, it can only be **fought**. Used both as Verb and Noun, 'fight' **needs no preposition**, e.g.

"These two are known to constantly fight each other." The preposition 'with' when accompanying 'fight' is grossly misplaced, e.g. "*The Allies fought with the Axis in the Second World War.*" When the preposition 'with' is used with 'fight' as Verb, it may indicate the opposite meaning and imply that instead of being opponents, the parties engaged in the fight were friends or allies and were together fighting a third person or force e.g. "Ram fought with Laxman against Ravana." If at all, a preposition must be used, then the most appropriate one is 'against' e.g. "Gandhiji **fought against** violence by using ahimsa" or better, 'Gandhiji **fought violence** using ahimsa." As Noun, it is easier to use 'fight', e.g. "Now be good friends and don't get into a fight."

LESSON 250

'Relief', 'Rescue' and 'Rehabilitation'

Relief, rescue, rehabilitation. These words, in this order, embody exactly what the citizens of Uttarakhand needed and what Kathmandu needs today after a calamity. "**Relief**" - a Noun - means the elimination of fear, anxiety, hunger and a host of other negative feelings. To those who cannot be transported because of difficult land circumstances, '**relief**' can be provided by delivering food, medicines, clothing and other necessary materials. All these can be air-dropped. "**Rescue**" implies bringing to safety those who are in great danger of losing their lives, e.g. "Those in danger of drowning were rescued by the erection of rope-bridges over swollen rivers." Finally, after relief has been provided and rescue operations successfully undertaken, those affected must be **rehabilitated**. Due to circumstances in Uttarakhand and Kathmandu, human lives were turned upside down leading to loss and injury. Adverse conditions leading to damage must be overcome. When earlier and better conditions are restored, it is known as **'rehabilitation'**. While man cannot restore natural conditions, it is necessary for the affected person to move to different surroundings and conditions which would help in his/her **rehabilitation**.

● LESSON 251

A pinch of 'Salt'

Some people like more **salt** than others in their food. For quite a few, consuming salt in higher quantities is dangerous as per the doctor's advice. It is however certain that without **salt**, life would lose quite a bit of its flavour. **Salt** is a crystalline substance that has a zingy taste. Generally known as **common salt**, it is used universally. What we put into our food is known as **table salt**. Nowadays, **table salt** is also available as **iodized salt**. **Iodine** in **salt** leads to prevention of the inflammation of the thyroid gland. The importance and value of salt, in addition to food, in languages too, can never be underrated. "**To be worthy of one's salt**" means that one is giving full value and consideration to one's own worth in all that one does in life. To take a statement made by someone "**with a pinch of salt**" is applied when we do not fully believe/support the person making it, especially a politician. "**To rub salt on someone's wounds**" is to make the situation for the injured person worse than before.

LESSON 252

'Salt' and 'Pepper'

Where **salt** is concerned, there are a number of other idiomatic expressions used effectively very often in English. "To be the **salt** of the earth" implies that the person being referred to should be considered an important element in the constitution of the social setup at a given point of time. This is a Biblical saying and today important for the entire world. If salt is an important ingredient, can **pepper** be far behind? A combination of the two is the most pleasant to the human palate. **Pepper** adds **spice** to food. **Pepper** is a group of condiments that are ground so as to lend a particular flavour to food. The word 'pepper' is also used as Verb to convey the addition of a particular kind of flavour, e.g. "His speech **was peppered** with humorous anecdotes." The **black and white** combination of **salt and pepper** is also used to describe a particular kind of appearance, e.g. "He looked very attractive in his natural **salt-and-pepper** appearance." A white beard and black hair on a man's head is considered to be extremely appealing by some.

LESSON 253

'Masala'

The word '**masala**' today is an English word (British English) and means the same as it does in the language of its origin. It is a Noun and has the effect of adding pungency to food. It must be noted that '**masala**', as we know it in India, is not a welcome ingredient in Continental food. Mexican food is the closest in taste to Indian food. Food in Mexico closely resembles Indian food in appearance as well as flavour. Mexican food also has a lot of '**masala**' in it. The word '**masala**' can also be used to indicate pungency, flavour or spiciness. The sentence from the previous lesson can be rewritten as "A number of humorous anecdotes added **masala** to his speech." While a number of words from various Indian languages today form part of the English lexicon, it would serve us well to remember that not every reader in the world may be familiar with the meaning of these words. Therefore, whenever such 'non-English' words are used, it is best to put them in inverted commas or *italicize* them.

LESSON 254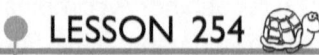

'Staple Diet' and 'Cuisine'

Man is the only animal who, because of his ability to control fire, **cooks**. Depending on which part of the world one lives in, particular **cooking styles** become extremely popular. These styles also depend on availability of ingredients, regional influences and the inclination of a generalized population towards a particular kind of taste. What is therefore eaten on a regular basis becomes what is known as '**staple diet**'. Rice and curry is the **staple diet** of South India. Bread, with beef, chicken and mutton forms the **staple diet** in many European countries as well as the American continent. The way an area adopts a **cooking style** gets described using the name of the place, e.g. Punjabi food, Maharashtrian dishes etc. The correct word used to describe a particular cooking style is '**cuisine**'. Pronounced 'kwi-zeen', the word '**cuisine**' is Noun denoting a specific method of cooking, e.g. "Many Indians do not like **Chinese cuisine** in spite of its popularity." "Unlike Indian meals, **Chinese cuisine** has very little to offer by way of **desserts**." Remember, the difference in pronunciation as well as meaning of 'cuisine' from 'cousin'. Both these words sound the same, but have different meanings. When saying 'cuisine' there can be a stress on 'quisine' and with cousin there can be stress on 'k-zin'.

LESSON 255

'Desserts' and 'Deserts'

The last word of the last lesson was '**desserts**'. "What did you have for '**dessert**' at that dinner?" is a common question when we require such information. The **sweet dish** that we consume after a full-fledged lunch or dinner is known as '**dessert**'. Many mistake it to be '**desert**'. The word '**desert**' indicates huge sandy areas of emptiness while '**dessert**' indicates fullness. The word 'desert' can also be used as a Verb, e.g. "She wanted a divorce because her husband had deserted her for a long period without a convincing reason." As Verb, 'to desert' means to keep away from or to be totally unconcerned about. The word '**desert**', as in the 'desert of Rajasthan' is pronounced '**de-zert**' whereas '**dessert**' is pronounced '**di-zert**'. If you are over-fond of eating sweets in any form, you can describe your inclination by saying, "I **have a sweet** tooth; that's why I'm taking a second helping of custard." When food tastes neither sweet nor salty, it is **bland**. Indians generally do not like Continental food because it is **bland** while Europeans aren't inclined towards Indian food because it is **spicy**. While it may not be compulsory to have **desserts** with every meal, generally people do consider it to be the final touch. If you look carefully at the word '**desserts**', it is '**stressed**' spelt backwards.

LESSON 256

'Criterion' and 'Criteria'

An individual's interest should not be taken as **a criterion** to judge her/him. A number of other factors should also be considered before they form **the criteria** to judge. As you can see, from the construction of these sentences, the word 'criterion' is singular whereas the plural is 'criteria'. Erroneous interchange of the two is common, and must not take place. Similarly, the word 'phenomenon' is singular and its plural is 'phenomena'. A phenomenon is a happening, an event or any occurrence in nature or man-made e.g. "The sun rising in the east is a natural phenomenon." A number of Nouns in English do not take the letter 's' to indicate plurality. The easiest way to recognize a person's incapacity to speak/write English correctly is when s/he says '*childrens*'. The word '**children**' itself is the plural form of '**child**' and the letter 's', when writing, without an apostrophe, must never be added. There are occasions when 's' is added to show possession. This is done using the apostrophe, e.g."Do you like the curtains in the **children's** room?" Similarly, the words 'sheep' and 'deer' are most commonly pronounced as '*sheeps*' and '*deers*' respectively. These errors too must be avoided at all costs. The best way to remember these plural forms of Nouns is by regular practice: **One child – many children; one sheep – many sheep; one deer – many deer; one aircraft – many aircraft.** Many uncountable Nouns have no plural e.g. 'information', 'equipment', 'data'.

● LESSON 257

'Publikcity'

Where pronunciation is concerned, difficulties faced by Indians over English get compounded when words are pronounced in a manner that conveys a different meaning. The word '**publicity**' is, more often than not, incorrectly pronounced as '*publickcity*', conveying that the speaker wishes to say something about the 'public' in a 'city'. The word '**publicity**' (pronounced without the 'k' sound) is Noun and indicates that the person concerned is trying to build a name using the media and wants everyone to talk about him/her. There is good publicity as well as bad publicity. However, even when publicity is bad, the person in question is happy for it leads to discussions on the person's character or actions. The word 'public' is also part of the word 'publish'. When we 'publish' a work as a book (hard copy), or transmit it in an electronic form through today's highly sophisticated technological avenues, we make the author's writing accessible at the same time to a huge number of people. No matter what final form an author's creation takes, it is important for every reader to concentrate on what the writer wants to convey.

LESSON 258

'Publicity', 'Advertising' and 'Commercials'

Although **publicity** and **advertising** are interrelated, there is a difference between the two. We have seen that **publicity** involves making matters **public**. An **advertisement**, on the other hand, is the **paid proclamation** in public of the **supposedly better features** of a product or service. This involves the effort of the **advertiser** to lure a buyer or consumer to buy the product/service being advertised. As Noun, **advertisement** is pronounced 'ad-ver-tis-ment' and the Verb 'advertise' is pronounced with 'tise' rhyming with 'rise'. It is generally believed that **advertisements** make us buy what we do not want. Very few **advertisers** make the products' qualities that they are advertising, noticeable. There is instead, more stress on showing the deficiencies of competitors' products' qualities. An advertisement on radio or on a television channel is known as a '**commercial**'. The musical outpouring extolling a product's better qualities on radio or television is known as a '**jingle**'. In today's highly consumerist market-driven economy, many **jingles** are catchy compositions and people remember them more easily than songs. **Commercials** on television are now so predominant that switching channels becomes futile.

● LESSON 259

'Medium' and 'Media'

There are various forms of communication through which a person wishes to get his creative effort across to the maximum number of people. A particular form that is chosen is known as a '**medium**'. The plural of '**medium**' in communications is '**media**'. **Media** can comprise various means of communication viz. books, pamphlets, blogs, websites, on the electronic media etc. **Media** also stands for television channels, radio talk-shows etc. that exploit any kind of electronic device to put across creative work to a huge number of people at the same time. The word '**medium**' is also used as an adjective denoting 'somewhere in the middle', e.g. 'the thief was of **medium height**'. Remember, '*mediums*' is not the plural of '**medium**'. Whenever a person wishes to put across his ideas or thoughts, he must choose the **medium** he feels would be the best-suited to communicate most appropriately whatever he wishes to communicate. Interchanging of **media** can lead to weakening of intensity. That is why, you will note that a film based on a highly successful book rarely appeals as much as the book does.

● LESSON 260

'Reach' – as Verb, as Noun

As we have seen in a few earlier lessons, **reaching out** to a number of people at the same time has become important where creative work is concerned. The word '**reach**' is both

Noun as well as Verb. When '**reach**' is used in the physical sense, many of us incorrectly attach '**to**' with it, e.g. *"When I reached to Indore, it was terribly hot."* This is incorrect. When the word 'reach' is used, the preposition 'to' must never be attached, e.g. '**When you reach Satara, please call me.**' The word 'reach' is also used as Adjective when it is part of 'far' as in 'The government's action will have **far-reaching** consequences.' It is very important to remember that both as Noun as well as Verb, the word '**reach**' need not use a Preposition. As Noun, it is preceded by a Noun/Pronoun, e.g. "The ball hit the ropes as it was beyond the fielder's **reach**."
"The book being high on the shelf was beyond her **reach**." The word '**reach**' also indicates a stretch or an extent of an area, e.g. "The garden had a wide **reach**."

LESSON 261

The silent 'b' after 'm'

Whenever a faucet (tap) in your kitchen or bathroom or at any other location develops a leak, you summon a **plumber**. The word '**plumber**' is **Noun** and denotes a person who handles and repairs equipment related to water supply and drainage. The word '**plumber**' is pronounced with '**b**' silent as '**plummer**'. Generally, a word containing the letter '**m**' followed by '**b**' has '**b**' silent. The words '**bomb**', '**tomb**' and '**womb**' are pronounced '**bom**' '**toom(b)**' and '**woom(b)**' respectively. As you can see, the letter '**b**' in '**tomb**' and '**womb**' is very lightly pronounced, whereas the '**b**' in '**bomb**' after '**m**' **is silent**. In case of words such as '**number**', '**slumber**' and '**umbrella**', the letter '**b**' is **not silent**. However, when a '**comb**' is used or described, it is correctly pronounced with '**b**' silent i.e. "**kom**" to rhyme with '**home**'. The word '**comb**', as **Noun**, denotes an article used to straighten, arrange or make hair neat. As **Verb**, the word '**comb**' is used to describe an action involving intense search, e.g. "The police **are combing** the slums for the thieves."

"In government offices, clerks **comb** drawers and racks when a particular file is required."

LESSON 262

'People' and 'Peoples'

One of the most difficult ideas to be explained to new students of English is that the word '**people**' can also be correctly used as '**peoples**'. However, '**peoples**' is used only in specific situations and circumstances. Let us see an example: "The **people** of India want peace. The people of Pakistan want peace. Therefore, the **peoples** of India and Pakistan together want peace." The word 'peoples' as a Noun involves a higher quantity. It also means that it has the representative function of standing for a bigger population. The word '**people**', being a Collective Noun, denotes a collection of **persons** who may or may not share a common purpose or identity. The word '**peoples**' can also be used as Verb indicating the formation of a huge quantity of some object or animals in a particular area, e.g. "This Library **peoples with** a number of books on Cultural Anthropology." The word '**person**' indicates '**a human being**'. As a common noun, the word '**person**' has '**persons**' as plural when we wish to talk about more than one of them. When the number is small, the word '**person**' is better than '**people**', e.g. "Only four **persons** can sit in this row." "When you talk to a V.I.P., you must show him/her due respect." **V.I.P.**, as you already know, stands for "**Very Important Person.**"

LESSON 263

'Dedicated to...'

"I want to **dedicate** this song to my parents." While this sentence is correct, the context in which the word '**dedicate**' is used is very often misplaced. When we '**dedicate**' something, we make it holy, or as is known in better language, we **hallow** or **consecrate** it. However, when we speak of being dedicated, we convey that we are committed to an issue. When Abraham Lincoln used the word '**dedicate**' in his famous Gettysburg address, he meant it as a tribute that would make the land holy for all those who had died in the American Civil War of that time. On a number of radio stations and television channels, when we hear people saying, "I want to **dedicate** this song to ………", it is clear that they are unaware of the appropriate use of the word '**dedicate**' and are doing it because they have seen/heard others do the same earlier. It would be best when playing the song for someone to say, "I would like this song played **for** my friend XYZ." This would clearly indicate that the person mentioned is alive, because '**dedicate**' can convey that the concerned person/s as the object/s of the dedication, is/are no more alive.

LESSON 264

'As' Simple 'As' That...

"Mary had a little lamb, its fleece was white as snow." Who has not heard of this nursery rhyme? The word '**as**', when used in this, indicates that the fleece of the lamb in its whiteness, was similar to the whiteness of snow. In this situation, the word '**as**', is clearly an Adverb. In many a comparative sentence, the use of '**as**' twice is necessary, so as to convey the similarity or **as** is known in English grammar, the Positive Degree. The use of '**as**' twice in "Ravi runs **as** fast **as** Rakesh" is clearly necessary because, when the capacity of the two runners is being described to be the same, then the word '**as**' before as well **as** after the Adjective/Adverb being compared, becomes mandatory. In this manner, there are a number of idiomatic expressions using '**as**', e.g. "**As far** as I can see, this project will not work." "She is as good **as** gold." Sometimes, we can use as with 'for', e.g. "**As** for the next lesson, you must wait till tomorrow." In this case, the word '**as**' combined with 'for' leads to reference.

LESSON 265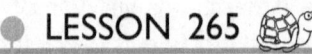

'As' – as Conjunction, as Preposition, as Pronoun

The word '**as**' also operates as a Conjunction e.g.: "**As** we were tired, we sat down to rest."; "We took along with us many bottles of water, **as** the weather had been forecast to become extremely hot." How can we distinguish whether '**as**', in a sentence, is an Adverb or a Conjunction? It is very simple. When '**as**' is followed by a comparative adjective or adverb, it is clearly an Adverb, e.g. "My bike, after repairs, was **as** good as new." (Adverb). When, a clause follows '**as**', then '**as**' clearly, becomes a Conjunction. In this case, the Conjunction can also begin a sentence, equalling the same function of **since/because**, e.g.: "**As** India is a poor country, many Indians die of starvation every year."

"**As** there is sufficient time for the train, let's eat at this restaurant."

The word '**as**' can also work as a Preposition, e.g. "When the

teacher is absent, Raju acts **as** a monitor."
We can also use '**as**' as a **Pronoun** e.g. "I have the same make of car **as** you have." Here, 'as' performs the same function as 'that'.

LESSON 266

'Cleanliness is next to godliness'

'Cleanliness is next to godliness,' is certainly the truth. When we feel that the world around us is **dirty**, both **literally and figuratively**, we strive to make sure that we ourselves remain **clean**. These two words – **clean** and **dirty**, playing an important part in our day-to-day existence, are **Adjectives**. The **Noun** form of '**dirty**' is '**dirt**', while that of '**clean**' is '**cleanliness**'. The more we strive for **cleanliness** in our lives, the surer we are to get to our goals. Both can also be used as **Verbs**, e.g. "Do not **dirty** the bathroom again." "**Clean** your room thoroughly before leaving!" We can also use them together as **Adjectives** when we wish to describe our surroundings, e.g. "Why is the kitchen of a **clean** restaurant in India so **dirty**?" In addition to the Verb **clean**, we have another Verb in English i.e. '**cleanse**'. The Verb '**cleanse**' implies the clearing away of any kind of unwanted dirt/mess/growth. '**Cleanse**' is pronounced '**klenz**'. **Cleansing actions** go deeper than **cleaning**, e.g. "Teenagers use **cleansing creams** to get rid of pimples and acne." "When a body is **dirtied**, it can be **cleaned**, but there must be cleansing of souls."

LESSON 267

'Weigh' your options

Have you, on any occasion, found that you are **overweight**?

Were you, at any time in your life, **underweight?** When was the last time you **weighed** yourself? **Have** you **weighed** the pros and cons of any action that you might have taken or did not take? Can you compare **the weight** of a feather with that of iron? The word **'weight'** is Noun and the Verb is **'weigh'**. Whenever you travel, your luggage has got to be weighed and checked that it falls well within acceptable limits. This is essential when travelling, especially by air. With the Verb weigh, we also have 'weigh in' describing a boxer/wrestler/athlete before events as "ABC weighs in at XYZ pounds/kilos." The weight of a person/object/animal is the heaviness in units that can be quantified. We generally do it in pounds or kilos and for smaller objects it is in ounces or grams. When we speak of 'weighing our options' it simply means that we are considering and deliberating as to what kind of decision to make/take so that the best result can be achieved.

- **LESSON 268**

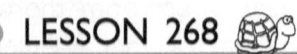

'With', 'To' and 'For': Associations with Verbs

The word **'meet'** is yet another Verb with which the Preposition **'with'** or **'to'** is unnecessarily added, e.g. "*I am meeting with him tomorrow.*" The correct sentence is, "**I am meeting him tomorrow.**" The Preposition **'with'** can be attached only with the Noun **'meeting'**, e.g. "I have **a meeting with** the Director tomorrow morning at 11.a.m." The Preposition 'to' also many times is incorrectly used with "meeting", e.g. "*I am meeting to the Deputy Director.*" When we attach the preposition **'with'**, it is only with the Noun **'accident'** e.g. "Their van **met with** an accident." Once again, as you can see, the word 'accident' is Noun and therefore use of the Preposition **'with'** is correct. Similarly, with the word **'request'** as **Verb**, the preposition **'to'** is never added, e.g. "*I want to request to you to please fill the tub* *tomorrow.*" The correct sentence is, "**I want to request you to please fill the tub tomorrow.**" When the word '**request**' is used as Noun, the Preposition '**to**' or '**for**' automatically follows e.g.: "I hope you will fulfil our request to bring the demonstration kit with you tomorrow."; "I hope our request for a break will be granted."

LESSON 269

'Move' and 'Shift'

A common error, when relocating from a home/office/city/site, to any other, is the use of the word, '**shift**'. In India, the incorrect use of '**shift**' instead of '**move**' is rampant, e.g. "*We have shifted to a new address.*" To make the sentence correct, it should be rephrased as "**We have moved to a new address**". The dictionary meaning of '**move**' is '**to cause to change place or posture**'. The dictionary meaning of '**shift**' is '**to change position**'. Moreover, in the case of human beings, when relocation is in process or has been completed, the word '**move**' is used, keeping ambulation or movement in mind. Human beings move of their own accord whereas things get **shifted**. The word '**shift**' is appropriate when connected with and to objects, e.g. "When you **shift** the gear-stick to the fifth, a car gains its maximum speed." The words '**move**' and '**shift**' are also used as Nouns, e.g. "That was a smart move." "Why don't you ask them to roster you in a day-shift?" Sumit was bored at the party and said, "**Let's make a move.**" Amit retorted, "I haven't brought my chess-board."

LESSON 270

'Trivial'. 'Trifle' and 'Truffle'

By and large, a number of students and professionals from the Commerce, Science and Engineering streams look down upon the studying of languages, especially English, as a **trivial** matter. They study it only because it is an **evil necessity**, a Subject that has to be studied because it is compulsory. The word '**trivial**' is Adjective and denotes the matter to be of no importance or significance. The Noun form is '**trifle**' and indicates an action or something that has no value whatsoever. The word '**trifle**' (pronounced to rhyme with '**rifle**') can also be used as Verb. When used as Verb, '**trifle**' denotes actions involving overconfidence, e.g. "Do not **trifle** with that dog, it can really bite." It can also convey the consideration of a particular act as being as easy as **child's play**. The word '**trifle**' should not be confused with '**truffle**'. The word '**truffle**' (pronounced to rhyme with '**ruffle**'), stands for a confection, somewhat like a pastry, made of chocolate. Generally eaten as dessert, it is more or less part of Continental cuisine. So as to remember the difference between the two, note the following: "It is certainly not a **trifle** to bake and sell a **truffle**."

LESSON 271

'Launch' and 'Lunch'

"You are invited to a program to **launch** our new product, followed by **lunch**." By adding 'a' after 'l', '**lunch**' becomes '**launch**'. We are aware of what '**lunch**' means, but what does the word '**launch**' (**pronounced 'lawnch'**) indicate? The word '**launch**' denotes the beginning of a new career, the introduction of a new product, or the initiation of any kind of activity. This activity may or may not be accompanied by fanfare. The word 'launch', as seen from the very first sentence, is generally used as Verb, always with an object, e.g. "He **launched** his production unit in a traditional fashion by lighting a lamp." When we use '**launch**' as Noun, it indicates an activity signifying commencement, e.g. "At the launch of the new syllabus, some senior teachers were unhappy." When using '**launch**' as Noun, it is advisable to ensure that an Article precedes it. The word '**launch**' is also used to indicate the movement or speed of a vehicle with great force, e.g. "The rocket **was launched** into space." A '**launch**' is also a motorboat that moves in water with great speed, sometimes also called a 'motor-launch'.

LESSON 272

'Mares', 'Vixens', 'Stags' and 'Peahens'

When a North Indian describes a Punjabi wedding, he invariably says that the bridegroom goes to the bride's premises on a horse. The bridegroom in a Punjabi wedding never proceeds on a horse, he rides a **mare**. The word '**mare**' stands for a mature, **female** horse. Similarly, many of us in India are unaware of the correct female names in English of many birds and animals. Did you know that a **female sheep** is a **ewe**? The word '**ewe**' is not pronounced 'eve' but strangely enough, as '**you**'. A female fox is known as a '**vixen**'. Did you know that '**goose**' and '**duck**' are female? The male forms are 'gander' and 'drake' respectively. A **peacock** is male and the female is known as a **peahen**. The **male** counterpart of a **hen** is known as a **rooster**. A **bull** is a bovine animal and its female is **cow**. Similarly, a female elephant is known as an **elephant-cow**. A fully grown **male deer** is known as a **stag** while its **female** is known as a **doe** (pronounced the same as **dough**). A party to which only men are invited is known as a '**stag party.**'

LESSON 273

'With due respect...'

"With due respect, I would like to state ...." What is the importance of the expression, '**with due respect**'? What does it mean? We are sometimes part of certain groups where experts and veterans, who have gained a reputation for being knowledgeable and expert in many matters, are also present. Nonetheless, there are times when we wish to point out a mistake made by any one of them or to direct attention to a point which might have escaped their attention. Whenever we put across our ideas in their presence, or point out an error, we need to be polite to these knowledgeable persons, seniors etc. and also give them **respect**. This **respect** has been earned by them because of their hard work and also because of the years of experience behind them. That is why, '**with due respect** …..' is added when we want to state what is on our mind, without fear of being ridiculed or questioned. The word '**due**', in this context, conveys what is deemed to be appropriate and fair. '**With due respect**....' is also used in debates and group discussions and becomes a convenient opening line for a speaker who wishes to challenge the earlier speaker.

LESSON 274

'Phobia'

Fear of the number thirteen in English is known as **triskaidekaphobia**. Many apartment blocks today in India too do not have the number 13 after 12, and instead use 12A or from 12 jump straight to 14. This is done clearly to avoid using the number 13. Great fear of some kind of a phenomenon in English is known as '**phobia**'. The word '**phobia**' is Noun with the adjective using the suffix '**phobic**'. When a '**phobia**' takes hold over a person's psyche, s/he makes great effort to avoid confrontation. **Phobias** are generally without rationale and form part of human psychology. A number of scientific studies are being conducted to analyze and cure different kinds of phobias. From the countless that exist, here are 10 strange kinds of phobias: (1) **myrmecophobia** – fear of ants; (2) **amaxophobia** – fear of cars/car journeys (3) **xocolatophobia** – fear of chocolates (4) **allodoxaphobia** – fear of being criticized (5) **iatrophobia** – fear of doctors (6) **gerascophobia** – fear of growing old (7) **athazagoraphobia** – fear of forgetting (8) melophobia – fear of music (9) **haptephobia** – fear of being touched - and the climax (10) **phobophobia** – fear of fear.

LESSON 275

'...between the cup and the lip'

"There's many a slip between the cup and the lip." What does this Proverb mean? In many situations, we assume that when things are going our way, the final outcome will also be in our favour. However, at the last moment, things change and we find that the outcome or result is the opposite, and not as per expectations. The analogy used is a cup containing a desirable drink. However by the time the drink reaches our lips, we find that the cup is empty. The cup could have been drained for a variety of reasons. The reasons are not for us to seek. Emptiness of the cup is of concern. This Proverb warns us that until and unless we have seen and experienced the final outcome to be in our favour, we should not make assumptions. Many students, on the basis of their documents, are granted admission to Universities in developed countries. However, celebrations shouldn't commence until and unless the Visa has also been obtained. A similar Proverb is, "**Don't count your chickens before they are hatched.**"

LESSON 276

Same word - different pronunciations

Where pronunciations are concerned in English, one has to note that a word's pronunciation in a different manner might demarcate it to be a different Part of Speech. Let us take the word **'aged'**. When the word **'aged'** is used as Verb, it is pronounced **'ay-jd'** – "Your dog **has** aged considerably in the past six months." The same word, when used as Adjective, gets to be differently pronounced as **'ay-jid'**, e.g. "His face wore an **aged** look." Similarly, when the word **'learn'** is used as Verb it has got to be pronounced to rhyme with **'earn'**. The Past Tense form of **'learn'** is learnt as well as **learned**. When we use and pronounce **'learned'** as **'learn-nid'**, then it indicates the word being used as Adjective, e.g. "He is a very **learned** man" i.e. he is a man who has great knowledge. As Participle, it is always better to use **'learnt'**. **Have** you **learnt** your Lessons?

LESSON 277

'Through' and 'Thorough'

"Have you been **through** this book in a **thorough** manner?" The addition of the letter **'o'** between **'h'** and **'r'** of the word **'through'**, makes for the formation of another word. When we use the word **'thorough'**, it is an Adjective and means to be extremely attentive to detail and to look at or to study something in a comprehensive manner. It can also mean **'wholly'** or **'to a great extent'**, e.g. "We enjoyed ourselves **thoroughly** at the party." The addition of **'ly'** makes **'thorough'** an Adverb and its use should be in accordance. What is of importance, however, is that when we use **'thorough'**, both when writing as well as when speaking English, we must convey it correctly. The word 'through', on the other hand, can be Adverb, Preposition as well as Adjective. In the sentence, "We were just passing through" the word 'through' is Adverb. In "We went **through** the garden to take a shortcut," the word 'through' is Preposition. In "When will you be **through** with that program?" the word 'through' is Adjective. I'm sure by now you must have understood 'through' in a 'thorough' manner.

LESSON 278

'Minute (mi-nit)' and 'minute (my-newt)'

Human beings have divided time into convenient segments of 'seconds', 'minutes', and 'hours'. The word '**minute**' in English however, has more than that one meaning that is connected with time. As a **Plural Noun** the word '**minutes**' also means a record of the proceedings of a formal meeting. If you live in a co-operative housing society, you must have, at some time, seen that minutes of the previous meeting are read out at the consequent formal general body meeting. The word '**minutes**' is simply a formal record. The word '**minute**' is also used as an Adjective, especially when we wish to describe something detailed or possessing much more than that what is visible to the eye, e.g. "This matter needs a **minute** inspection." Here, the word '**minute**', being Adjective, needs to be pronounced 'my-newt'. As Adverb, it becomes '**my-nyootly**' i.e. minutely, e.g. "He looked minutely at the clock." The word '**minute**' is of course pronounced '**min-it**' when we mean it to be a division of time, e.g. "An hour has sixty **minutes** in it, a **minute** has sixty seconds in it."

LESSON 279

'Body Language' and 'Gestures'

While awaiting your turn at a personal interview, do you bite your nails? Do you constantly knock your knees against each other? Do you scratch yourself even when you're not itching? These actions display nervousness and form part of what is known as **body language**. When we make certain actions, we indicate certain emotions. These actions are known as **gestures** (pronounced '**jes-chers**'). The word '**gesture**' is both Noun and Verb. '**To gesture**' can also mean to make a sign, e.g.: "The African, unable to speak English, **gestured** to the white man to eat." The same sentence can be rewritten with the word '**gesture**' as Noun as "The African, unable to speak English, made a **gesture** with his hands, asking the white man to eat." The words, '**gesticulate**'(pronounced '**jes-ti-kyu-late**') and '**gesticulation**' can also be used and have the same meaning as the Verb '**to gesture**'. When '**gesticulate**' is used instead of '**gesture**', it conveys excitement. This excitement may or may not exist in '**gesturing**',e.g. "The lost children wildly **gesticulated** toward the woman identifying her to be their mother."

LESSON 280

'Picture' and 'Pitcher'

Have you ever heard the word '**picture**' being pronounced correctly? Invariably, you get to hear it as '**pitcher**'. The meanings of both these words are vastly different from each other. Through the correct pronunciation, we should be able to convey correctly what the meaning is. However, due to association of ideas and our own indifference, we generally overlook such oral misdemeanours. The letter 'c', we have seen on so many occasions, is pronounced 'k', and the correct pronunciation of 'picture' is 'pick-cher'. A picture, an image, is the representation of reality on a surface. The word 'pitcher', possessing more than one meaning, stands for a large jug or container generally with a handle. The word 'pitcher' also stands for a person who throws a ball using a particular throwing style to the 'batter/hitter' in baseball. The word 'picture' can also be used as Verb, e.g. "I cannot picture this plain Jane as a glamorous woman."

"How do you picture your life, say, three years from now?" The word 'pitcher' is only Noun and cannot be used as Verb.

LESSON 281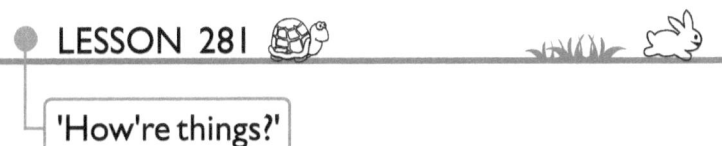

'How're things?'

When we do not specify the Subject of a sentence, we tend to be **vague, ambiguous, confused,** or **unclear**. Constant use of the word 'things' is a clear indication that the speaker does not know the exact word required or is generalizing, e.g. "Please pick up your **things** when you leave." Here, the word 'things' obviously implies some items or luggage or clothes or other belongings of the person concerned. At times, you hear the question, "How're **things**?" Here, the word 'things' implies circumstances or situations that govern one's life in general. The answer may be "**Things** aren't so good" or "**Things** are looking up" or "**Things** are really bad." While the use of the word 'things' in such contexts is acceptable, especially where spoken English in colloquial terms is concerned, its use in formal situations and in written English is unacceptable. English has the richest Vocabulary in the world. There are clear and correct words for facts, items, phenomena etc. Imagine the confusion if Einstein's famous equation had been described as - "E is equal to the square of this thing multiplied by that thing." One must, therefore, continually keep looking up the dictionary and enriching one's Vocabulary.

LESSON 282

'Cynical', 'Pessimist' and 'Optimist'

Just when you are being highly **optimistic** about your career with the company taking an upswing, a colleague paints a **cynical** picture of your company's and related with it, your prospects. His/her comments obviously burst your balloon. Who is a **cynic** (pronounced 'si-nick')? What does **cynicism** (**pronounced** 'sini-sism') imply? A cynic is a person who believes that every human action, including charity, is motivated by selfishness. Sometimes, being **cynical** does help, especially when confronting ground realities. **Cynicism** is not the same as **pessimism**, although many assume it to be so. **Pessimism**, the opposite of **optimism**, involves disbelief in the positive aspects of development and emphasizes that the negative is overwhelmingly present. **George Bernard Shaw** described a **pessimist** correctly, by stating that 'A **pessimist** is a person who feels bad when he is feeling good because he is afraid that he might feel worse if he is feeling better.' There are many clichéd descriptions of **optimists** and **pessimists**. However, one of my favourites is, "The **optimist** sees the doughnut, the pessimist the hole."

LESSON 283

'Skeptic', 'Specious', 'Agnostic' and 'Atheist'

Continuing with negative developments that some people feel are more important than positive ones, the next word is 'skepticism'. A **skeptic** or as is written in British English, a **sceptic** (pronounced 'skeptic', as in American English), is a person who doubts the truth behind a stated fact or phenomenon. For a **skeptic**, every argument is **specious** (pronounced '**spee-shee-yus**'). In earlier times, the word **skeptic** was used to describe a person who did not believe in the origin of many happenings, developments and miracles as described in Christianity. The word '**specious**' is Adjective and means that although an argument or some kind of reasoning appears to be sound, it has absolutely no truth in it. This word is very often used in courtrooms by lawyers when arguing in English. It is a very useful word when you wish to point out in an essay or a debate, the flaws in an argument. Coming back to non-believers, where religion is concerned, a person, who accepts the existence of a supreme being, but does not believe in God in currently accepted forms, is known as an '**agnostic**'. A person who totally disbelieves in the existence of God is known in English as an '**atheist**'.

LESSON 284

'Rapport' and 'Vibes'

Can the word '**rapport**' be preceded by the Adjective 'good' or 'bad'? Most definitely not! The word '**rapport**', an Abstract Noun, denotes 'a very good relationship' or a 'harmonious relationship between one individual and another or between an individual and a group'. Being Abstract Noun, the word 'rapport' cannot be quantified or further qualified. Due to the weight of its meaning being connected with a positive aspect, a negative perspective cannot be attached to it. Pronounced 'ra-poh', the word 'rapport' is used to describe the development of a wonderful relationship between two or more individuals, e.g. "The **rapport** developed between the teacher and her students helped improve their Communication skills."

"In a call-centre, the local employee is so busy building **rapport** with overseas customers that s/he is hardly aware of his/her immediate neighbour." The closest that another word comes to 'rapport' is '**vibrations**' or as is spoken in colloquial English as '**vibes**', e.g.: "In spite of the difference in their ages, there are great **vibes** between them." Here, 'good' or 'bad' or any other quality is possible as '**vibes**' is a Common Noun, e.g. "Events outside the office premises led to **terrible vibes** between the Process Manager and the Team Leader."

LESSON 285

'Beware', 'Aware' and 'Wary'

"Beware of the dog!" This is a common signboard very often seen on the door or the main gate of a big house, especially a bungalow. The signboard also deters thieves from making any attempt at stealing from such premises. To '**beware**' is to 'make someone **become aware of**'. Let us first take the word '**aware**'. To be '**aware**' is to be informed, or to be conscious of any kind of happening, instance, etc. An '**aware**' individual is armed with information that may be general or have a specific background. The word '**beware**' is Verb in the imperative form and acts more as order or warning rather than request. The word '**beware**' warns the reader/listener to be on guard or to be cautious against some kind of danger. The consequence of '**Beware!**' is that the concerned person becomes wary. When a person is wary, he is more than aware i.e. he is cautious and extremely watchful. '**Wary**' and '**aware**' are Adjectives, while '**beware**' is Verb. So, as you go on becoming aware in the oceans of English, you will hopefully become wary of mistakes and avoid them. **Beware!**

LESSON 286

'Loot', 'Plunder' and 'Pillage'

The word '**loot**', coincidentally, means the same in English as it does in Hindi. As Verb, '**to loot**' means to take things in great quantity that do not belong to you. As uncountable Noun, it stands for the material objects illegally and immorally taken from someone. When used as Verb, the word '**loot**' can be used with/without an object, e.g. "The thieves **looted** cash and other valuables from the locker." "They went on **looting** and **plundering** leaving nothing of value behind." The word '**plunder**' adds the element of force, by robbing without obstruction or committing frauds without fear of punishment. The word '**plunder**', like '**loot**', is both Noun as well as Verb, e.g. "The **plunder** committed by them had no parallel."

"After the town **had been plundered**, it was virtually unrecognizable."

The word '**pillage**', is of the highest degree in a negative manner with '**pillage**' denoting looting and plundering with force and violence and no obstruction or resistance whatsoever, e.g. "After **pillaging** it, the criminals set fire to the village."

"The **pillaging** turned the village's prosperity into poverty."

The former sentence uses '**pillage**' as Verb, the latter as Noun.

LESSON 287

Synonyms and Antonyms – Some exact, some approximate

The opposite of 'genuine' is 'spurious', not 'duplicate' or 'fake'. The word 'duplicate' is the opposite of 'original' and the word 'fake' the opposite of 'real' or 'authentic'. Many a time, the synonyms of a word do not convey similarity in an exact manner but are approximations. So is it with antonyms. Where an antonym is concerned, there may not be a word that is **exactly** the opposite but **roughly** the opposite. In the above examples and elsewhere, we have seen overlapping of words on so many occasions. Let us look at the opposites of certain words that we regularly use or need. (1) **Cheap – expensive** (2) **light – dark** (3) **fair – unfair** (4) **small – big** (5) **slim – fat** (6) **neat – untidy** (7) **pure – impure** (8) **safe – dangerous** (9) **beautiful – ugly** (10) **secure – insecure**. In the above examples, you could easily swap words and be none the wiser. Of course, once again, the context is of prime concern. When the context is clear, then the word chosen is bound to fit in a most appropriate manner.

LESSON 288

Synonyms and Antonyms: As per the Context

On careful examination of the previous lesson's ten paired examples, in each chosen word's case, there can be another synonym/antonym depending on the context. The word '**cheap**' also implies a lowly behaviour, e.g. "That was a **cheap** trick to do." '**Light**' can be used in a context related also to weight, with '**heavy**' being an antonym. '**Fair**' has been used in the context of justice. It can also be related to '**complexion**' with the opposite being '**dark-skinned**'. 'Small' has so many contexts that it would take a whole chapter. Two of its many antonyms are '**big**' and '**large**'. '**Slim**' is synonymous with '**thin**' and its antonym '**fat**', being Noun in addition to an Adjective, can also mean extra flesh. '**Neat**' has more than one meaning, and besides cleanliness, also implies skilful actions. When associated with alcohol, '**neat**' means drinking an alcoholic drink without adding soda/water. The opposite of '**pure**' together with '**impure**' can also be '**adulterated**' or '**debased**'. When '**safe**' is used in particular contexts, its opposite can also be '**risky**'. '**Safe**' is also a Noun and means a large box/container to store valuables. The word '**beautiful**' has quite a few synonyms and its antonym '**ugly**' too has more than one, e.g. '**unattractive**', '**revolting**' etc. '**Secure**', when used as Verb, has '**free**' or '**untie**' as its antonyms. Where English is concerned, context is of prime concern.

LESSON 289

'Compatibility' and 'Congeniality'

Before plunging into matrimony, the concerned man and woman must find out if they have '**compatibility**' and '**congeniality**'. What do these words mean? Why are they necessary for a happy marriage? Their Adjective forms are '**compatible**' and '**congenial**' respectively. The word '**compatible**' stands for a quality that shows its possessor to be able to live in harmony and co-exist peacefully with another human being. **Compatibility** leads to happiness in marriage. Before getting married, potential spouses must seek to know from a psychologist/counselor their **compatibility quotient**. The word '**compatible**' is also used with computers and electronics and means the ability of any system/device to be used in/on another computer (both software and hardware) or appliance without change or modifications. The word 'congenial' means possessing the quality of being agreeable, and by and large, disinclined to creating conflicts in disturbing circumstances. It is important for a spouse to be **congenial** so that s/he can be compatible. The word **'congenial' should not be confused with 'congenital'**. The word **'congenital'**, an Adjective, means any quality or impairment, defect or disorder present in an individual, from the time of his/her birth.

LESSON 290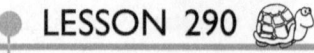

'Potable' and 'Edible'

Water is the elixir of life. When not respectfully treated, it gets contaminated. When contaminated, it may lead to serious ailments. A disease caused through intake of contaminated water, is known as a **water-borne** disease. Illnesses may also occur due to bathing in polluted waters. When we drink water without filtering or boiling it, dangerous micro-organisms get into our bodies and create deadly ailments. These may even lead to death. Therefore, water, before being drunk, must be made **potable** i.e. **fit for drinking**. The word **'potable'** is **Adjective** and has the same meaning as **'drinkable'**. However, **'potable'** must not be confused with **'portable'**. The correct Adjective with food is **'edible'** (as in food that is fit to be eaten). School-going children must never eat food cooked in unhygienic conditions sold in streets. The word **'eatable'** is Adjective and carries the same meaning as **'edible'**. When s is added to **'eatable'** it becomes a plural Noun. The plural **'eatables'** means a number of food items. Remember, not all eatables may be **eatable**. Use of **'edible'**, therefore, is advisable because it eliminates confusion. You must always ascertain before drinking and eating, that the water is **potable** and food is **edible**.

LESSON 291

Anagrams and Palindromes

We have seen "**stressed**" earlier to be an anagram of "**desserts**". "A **leader** is a **dealer** in hope." If you look carefully at **leader** and **dealer**, both contain the same letters albeit in a different order with each letter used only once. Now look at the words in bold in the following sentence: "A **teacher** is a **cheater** of ignorance." The word '**orchestra**' when rearranged becomes '**carthorse**'. An **anagram** is a word using all the letters of another word without repeating any letter. The system of spelling being so difficult, makes it important for us to know how words use letters and in what kinds of sequences. Apart from entertaining us, recognizing **anagrams** makes us sharper. An **anagram** means the creation of another word. When a word reads the same when spelt backwards then it is known as a **palindrome**. A famous palindrome involving more than one word is "**Madam, I'm Adam**". Here are some **palindromes** in English, and it would help if you read and remember them so that you don't forget when you write: **civic, dad, eye, kayak, level, Malayalam, mom, peep, pip, and tot.**

LESSON 292

'Grinning' and 'Smiling'

When circumstances turn difficult, one is advised to '**grin and bear it.**' This advice is so that one doesn't cave in because of the difficulties. It also inspires one to keep on making efforts to overcome those difficulties. The word '**grin**' stands for a big smile and when used on its own, means that one is amused or very happy on seeing or meeting someone, e.g. "Your **grin** clearly shows you are up to some mischief." "Her classmates were grinning from ear to ear when she fell on the chair being pulled away from beneath her."

The word 'grin', instead of 'smile', with 'bear it', indicates the fact that in spite of the number of difficulties involved, intensity of effort is doubled. There are a number of expressions, sayings and idioms in English that help one face difficulties. Another significant expression toward surmounting obstacles is 'take it in your stride'. Use of the word 'stride' rather than 'step' is certainly a booster. "Having resolved to be a successful actress, she took the string of flops in her stride."

LESSON 293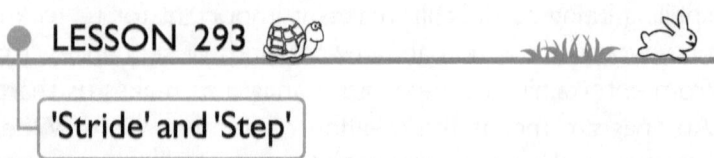

'Stride' and 'Step'

The word 'stride' ended the last Lesson. A 'step' is a small movement towards a particular place while 'stride' (pronounced to rhyme with ride) stands for a longer distance covered in one movement as compared to 'step'. The word 'step' is Noun as well as Verb. And so is 'stride'. When we 'step' toward a place or an object, we make a movement and this movement does not cover a large distance. This movement is smaller compared to the one involved when taking a stride. While we can make as well as take a 'step', 'stride' is generally used only with the Verb 'take'. In many fairy tales one comes across giants and demons taking huge strides, i.e. a step that may equal two ordinary steps or even be of much greater length. Generally, taller individuals take strides, while shorter ones take steps. The Past Tense of 'step' is 'stepped' while the Past Tense of 'stride' is 'strode'. The word 'step', as Verb, combines with Prepositions to become Phrasal Verbs. These are commonplace and seen in routine events, e.g. (1) to step down - "After so many years as Managing Director, he has finally stepped down." (2) **to step up** – "With the possibility of being deprived of their bonus, the workers have **stepped up** their agitation." (3) to **step into** – "As her mother is abroad, she has **stepped into** her mother's shoes, looking after her younger siblings."

- LESSON 294

'Step On', 'Being in Step' and 'Keep in Step'

"You're going too slow, step on the gas." In this sentence, the word 'step' is Verb and indicates that the listener must press the accelerator pedal so as to increase speed. Incidentally, this is American slang. The word 'gas' does not imply gas, but is short for 'gasoline'. Fuel (petrol/diesel) in American English is known as 'gasoline'. We have seen some Phrasal Verbs with 'step'. Here are some idioms: (1) to break step – "The section behind the flag-bearer broke step as soon as the salute was over." (2) To be in step – "The song being simple made it easy for many to be in step with its rhythm." (3) To keep in step – "Not many industries have kept in step with the phenomenal growth of the IT industry in India." We are aware of the expression 'step by step' and have many a time been confronted with its application in life. 'Failures are stepping stones to success' is a frequently-given topic for classroom essay-writing. The most famous sentence with the word 'step' was spoken by Neil Armstrong, when he, being the first human being to land on the moon, said, "A small step for man, a giant leap for mankind."

LESSON 295

'Scope', 'Periscope' and 'Kaleidoscope'

As school students, we make various kinds of articles for our Art/Craft classes. The word 'scope' is part of two of these very common articles. One of the easiest items to be made is the periscope. A long square tube with a flat S-shaped hollow made of cardboard with two mirrors facing each other at crucial angles of 45 degrees each. From one end of the periscope we can see the person standing at the other end. This is due to the laws of reflection and a periscope is an extremely important instrument in a submarine. A kaleidoscope is a hard cylindrical tube, approximately six to seven inches in length, with an eyepiece on one end and broken bangle pieces on the other larger end. When the tube is rotated, the colourful broken bangle pieces move and through the eyepiece appear to be forming attractive and intricate patterns. The word 'scope' stands for range, limit or extent. It is used in a variety of areas and its extent may or may not be limited, e.g. "Whether the miracle occurred or not is beyond the scope of human enquiry."

LESSON 296

'Won't'-'Wont' and 'Can't'-'Cant'

The moment the word '**don't**' is typed on your computer (MS-Word), the apostrophe, by default, jumps to its position between *n* and *t*. The apostrophe, however, doesn't automatically jump in between *n* and *t* when you type '**wont**' and '**cant**'. Why? That is because **wont** and **won't** are two separate words, and the same is true of **cant** and **can't**. '**Wont**' is pronounced '**want**' and '**cant**' is pronounced the same as '**can't**'.

The word '**wont**' indicates an **inclination toward** or being accustomed to any particular act, generally negative, e.g. "Don't give the watchman a five-hundred rupee note, he's **wont** to keep the change."

"Some schoolboys are **wont** to ask for a lift from passing vehicles." '**Cant**' is used to describe any irritating manner, using which, some people speak. These may be members of the underworld or anti-social elements or even beggars, e.g. "I can't stand the **cant** of these beggar-women at traffic lights."

"In Hindi films, the hero as underworld don uses a peculiar **cant**." The word '**cant**' isn't the same as '**chant**'. Remember, '**won't**' and '**can't**' are contractions of '**will not**' and '**cannot**', respectively. Remember, '**cannot**' is one word.

LESSON 297

'Chant', 'Prostrate' and 'Kneeling'

"I can hear devotees **chanting** Hare Rama Hare Krishna." The word '**chant**' is used to describe a particular kind of singing used especially when praying. You can hear devotees **chant** hymns to Christ in a church or when the devout are in a mosque, they **chant** a call to Allah. The word '**chant**' is Noun as well as Verb. When one prays to one's God, especially in the company of other devotees, there is an element of chanting involved. When Hindus pray in a temple, many pay **obeisance** (deep respect) to their God by lying prostrate on the floor. The word '**prostrate**' is both Verb as well as Adjective, e.g.: "The minister **prostrated** himself in front of the lady Chief Minister."

"Long after the others had gone, this devout Hindu was still **prostrate** before Lord Krishna."

The word '**prostrate**' means 'to lie, face downwards in humility to pay respects or homage to someone, especially your God.' In a mosque, Muslims do not **prostrate**, but **bend forward** together to touch the ground with their foreheads. Christians pray sitting on benches in a church, with no need to remove footwear outside, and some of them, when near the altar, **kneel** to pray in silence.

LESSON 298

'Breed', 'Bred' and 'Pedigree'

The word '**bred**' has nothing to do with '**bread**'. When we speak of upbringing using the Past Tense, then '**breed**' becomes '**bred**', e.g. "He was born and bred in a small town of Madhya Pradesh." The word '**breed**' is **Noun** as well as **Verb** and can therefore be used in relative contexts. As **Noun**, it is generally used for animals or any other creature that is nurtured and brought up by human beings, e.g. "This horse is of a fine **breed**." When we speak of the superior background of a particular horse, we also say, "He is a **thoroughbred**." When used as Verb, the word '**bred**' informs us as to how someone has been **raised** (American English) or **brought up** (British English). The word 'breed' is very commonly used when people wish to keep or buy a particular kind of dog or any other domesticated animal as pet. e.g. "What breed dog do you wish to buy, a cocker-spaniel or an Alsatian?" In such cases, the word '**pedigree**' is also used to describe the historical and genealogical background of the concerned animal/human being, e.g. "Hitler considered only a particular **breed** of Germans to be of fine Aryan **pedigree**."

LESSON 299

'Fast', 'Feast' and 'Banquet'

Where eating is concerned, the word '**fast**' denotes **abstaining** i.e. **not indulging in** or refraining from eating. Being an important aspect of our control over the desire to eat, '**fasting**' is integral to many religions. All over Maharashtra, you find men and women fasting on selected days of the week. The opposite of '**fasting**', in a way, is '**feasting**'. When we speak of '**feasting**', it is generally done on festivals or weddings or occasions that warrant great joy and happiness. Both, '**fast**' and '**feast**', are Nouns as well as Verbs, e.g. "I'm not having lunch for I'm on **a fast** today.";

"Muslims **fast** in the month of Ramadan.";

"Christians have **a feast** during Christmas.";

"Parsis **feast** during Pateti." Where feasting is concerned, there is a tendency to hold a **banquet** (pronounced **ban-quett**). A **banquet** is generally the serving of food to a number of guests. These guests help themselves to servings from a table or sit at a table and are served delicious food. Food served at a banquet includes a huge number of dishes that are richly cooked and flavoured.

LESSON 300

> True Education – Application of Knowledge and Skill of Comprehension

On a number of occasions it has been noted that students who did not study at English-medium schools, complain of having been deprived the opportunity of having got to study and learn English well. Ironically, a great number of students who have passed out from English-medium schools also do not possess as much fluency over English as they would like to imagine they do. Not using the language outside academic premises is the main reason for this predicament. Many students are in the odious habit of referring to guides and do not read the text at all. Behind every Lesson in the text, a number of exercises involving grammar and showing its correct use in English are conveniently placed for the serious student to work on. These exercises use textual matter that the conscientious student can easily understand and consequently apply. True education lies in the development of a student's abilities to correctly apply knowledge gained, in addition to the gradual development of comprehension skills. Remember, the heart of education lies not only in education of the heart, but more importantly in educating the mind.

LESSON 301

> 'Enough' and associated prepositions

The word '**enough**' (**pronounced e-nuhf**) is generally used with the word '**to**'. Even if the word '**to**' is not spoken or written, it is most certainly implied, e.g. "I was so hungry, I have had food enough to last me two days." As Adjective, the word '**enough**' is generally used **after the Noun** in order to create emphasis. This

is clear from the above sentence and in the following sentence too, it follows the same pattern:
"The auditorium being full, there wasn't **room enough** (to seat so many) with people standing in the aisles to watch." The word 'enough' conveys the quantity or extent of the said subject to be **sufficient** or even **more than sufficient**, e.g. "You are **old enough** now to earn." With the word 'to' (implied) as an accompaniment, the word 'enough' shows what kind of effect the extent would have. However, when 'of' is used after 'enough', it conveys displeasure, e.g.:

"**Enough of** your nonsense!" When followed by 'of' the word 'enough' becomes an interjection, and is a declaration of some kind of limit having been reached.

LESSON 302

'Valid-Invalid'

When we look at documents or facts that need no further verification the term '**valid**' stands for its applicability at the moment in force. The word '**valid**' implies that a fact or rule or law fulfils all conditions. It can also mean that there cannot be a challenge to such a fact, rule or law. '**Valid**', an **Adjective**, gives sanction or force to the Noun that it is qualifying or governing, e.g. "The student raised a **valid question** regarding allotment of scores, where more than one answer was possible in the Speaking test."

Where validity is concerned, it is also used in and on documents to declare conditions or a period during which a particular document is in force, e.g. "Valid from January 2013 to June 2016."

The word '**invalid**' is used as the opposite to '**valid**', making facts, rules and laws subject to question.

The word '**invalid**' is also used to denote a physically challenged individual. When applied to indicate or describe a person with physical disabilities, '**invalid**' is pronounced '**in-vuh-leed**'.

LESSON 303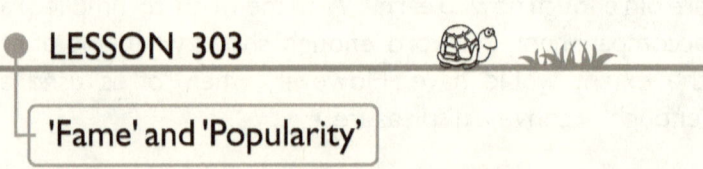

'Fame' and 'Popularity'

Do you wish to become famous? Do you desire your share of fame? Have you ever taken steps to become a celebrity? The word '**famous**' is Adjective, and indicates that a famous person is one whose name is widespread in a particular profession or who has a skill of high caliber. This person, because of the fame attached to his/her name, is a **celebrity**. The words '**fame**' and '**celebrity**' are Nouns. Those who are famous have a reputation for being able to do things that ordinary people generally do not or cannot. It is because of the fame a person possesses that s/he also gets access to money. Those who are famous are also **renowned**. Remember, **being popular is not the same as being famous**. A popular person is one who is well-liked for certain qualities, and may also achieve a name. This achievement, however, gets to be limited, e.g. "Nazia Hassan, Runa Laila, and Salma Agha became popular singers but could never become as famous as Lata Mangeshkar." The Noun form of '**popular**' is '**popularity**'. As you might have by now guessed, popularity is a short-term phenomenon whereas one is famous over a longer period of time.

LESSON 304

'Notorious'. 'Notoreity' and 'Goodwill'

The words **'famous'**, **'fame'** and **'celebrity'** describe an individual and his/her achievements in a positive manner. When someone becomes famous for the wrong reasons, the correct Adjective to be used is **'notorious'**. Both 'famous' and **'notorious'** can be used in the same sentence to describe these two opposing qualities, e.g. "India is not only famous for spirituality, but also notorious for corruption." When a person, city, capital, or country etc. becomes well-known for a negative quality, the word **'notorious'** is most appropriate to describe that quality, e.g.: "Shyam is notorious for being late to school every day."

The Noun form of 'notorious' is 'notoriety'. e.g. "The notoriety of Las Vegas as a gambling city runs across internationally, making it the gambling capital of the world."

"Mumbai is famed to be a safe city for women but recent crimes might earn it notoriety." A famous person has a reputation to take care of whereas a notorious person has got stuck with a bad name. When it comes to businesses and commercial setups, a firm's reputation results in the firm earning what is known as 'goodwill'. The word **'goodwill', is not a synonym of 'famous'** but makes the company that possesses 'goodwill' well-known for its dealings to be above board, i.e. clean, clear, fair and in a legitimate manner.

LESSON 305

'Saloon' and 'Salon'

"I'm going to the saloon." So often you hear people using English to refer to the place where they would be getting their hair cut as '**saloon**'. The word '**saloon**' is incorrect with the correct word being '**salon**' (pronounced '**suh-lon**' or '**sa-lawn**' with the '**law**' being of a slight nasal sound). A **saloon** is a place that is frequented by people who wish to drink. **Saloons** came into existence as resting-rooms in the USA where cowboys on horseback had to stop for rest on long journeys. The cowboy's horse was given water to drink outside while the cowboy quenched his thirst inside. The word '**salon**', on the other hand, denotes an area in which a client's, either a gentleman's or a lady's, physical appearance is catered to. A '**salon**' is generally a place where different kinds of beauty treatments, including haircuts, are performed. The word '**salon**' can also be used to describe a large waiting area. Remember, a **saloon** may have a **salon** but a **salon** cannot be used as a **saloon**. A sophisticated **salon** nowadays may also describe and advertise itself as a health **spa**.

LESSON 306

'White Elephant'

Many expressions in English have their sources spread all over the world. One such expression - '**white elephant**', originated in Thailand (formerly Siam). White elephants, although a rarity in most elephant-inhabited forests of Africa and Asia, were found in Siam. It is said that when the king of Siam wished to punish someone, he would present the wrongdoer with a white elephant. An elephant that was white was deliberately chosen to symbolize the king's command. As refusing or returning it would be insulting the king, its recipient was forced to take the white elephant home. Maintaining **a white elephant** at home involved **huge financial expenses which were frightfully burdensome.** Soon, the wrongdoer would become penniless because of the maintenance and upkeep of the elephant. The king's punishment ensured the maintenance of the elephant as penalty leading to financial ruin and poverty of the wrongdoer. The expression '**white elephant**' today is used to describe an economic exercise leading to huge financial losses, e.g.:"This Plan, subsidising prices of cooking gas, food-grain etc. will soon become **a white elephant.**"

"That vintage car with a mileage of four kilometers per litre is **a white elephant.**"

● LESSON 307

'Custodian' and 'Custody'

Recently the word '**custodian**' was in the news for all the wrong reasons. A '**custodian**' is someone who has been entrusted the guardianship of a person or of a document or any item of value. The word '**custodian**' is **Common Noun** with '**custody**' being another. When an accused is taken into '**custody**' he is first '**arrested**' and then kept in an area where necessary security arrangements have been made to keep an eye on him/her. When important documents such as files, deeds, agreements, ornaments etc. of great value are to be looked after, they are handed over to a person who is deemed to be its/their **custodian. The custodian is supposed to keep them** safe in his/her **custody.** When the owner or any authorized person or anyone connected with an item or document wishes to have them back or checked, the **custodian** must hand them over. In earlier days, a person known for his honesty, integrity and sense of fairness was handed over many kinds of objects, even children, to be their custodian. The owner, or the concerned individual, was certain that on demanding them back, the custodian would hand back the objects/children in a sound condition.

LESSON 308

Safe and 'Sound'

"Fortunately, they weren't hurt and got out of the accident **safe and sound.**" The word '**sound**' in this sentence, means that the persons being spoken of were uninjured and in a healthy condition. The word '**sound**' is **Noun, Verb** and **Adjective**. When '**ly**' is added, it becomes **Adverb**. It must therefore be correctly placed according to what meaning the speaker/writer wishes to convey. Generally, when it is used to convey that no harm has been done, the word '**sound**', being Adjective, is used together with '**safe**' i.e. '**safe and sound**'. The word 'sound' can however, also be used by itself. e.g. "It was a sound decision not to sell those shares now that their price has doubled." As **Noun**, the word 'sound' is known to us all as denoting an aural signal that registers in our ears, e.g. "I don't like the sound of that cough." **Please note that 'sound' does not mean 'voice'. A voice has a sound (pleasant or unpleasant) but a sound has no voice.** When '**sound**' is used as Verb, it indicates communication e.g. "Have you sounded the students out regarding next week's picnic?"

LESSON 309

'Discoveries' and 'Inventions'

Many students of English assume a **discovery** to be an **invention**. What is the difference between the two? The word '**discovery**' means uncovering or revealing that what is already in existence. An **invention** is the making of something that is new, i.e. something that did not ever exist earlier. Columbus was on his way to the land he imagined would be India, but went on to **discover** America. A **discovery**, i.e. the Noun form of the Verb '**discover**', is the result of a search whereas an **invention** is the result of experimentation through perseverance. Benjamin Franklin **discovered** electricity and it was Thomas Edison who **invented** the light bulb. Similarly, there have been instances of so many scientific laws, rules and facts being **discovered**. While in a bathtub Archimedes **discovered** what is now known as the Archimedes' Principle. Similarly, Newton's laws of motion and principles to do with gravity are clearly **discoveries**. The Wright brothers **invented** the airplane and Henry Ford **invented** the motor car. Likewise, **inventions** such as trains, telephones, computers, spacecraft etc. are not **discoveries**. On a philosophical note, no matter how many **lies we invent, the truth always gets discovered.**

LESSON 310

'Clever' and 'Intelligent'

On securing a higher than average score in a test, do you feel **clever**? Or do you feel that you are **intelligent**? What is the difference between being **clever** and being **intelligent**? The word '**clever**' has more to do with **skill** or **ingenuity**. When describing someone as being '**clever**', we are showing that that person is a good learner. He is therefore considered to be able to do what is asked or required of him. For a servant to become the boss, and ensure that he remains boss, he has first got to be **clever** and then become intelligent. An individual able to reason out solutions, think his way rationally out of difficulties or move steadily toward success certainly possesses the attribute of being **intelligent**. A monkey is generally considered to be clever, while an elephant is supposed to be intelligent. Both **clever** and **intelligent** are **Adjectives** with **cleverness** and **intelligence** being their **Noun** forms respectively. When describing someone as '**clever**', the speaker/writer may be using sarcasm, but being described as '**intelligent**' is definitely being praised, e.g. "How **clever** of you to win that game on your phone!" "Dhoni's **intelligence** has seen India emerge successfully out of many tight corners."

LESSON 311

'Been': A Unique Time-Frame

It is quite difficult to teach new students of English the meaning and correct usage of the word '**been**'. The word '**been**' conveys a time-frame that has no equivalent in non-English languages. Transliterations used to explain '**been**', therefore, are **futile**. The use of '**been**' clearly shows completion of action e.g. "Have you ever **been** to Hawaii?" The listener/reader may now be interacting with the speaker either personally or on the phone. Use of the word '**been**' implies completion of the journey to Hawaii, if at all undertaken earlier. Action **being** over, brings the conversation back to wherever the listener/reader now **is**. Remember, '**been**' cannot be used without the addition of 'has/have' (Present Participle) or had (Past Participle), e.g. (1) "It **has been noticed** that there are too many holidays in India." (2) "When I reached my friend's office, her work **had been** done." When 'been' is used, the sentence goes into the **Passive Voice** mode with the agent 'by' being used. In (1) & (2), the word 'by' is implied: (1) noticed **by** someone and (2) done **by** her.

LESSON 312

'...ing' – Proper/Improper Use

We saw the use of 'been' in the earlier Lesson with the **Perfect** form of the tenses, both the **Present** as well as **Past**. The word 'been' is also used in the **Present Perfect Continuous** as well as the **Past Perfect Continuous**, e.g.: "I **have been reading** since 7 a.m."; "They **had been dancing** for over five hours when the police arrived." Once again, it is important to emphasize that in the Present Perfect and the **Present Perfect Continuous Tense**, **'has/have' is used** and in the **Past Perfect** and in the **Past Perfect Continuous Tense**, 'had' is used together with the Verb. It is very important here to understand that the following verbs must **never be used** in the ...ing form: **appear, believe, belong to, care, consist of, contain, dislike, feel (that), forget, forgive, gather, hate, know, like, love, matter, mean, own, possess, recollect, refuse, remember, seem, suppose, think (that), understand, want, wish.** These Verbs must be used only in the **Present Simple** (as given above) or **Past Simple Tense** forms. When used in their ...ing forms by themselves, these Verbs are **Adjectives**, or **Nouns**. To give an example, **'loving'** is **Adjective** whereas **'living'** is **Noun** – "He has always been a loving husband." "He sells computers for a living."

LESSON 313

'Heir', 'Inheritance' and 'Erstwhile'

The words 'air' and 'heir' are **homophones** i.e. both are differently spelt, but pronounced the same. It is how each is used that conveys its correct meaning. The word '**heir**' must never be mispronounced as '**hair**'. When we use the word '**heir**', we mean the person who is next in line to take up the position of power. It generally also means the eldest child who would be getting a chance to become a leader/king/minister/owner/etc. When the word '**heir**' is used, it clearly conveys to the reader/listener the person who is going to '**inherit**' power. The **Noun** form of '**inherit**', a **Verb**, is '**inheritance**', e.g. "The property came his way as a matter of **inheritance**." Here, the word '**erstwhile**' is also used to indicate the former owner. The word '**erstwhile**' is Adjective and clearly denotes chronology, e.g. "The **erstwhile** Chief Minister of Haryana wanted his eldest son as **heir**, to take over, but had to wait for the elections."

When a **sibling** (brother/sister) would want his share, it could lead to a clash for power. An heir is also known as 'scion' (pronounced 'sion' - 'c' silent).

LESSON 314

'Symptom', 'Syndrome' and 'Diagnosis'

When you visit a clinic in the event of some physical discomfort, the doctor first puts a **thermometer** into your mouth. If you have **fever**, i.e. your body temperature is more than 98.4 degrees C, the doctor considers it to be a '**symptom**'. The word '**symptom**' stands for a sign or an indication of the presence or the development of some kind of an illness, disease or sickness. The word 'symptom' is Noun with 'symptomatic' being its Adjective form and can be thus used: "The patient's continuous coughing was symptomatic of asthma." When there are more than two symptoms, the collection of all of them together is known as 'syndrome'. The word 'syndrome' is Noun and is generally not used in any other form e.g. "Physical weakness, high fever and a yellowish tint were part of a jaundice-syndrome in the patient." At times, a doctor is immediately able to ascertain what kind of sickness a patient has from a single symptom or takes into consideration the syndrome. When a doctor, after examining the patient and studying the symptoms/syndrome, declares the name of a patient's illness/sickness/disease, it is known as a 'diagnosis'. For a doctor to correctly reach a 'diagnosis', he must first thoroughly examine the patient. The entire process involved in reaching a conclusion for a doctor is known as 'to diagnose an illness.'

LESSON 315

'Sympathy' and 'Empathy'

When you see someone you know or even a stranger suffering or in great difficulty, do you cluck your tongue "tch, tch" in sympathy? Or do you do something to help that person? The word 'sympathy' is used when we wish to show that we have been or are touched by the misfortune suffered by someone. We then try to console that person or give him/her some kind of assurance that things will get better soon, e.g. "I extend my sympathy to the riot victims in Muzzafarnagar." Feeling sorry is displaying sympathy. The word 'sympathy' is Abstract Noun and the Adjective is 'sympathetic' with 'sympathize' being the Verb. However, when someone's suffering affects us to an extent that we imagine ourselves in his/her place, then we display '**empathy**' e.g. "Many women in the audience wept in **empathy**, seeing Rajesh Khanna in 'Avatar' reduced to poverty." When the word '**empathy**' is used, it indicates a stronger emotion than '**sympathy**'. It can also lead to concrete action giving relief to the sufferer. We know how Mother Teresa **empathized**, by not clucking her tongue but actually doing a lot to help those who were suffering.

LESSON 316

'Synchronization' and 'Chronology'

Switching from one channel to another to avoid a commercial, you find, to your frustration, the other chosen channel too showing advertisements. TV channels obviously have **synchronized** their clocks forcing advertisements on viewers. The word '**synchronize**' is Verb and means to match time on two or more time-telling mechanisms, ensuring that movements in two or more persons/locations occur at exactly the same time. For **synchronisation**, one must make sure that the watches etc. are of high quality with exactly the same settings. **Synchronized swimming** is an exciting event at the Olympics. When two swimmers dive together, and while diving, as well as when in the water, perform the same actions at the same time, it is a treat to watch. High degree of practice has obviously been undertaken and perfect coordination between the two leads to a breathtaking performance showing how well they synchronized their actions. The word '**synchronize**' has everything to do with '**chronology**' i.e. the movement of time. By a '**chronological**' order is meant the movement of time in a fixed order, towards the future. Moving behind towards the past is known as going in an **anti-chronological** manner.

How Not to Speak English

LESSON 317

'Bore' – different meanings, different forms

Considering the number of channels offering the same stuff, don't you get '**bored**'? The word '**bore**' has different meanings and one must use it carefully in one's conversation as well as writing. The word '**bore**' is **Noun, Verb** and in the '....**ing**' form i.e. '**boring**', it is **Adjective**. The word '**bore**' indicates the drilling of a hole in the ground or in a wall or through any other surface, e.g. "He **bored** a hole through the centre of the cardboard to make a replica of a long-playing record." A '**drill**' (electrical or manual) with a drill-bit is used to bore a hole. The word '**bore**' also indicates extreme dullness arising out of an interaction. When we encounter dullness in a book/movie/TV program/lecture etc, we describe it as '**boring**'. The word '**boring**' is antonymous to '**entertaining**' or '**interesting**'. When boredom gets to be extremely tiring and tedious, it is known as '**ennui**' (pronounced '**ahn-wee**'). The word '**ennui**', French in origin, stands for great '**boredom**'. Both **boredom** and **ennui** are Nouns and can be used thus: "You think the doctor will call you in soon, but **boredom** grows to **ennui** when your wait keeps on getting extended."

LESSON 318

'Ignition', 'Dashboard', 'Rear-View Mirror'...

The key that starts a car is known as the **ignition key**. To **ignite** is to spark or light a fire, which the key does by sparking life into the engine. Earlier, cars had separate keys for the '**boot**' (**dickey** in Indian English), and for the door handle (especially of the door to the driver's seat.) A handle just below the extreme right hand section released the lock of the '**hood**' ('**bonnet**' in Indian

251

English.) The toughened glass through which a driver views the road ahead is known as a 'windshield'. The console or the cluster of gauges etc. or meters is advantageously installed so that the driver can view them all while driving. All these become part of the 'dashboard'. The mirror through which you can view traffic behind your vehicle is known as the 'rear-view' mirror. Nowadays cars have rear-view mirrors on front doors also. The latest cars have indicator lamps too mounted on these front-door rear-view mirrors. An 'indicator' lamp, as the word suggests, 'indicates' when a driver wishes to turn the vehicle right or left. When both indicator-lamps are made to flicker (go on-off) simultaneously, it indicates break-down of a vehicle or some activity that may lead to traffic-inconvenience.

LESSON 319

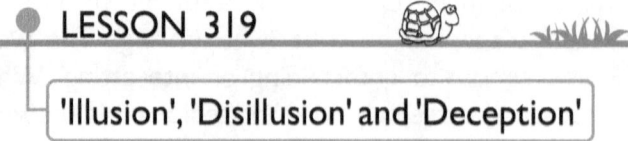

'Illusion', 'Disillusion' and 'Deception'

Rear-view mirrors mounted on front doors of cars and on handlebars of two-wheelers have the following **legend** on them: "**Objects in the mirror are closer than they appear.**" When we see something that is not what it actually appears to be, including the distance it is supposed to be at, then what we see is an '**illusion**'. In medical terms, an **illusion** is connected with our faculty of seeing and is classified as '**optical illusion**'. The word '**illusion**' is **Noun** and has no **Verb** form. The opposite i.e. '**disillusion**', however, exists in Verb form. When an illusion is no longer able to deceive a person bringing him/her face to face with the truth, then the word '**disillusioned**' is used, e.g. "He fell in love but got quickly **disillusioned** on discovering that she did not belong to a rich family." When we go on believing that something is true in spite of knowing in our heart of hearts that it isn't, then we '**deceive**' ourselves. To '**deceive**' is to '**cheat**' and the Noun form is '**deception**'.

LESSON 320

'Rest', 'Restless' and 'Restive'

"The manager will not be coming today, he is taking *a rest.*" It is advisable not to precede the word 'rest' with the article 'a'. The word 'rest' indicates a situation involving a period of relaxation or sleep after physical or mental exertion. The word 'rest' is both Noun as well as Verb and can be used in different ways, e.g. "I hope you don't mind my leaving right now, I need **to rest**." (Verb);

"The eight-hour **rest** he got after that tiring trip was quite refreshing." (Noun).

The word 'rest' also indicates what remains after subtracting a quantity. When used thus, 'rest' is Noun and must be preceded by the definite Article '**the**', e.g. "Those who wish to perform, may stay, **the rest** may leave." The word 'rest' has '**restless**' as virtual antonym indicating nervousness or anxiety, e.g. "Tension before the announcement of the results was making her **restless**." The word 'restless' is Adjective with '**restlessness**' its Noun. Please remember that '**restive**' has nothing to do with 'rest', and '**restive**' indicates nervousness or even loss of control. The word '**restive**' is very often used with animals, e.g. "The dog's meal was delayed, making her extremely **restive**."

LESSON 321

'Ghostwriters' and 'Pseudonyms'

Many people doubt the existence of **ghosts**. But, have you ever heard of **ghostwriters?** A ghostwriter actually exists. The name of the ghostwriter however, will always remain a mystery. That is because, whatever has been written by him/her has been credited to someone else's name (for a fee of course). When a book/article/essay etc. is written by someone other than the person whose name appears on it as author, then it is known to have been **ghostwritten.** There are thousands who wish to show that they can write (especially in English), so they hire the services of a ghostwriter. There are also writers who wish to stay hidden for reasons of their own. That is why they write under some other name. This name is known as **pseudonym** (pronounced '**sew-do-nim**'). **Samuel Langhorne Clemens** wrote under the **pseudonym Mark Twain.** At times, the term **pen name** is also used. The term **nom de plume (French in origin)** is also a synonym of **pseudonym.** When the author is unknown then the word '**anonymous**' (pronounced '**a-non-e-mus**') is used to declare that the creator of this piece of writing is unknown.

LESSON 322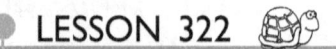

'Plagiarism' and 'Intellectual Property Rights'

Some people use lines by famous authors, writers, novelists and poets, and try to pass these lines off as their own. When a prose piece or part of a poem has been written by someone else, then the one under whose name the 'stolen' material appears is guilty of '**plagiarism**'. The word '**plagiarise**' (pronounced '**play-jee-a-rise**') means using somebody's work without acknowledging the original creator's name. It is a serious offence, and when detected, can lead to punishment. Attempts are regularly made to show that the original has been written by the **plagiariser.** Today, cyber access in a highly techno-savvy world makes the committing of such crimes extremely easy. People especially in developing countries, copy, cut and paste rampantly from the Internet. Plagiarism is also known as violation of **IPR (Intellectual Property Rights).** If you have unknowingly committed such an crime, you can find out the original source i.e. the holder of the **copyright**, and acknowledge the original work publicly. Besides, before publication, you can avoid such a crime by passing your work through a **Plagiarism Checker** on Google. Remember, stealing somebody's work deprives the original owner of the copyright his legitimate right to money. Do not cheat the world and yourself by saying that you are the creator when you are not.

LESSON 323

With a Sense of Humour

A **sense of humour** is an essential element that one needs to develop in a world full of stress and strain. What is it that exactly constitutes **a sense of humour**? Is it the ability to crack jokes at the drop of a hat? Is it the ability to laugh at oneself? Is it the ability to laugh with others? Many a time you must have noticed that even though you do not like or appreciate a joke, you smile or laugh to display politeness. When the teller of the joke is your boss, then you force yourself to laugh. In earlier days, the word **humour**, **Noun** as well as **Verb**, was thought to be one of the many constituents of human blood. Later on, it was spoken of as an invisible entity that had to be developed. A sense of **humour**, when developed, gives one a balanced approach to life and the ability to take difficulties in one's stride. The word '**humour**' is also used as Verb and the following is an example: "When our six-year old son pretends to be Batman, we **humour** him." As Verb, '**to humour**' means '**to tolerate**'.

LESSON 324

'Tolerate', 'Tolerant' and 'Tolerance'

When someone is described as being '**tolerant**', then it is clear that this person possesses the ability of allowing others to do what they want without opposing them. The person concerned may be accepting of a number of incidents and events that show that s/he is willing to accommodate another's viewpoint. The word '**tolerant**' is Adjective and can be used thus: "Hinduism is a **tolerant** religion." The quality of being tolerant makes its owner possess tolerance. The word '**tolerance**' is **Noun (Abstract)** and can be used thus: "When he obeys her all the time, it shows a husband's tolerance towards his wife." The Verb form of tolerant is '**tolerate**' and is very often used in situations that show continuation of acceptance, e.g.: "Miss XYZ continued **to tolerate** the students' indiscipline with a smile."

"He was surprised when she switched the fan off for he knew that she generally couldn't **tolerate** the heat."

The antonym of '**tolerant**' is '**intolerant**'. The Past Tense of '**tolerate**' is '**tolerated**' as it is a **Regular Verb**, e.g. "I've **tolerated** enough of your nonsense and am now going to complain."

LESSON 325

'Patrol' and 'Petrol'

In many English answer sheets, the word '**patrol**' is incorrectly spelt '**petrol**'. The word '**patrol**' is both **Noun** and **Verb**. As Noun, it means the formation or existence of a unit that is oriented toward guarding of an area or property, e.g.

"The Police **Patrol** Unit reached the scene of the crime within minutes.";

"The Coast Guard **Patrol's** boat chased and caught the smugglers within no time."

As Verb, '**to patrol**' is to guard either in a stationary or a moving position, e.g.:

"A police van **patrols** the entire 4 km stretch of sensitive areas."
"The army has been called in to patrol communally tense areas."

In many developed countries, a **Police Patrol Unit** continually surveys a designated area. This **patrolling** therefore results in preventing the outbreak of crime. The word '**patrol**' as compared with the word '**guard**' has a sense of greater responsibility and purpose. The word '**petrol**' is Noun and cannot be used as Verb. The word '**petrol**' is used to describe a liquid that enables an internal combustion engine to run. The other liquid used is '**diesel**'. Both, '**petrol**' and '**diesel**' are '**fuels**' that run an engine.

LESSON 326

In a 'Spot'

"Now that it's known he has sold his textbooks, this schoolboy is in a **spot**." In this sentence, the word '**spot**' is Noun, and means that having been caught, the schoolboy is in for punishment. The word '**spot**' has many meanings and in different contexts can be used as **Noun, Verb** as well as **Adjective**. "She put us in a **spot of bother** as we had to go out of our way to drop her at the airport." As Verb, the word '**spot**' can be used thus: "You can't miss him, her brother's so tall, you could **spot** him from anywhere." The word **spot** also stands for a particular location or site, e.g.

"When the police reached the **spot**, the body was not to be seen."

The use of **spots** in designs is quite popular, e.g.:

"She looked very pretty, wearing a **spotted** t-shirt." Here, '**spotted**' is Adjective. The word '**spot**' is an indication of a **dot** or the focusing on a particular area or a feature. The expression, "A leopard doesn't change its **spots**" is used to show that no matter how many claims a person makes of having changed, deep within herself/himself, s/he remains the same.

LESSON 327

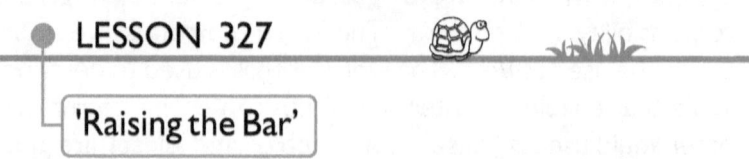

'Raising the Bar'

Time and again, when we read of successful people, we learn how they, on achieving small successes, used to '**raise the bar**'. What does '**raise the bar**' mean? When someone talks about '**raising the bar**', s/he conveys that a certain amount of success has been achieved. The person having decided to go further, desires to achieve a lot more. On the path toward greater success, the standard or measurement level of the next achievement to be gained has also been increased so that the increased level would inspire the person further toward greater glories and more difficult challenges. In Olympic events such as the **High Jump** and **Pole Vault**, each time an athlete is successful **the bar is raised** and placed at a higher slot/level/notch for the next attempt. Hence, the expression, '**raise the bar**'. A lesson in a 10th std. (SSC) English textbook, inspiringly describes a girl athlete Jyoti Maggu's achievements. She represented India at the International Blind Sports Association, Quebec, Canada. When a **visually challenged** Jyoti can say, "I believe in constantly raising the bar for myself," **(figuratively, not literally)** then we who are blessed with normal eyesight must make **'raising the bar'** a regular feature of our lives.

LESSON 328

For a 'Drive'

A word regularly used in English that easily conveys how a **Noun** can become **Verb** is 'drive'. "How would you like to go for a drive?" At today's petrol prices, it is doubtful whether many people actually do. A **'drive'** is a journey undertaken for pleasure in a car. The owner of the car generally drives his own vehicle. Rich Indians employ **'drivers'**. A person employed **to drive** a car is known as a **'chauffeur'** (pronounced **'shof-fer'**- with/without uniform). The word **'chauffeur'** too, like **'drive'**, is both **Noun** and **Verb**, e.g. "What time is the **chauffeur** expected?" (Noun). "Why doesn't your wife learn **to drive?** How long will you **chauffeur** her around?" (Verb). The word **'drive'** is used in many contexts to show the steering or the path of a vehicle or any other situation, e.g. "I doubt if he'll be successful, he doesn't have the **drive**." Here, the word **'drive'** is used as an inclination or tremendous urge to succeed. When somebody is spoken of as being in **'the driver's seat'**, then it is clearly indicated that s/he is a leader, taking an organization toward success or failure.

LESSON 329

'Clerk', 'Maidservant', 'Office-Boy' and 'Peon'

We Indians generally do not give much respect to those who do **menial jobs**. A **menial** job is one which is obviously not high-paying and done by millions who were not able to get a better one, either due to lack of education or any other reason. A **maidservant** is a menial worker; a **peon** is also a menial worker, and so is an **office-boy**. Similarly we have a **clerk**. The word 'clerk', a Common Noun, is used to denote a worker in an office who does all kinds of writing jobs required in an office. He may be maintaining records, noting down details or looking into **administrative matters** required every day. The word **clerk** is pronounced 'clark' in British English and 'clerk' in American English. Although not considered a **menial** job, **clerks** are not given much respect. In many government offices, we can see even today a huge number of **clerks**. These **clerks** are part and parcel of a huge **bureaucratic** system prevalent in the functioning of **government offices** (State as well as Central) in India. Premchand's Hindi short story in an English translation ("**Resignation**") most appropriately describes a **clerk** Fateh Chand's life in British India.

LESSON 330

Child Labour and Superpower

In many books containing stories on children, especially those by **Charles Dickens**, one gets inspired by the courage and determination of young boys. A boy who shines shoes to earn money is known as a **shoeshine boy** in English. On railway platforms in Mumbai and at street corners in many cities, even today, one gets to see these boys hard at work polishing shoes for a living. Now, with **child labour having** been banned and the **Right to Education** having become a **Fundamental Right** in India, there is hope that these **boys and girls** will have a much better future. A Fundamental Right is a basic right that every citizen born in a country is entitled to. A nation cannot be considered to be a **superpower** because of the huge quantity of arms and ammunition that it possesses, but because of the **quality of life and the potential of a comfortable livelihood** it provides its citizens, especially those of the future i.e. its children. Literacy i.e. the ability to read, write and study, is the first step towards sound education. We still have a long way to go before we can even begin to consider ourselves to be on the path to becoming a superpower. If we can teach every child to read, write, correctly understand and use English, then and only then shall we be on the right path toward becoming a superpower.

LESSON 331

'Juggernaut' and 'Jagannath'

Learners of English sometimes react with great astonishment on being made aware of the connection of the etymology (source of origin) of the word '**juggernaut**' with Orissa. First, let us look at what '**juggernaut**' means. The word '**juggernaut**' is used to indicate a vehicle with enormous power. It can also be used to denote a tremendous force by itself. This powerful vehicle or force is so strong that no obstacle can cause it to stop. No hurdle or impediment in its path can make the slightest difference in its smooth journey toward its destination. 'Destination' may also be equated with success. The word 'juggernaut' comes from the temple of Jagganath in Puri in Orissa and symbolizes the gigantic chariot requiring more than two hundred devotees to pull it onward. Every year, as a ritual, the chariot is pulled and devotees not strong enough are pushed aside or sometimes even crushed, hence the word, '**juggernaut**'. The word '**juggernaut**' therefore clearly denotes the onward journey of a vehicle or enterprise toward phenomenal success. The word '**juggernaut**' can be used thus: "His newly established business flourished, moving like a **juggernaut** crushing all competition." "Hollywood faces stiff competition with the juggernaut of Bollywood achieving international fame."

LESSON 332

'Morale' and 'Moral'

Very often, after a spate of defeats, or after facing unfavourable circumstances, we get to hear that the '**morale**' of a person, team, organization etc. is not very high. What is the meaning of '**morale**'? How is it different from that what we know as '**moral**'? Let us look at the word '**moral**' first. Many fables carry what is known as a '**moral**' at the end. Here, the word '**moral**' stands for a lesson learnt or inferred through the story by the reader. The word '**moral**' also means not compromising with one's conscience. The antonym of '**moral**' is '**immoral**'. "Stealing is an immoral act." The word '**immoral**' is Adjective as is the word '**moral**' when preceding 'acts/actions'. When used as Noun, the word '**moral**' is generally used in the plural, i.e. '**morals**', e.g. "These people have no **morals**." The word '**ethics**' is a synonym of '**morality**' (Abstract Nouns) and the adjective '**ethical**' has '**unethical**' as its antonym. '**Morale**' (pronounced '**mo-raal**') is Noun and has no Adjectival form. It stands for a feeling deep within an individual or together in many as a unit. The word '**morale**' is also used to show the spirit of a person, considering what s/he, or a group of persons as a team perhaps, is going through because of circumstances, e.g. "His consecutive

failures have led to a low **morale**."
"The team, having won the preliminary rounds, with a very high **morale**, is eagerly awaiting the final."

LESSON 333

'Scruples', 'Values' and 'Principles'

The word '**morals**' is closely connected with '**scruples**'. How is '**scruple**' different from '**moral**'? The word 'moral', as we saw in the previous lesson, is an Adjective as well as a Noun. The word '**scruple**' is a Noun and means a feeling/thought/emotion that is loaded with a sense of morality, e.g. "She kept the money that was to be donated, for she had no **scruples**." The Adjective form of **scruple** is '**scrupulous**' and it is generally used in its antonymous form, e.g.

"They decided to kidnap the child for they were **unscrupulous**."

Closely connected with **morals** and **scruples**, are the words '**values**' and '**principles**'. When we speak of a value, we mean the worth of any item. This word is very often utilized to describe mathematical terms. As a **moral**, the word '**value**' has greater significance, e.g. "A thief has no **values**, and can go to any extent to make money." We also have the word '**principles**' that is again connected with 'values'. The word '**principles**' is also used to denote the physical aspects of systems or a set of rules that have been adopted e.g. "The **principles of arithmetic** do not accept that two and two can be five." When associated with '**morals**', we can describe 'principle' thus: "He was a man of **principles**, and will never compromise on the quality of his products." This word, i.e. 'principle' is different from 'principal' which means the head of an institution imparting education.

LESSON 334

'Hospital' and 'Hospitable'

"If you wish to work in the Hotel industry, then you must be **hospitable.**" What does the word '**hospitable**' mean? How is it different from the word "**hospital**"? The word '**hospitable**' is Adjective and means **the quality of being warm and generous** when welcoming **guests**, including strangers to your house. You must have been invited to many homes, but were disappointed when the **host** was not **hospitable** enough to look after the **guests'** comfort. The quality of being **hospitable** can't be considered universal and varies from place to place, region to region and also from person to person. The ability to look after people, including strangers, will depend on an individual approach and it is incorrect to generalize it by saying that such and such people are more hospitable than others. The Noun form of '**hospitable**' is '**hospitality**' and being a quality in behaviour is obviously an **Abstract Noun**. Over here, it is also important to remember that when you are invited to someone's house, you are a '**guest**'. The person who invites you to his/her house is known as '**host**'. The word '**guest**' has no feminine form. The word '**host**' however, has the feminine form i.e. '**hostess**'. As you, by now, must be aware that the word '**hospital**' has nothing to do with '**hospitality**' The word 'hospital' is related to sickness and health.

LESSON 335

'Hospital', 'Patient' and Use of Articles

A **hospital** is a place where the sick are looked after, where the injured are treated, and where preventive health measures can also be explained and adopted. You will, however, hear people in India using incorrect English when describing certain situations related to hospitals. When a person is a patient and has been admitted, then the correct expression is, "**He is in hospital.**" As you can see, the article '**the**' is not used. If the sentence is, "**He is in the hospital**", then it means that this person is not a patient and **is in the hospital** for some other purpose, i.e. he may be a doctor there, or a supplier, or is visiting the hospital for any other purpose. Nowadays, big hospitals in many cities in India are like five-star hotels with sophisticated medical and surgical equipment and a high level of comfort is provided, especially after surgical and operative procedures. Many times, incorrect English is used when someone meaning that s/he is being treated for an illness, says, "**I'm patient.**" Here, the sentence means that this person is projecting his/her quality of being patient. When related to treatment for an illness, the correct sentence is, "**I'm a patient.**" The correct use of Articles in English can never be overemphasized and one must always use them in the correct position to convey exactly what one wishes to.

LESSON 336

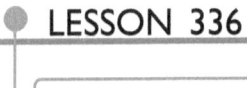
'Opposite to...'

When we provide directions to someone, we generally say, e.g. "As soon as you turn left, you will see a bank; my house is *opposite to the bank*." The preposition '**to**' must not be used with the preposition '**opposite**' when providing directions. The word '**opposite**', as Preposition, means, '**standing or situated in a position facing each other.**' The correct sentence, therefore, is, '**My house is opposite the bank.**' The Preposition '**to**' may be used with '**opposite**' when describing the contrariness of two abstract ideas, e.g. "The theory put forward by Nicholas Copernicus was **opposite to** the established theory of the Church." The word '**to**' is always used with the word '**apposite**' which means – 'suited to each other', e.g.: "Salt and pepper appear to be contrary but are **apposite to** each other."

● LESSON 337

'Agree with' and 'Agree to'

While using the verb **'agree'**, we generally use **'with'** and **'to'**. The use of both these words is correct, but the meaning conveyed differs when we say **'agree with'** as compared to **'agree to'**. Let us see the difference in the meanings conveyed: **(A) agree with** means "to have the same opinion as someone regarding a particular issue", e.g. "I **agree with** the Prime Minister that education is the path to India's success." **(B)** The word **'to'**, when used after **'agree'**, implies obedience or compliance. e.g. "My friend is a loving husband and gladly **agrees to** take his wife shopping." Over here, we must remember that **'with'** is a Preposition whereas **'to'** is used as the Infinitive whenever it follows the verb **'agree'**. When using the word **'compare'**, the correct word is **'to'** as Preposition. e.g.: "When compared to my aunt's degree, my uncle does not possess a very high qualification."

● LESSON 338

How's the 'ambience'?

"The food was okay, the music was not very good, and I also did not like the **ambience**." The word **ambience** (pronounced **am-bee-yuhnce**) conveys the décor, the furniture, and the way things have been arranged in order to create a particular effect on a visitor. Loosely connected with the words **atmosphere** and **environment**, the word **'ambience'** stands for the effect of or the result of a number of factors taken together as a sum-total, e.g. the furniture, the tapestry, the wood-work, the paintings on the walls, the upholstery, as well as the quality of the cutlery and the crockery, if we are speaking about a particular eating place. When we speak of 'ambience', many of us assume it to be loosely connected with the atmosphere or the environment of a particular area. It is, however, the effect that is created by arranging or rearranging a number of factors within a specified area. You will generally hear of 'ambience' being connected with a restaurant or a hotel, but even a hospital room or a well decorated residence can have an ambience. The kind of people frequenting a place may also be responsible for making its ambience attractive or unattractive.

LESSON 339

'A pat on the back'

How many times have you given yourself **a pat on the back** for a job well done? Do you also do it when someone else does a good job? The correct expression is **'give a pat on the back.'** Unfortunately, you will find this idiomatic expression being the most misused with many of us saying, 'he patted himself on his back for doing that task well.' When spoken thus, it is putting forward the *physical* act of patting your own or someone else's back. Whenever the expression needs to convey an idiomatic/figurative meaning, it must be used correctly i.e. 'give **a pat on the back.'** Similarly, there are a number of expressions, especially idioms, that are constantly being changed by us to suit our convenience. The user of a language must remember that excellence in communication is the hallmark of a fluent speaker of a language and this excellence must never be sacrificed at the altar of convenience.

LESSON 340

'Use' and 'Utilize'

Students, when confronted with the word **'utilize'**, are unable to distinguish it from the word **'use.'** What is the difference between the two? For those who study Economics, the difference is easier to understand. Let us look at the meaning of the word **'utilize.'** The word **'utilize'** means 'to put into application or serve a purpose in a productive manner.' When the word 'utilized' is applied, it goes further than **'use'** and puts across the idea that the maximum amount of profit has been derived from that kind of exploitation of that product or service. When we put the word **'use'** before products or services, we mean how we are able to exploit what it can do for us. The words **'useful'**, **'usefulness'** and **'usability'** are the variations of **'use'** and can be placed in proper positions in a sentence. When you finish reading this book, see that you **utilize** the Lessons written within.

LESSON 341

Not

The adverb 'not' when added to a verb makes it negative e.g. "You *must not take* what *does not belong* to you."

"Please *do not be afraid* of the dog, he barks but *does not bite.*"

At times the placement of 'not' after the Verb converts the sentence into the imperative mode, e.g. "Take not (that) what does not belong to you!"

"Be not afraid (of the dog)!" Whenever the negative is used, many of us in India, have a tendency to use the Verb form of the Third Person Plural Pronoun in place of the Verb form of the Third Person Singular, e.g. "*He don't sing well.*"

The correct form of the Verb in the Third Person Pronoun Singular will make the sentence correctly read:

"He doesn't sing well."

The easiest way to eliminate such errors is by practicing the correct Verb form of the Third Person Pronoun Singular, i.e. "he, she, it" in a number of sentences so that you always speak correct English e.g.

"She cooks well"

"She does not / doesn't cook well."

"He drives well."

"He does not/ doesn't drive well."

"It is/ it's very cold today."

"It is not/ isn't very cold today."

LESSON 342

Back of me?

"*Why you are always back of me?*" The person saying this in a complaining fashion is unable to frame the correct question in English and so conveys utter nonsense. The person speaking this sentence wishes to tell someone to stop irritating him/her by constantly picking on him/her. Unfortunately s/he is only transliterating. S/he means that the person the question is directed at, should stop irritating/teasing/harassing him/her. The correct question therefore is, "Why are you constantly after me?" Whenever we feel someone is constantly picking on us for the purpose of irritating/teasing/harassing us, the question should involve the word 'after' and not 'back'. The question can also use the word 'pick' e.g.

"Why are you constantly picking on me?"

LESSON 343

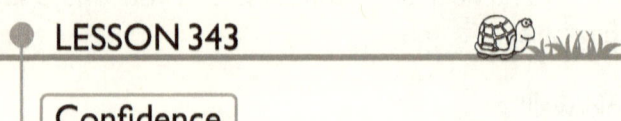

Confidence

When students are asked to point out what they feel they are the weakest in, where English-related skills are concerned, they invariably point out 'confidence'. The word 'confidence' does not stand for a skill, but is a feeling of assurance from deep within ourselves that tells us that we now possess adequate proficiency over a skill to be able to apply or use or, combining it with our talents, are ready to perform in public. Confidence is developed after we work hard and practice harder. While learning a skill, if we do not practice it to perfection, or work hard on it, then the level of confidence does not rise within us. Many of us assume that 'self-confidence' is a different word with a different meaning. The word 'self-confidence' has no relevance for confidence is all about the self. When we speak of 'confidence' related to others, then who we are referring to, is clearly evident from the sentence, e.g.

"I'm confident that although I'm not playing, my team will win."

The word 'confidence' also has to do with information we give to someone we trust. This trust makes us believe that this person will not reveal this information to anyone else, and the expression is 'to take into confidence' e.g.

"She took her cousin into confidence regarding her romance with his friend."

In such a situation, the Verb is 'confide' and can be used thus: "Make sure he is trustworthy before you confide in him."

LESSON 344

Trust

The last sentence in the previous Lesson has the word 'trustworthy' in it. Many of us, when describing someone in whom we can place our trust say, "He is very trusty." While the word 'trusty' is not incorrect, it is better to use 'trustworthy'. As the second half of the word says, this person is worthy of being trusted. What does 'trust' mean? By 'trust' is meant the feeling that we have when we believe that someone has a high sense of integrity regarding what we expect that person to do for us e.g.

"We have trust in the ability of our employees." Here, 'trust' is a level higher than 'confidence'. The word 'trust' can also be used as Verb, and when used as Verb, it conveys a feeling of hope and also, of belief, e.g.

"I trust you must have received the gift I sent."

"I trust you will keep this information to yourself." The word 'trust' can be used both as Noun and Verb in the same sentence, e.g
"I trust you will not betray my trust."

LESSON 345

Conserve / Converse

The conservation of our environment is now of the utmost importance and the sooner we understand how to conserve it the better. What does 'conserve' mean? If you notice carefully, the word 'conserve' is an anagram of 'converse' and very often mistakenly written as 'converse'. To 'conserve' means to make efforts to prevent damage to a structure or system of practices or any natural phenomenon of importance to human life. When we say to 'converse' we mean the act of speaking with others. The word 'converse' as an Adjective means 'as or in the opposite position.' Many scientific theories, theorems, mathematical paradigms etc have the 'converse' too so that your level of understanding of such concepts increases by leaps and bounds. The word 'converse' when used as Verb related to the act of speaking, has 'conversation' as the Noun; when 'converse' is used as an Adjective to mean 'the opposite' it has 'conversely' as its adverb, with 'converse' as a noun e.g. "The converse of this theory has not been tested as yet." Note, the word 'inverse' refers not to the opposite but to the reverse. The Figure of Speech known as Inversion, clearly illustrates the meaning of this word. The Subject and the Predicate are reversed, e.g. "In the forest, a sage lived."

LESSON 346

Zest Gusto VIM & Verve

"I liked the performance for it had a lot of zest." What does the word 'zest' mean? Does it have a synonym? What is its antonym? The word 'zest' means energy and has the word 'gusto' as a synonym. Both 'zest' and 'gusto' are near-synonyms of 'vim' and 'verve'. With the word 'vim', there is eagerness involved. It can therefore be safely said that 'zest' has power but 'vim' has more of enthusiasm in it. With the word 'verve' there is a greater sense of liveliness involved. As you will notice, and when you come across these words in different kinds of writing, they will appear to have the same meaning but there will always be a slight difference. That is where the skill of a writer/speaker lies, using the most appropriate word in a particular context or situation. The opposite of 'zest' is 'dullness'.

LESSON 347

Nurture & Nourish

Very often you see these two words together in a combined format "nurture and nourish" or as 'nourish and nurture". The combination in the former format is better. When we 'nurture' we bring up. The word 'nurture' is a Verb and it means to create an environment so that the growth of an individual or an aspect of human life takes place in an ideal manner. When we 'nourish' someone or something we provide adequate means of survival as well as growth. 'To nourish' has more to do with food, especially that food which gives the maximum amount of benefit by way of energy, to the person or creature or being or phenomenon consuming it. The word 'nurture' has 'nurturing' as Noun and the word 'nourish' has 'nourishment' as Noun. Both can be used together thus: "She makes sure that she gives her best to the nurturing and nourishment of her plants."

LESSON 348

> **Mature**

Many words in English with the letter 't' in the middle of it, use the 'ch' sound to make its pronunciation correct, e.g. adventure-pronounced 'ad-ven-cher'; nurture-pronounced 'nur-cher', creature pronounced 'cree-cher'. Some words also have the 'sh' sound for 't' – e.g. station as 'stay-shun'. Due to this peculiarity, we have a tendency to pronounce words with 't' in the middle by using the 'ch' sound. There are however exceptions, e.g. 'mature' which does not take the 'ch' sound for 't'. We must pronounce the first three letters of 'mature' as we say the word 'mat' with a very short 'a' sound and the last three letters 'ure' to rhyme with 'cure'. The word 'mature' stands for a person with a fully developed body and/or mind or any plant, or animal with all physical characteristics showing full development. To be 'mature' also means 'to be in a position of full adulthood' and involves, very often, a sense of responsibility, e.g. "When she lost her father, she displayed maturity, taking charge of the family's financial requirements." The word 'mature' is Adjective as well as Verb and having seen it in its Noun form, 'maturity' let's see it in the other two forms e.g. "The mature mangoes have a tendency to fall on their own." "Animals and birds generally take a shorter time-duration to mature as compared to the period of time taken by human beings to develop."

LESSON 349

> **T-o - To, D-o - Do**

In the Hindi film "Chupke Chupke" (1975) its hero Dharmendra asks, "if 't-o' is 'to' and 'd-o' is 'do' then why is 'g-o' 'go' and not 'goo'? The question, supposedly rhetorical, elicits no answer. The audience too laps up the question in its blissful ignorance with peals of laughter. If you are a serious student of English, you will surely know that 'g-o' is 'go' because in English 'g-o-o' is 'goo'. And yes, 'goo' in English means exactly that what it does in Hindi. The only difference in usage is that in English it is more used in its adjectival form 'gooey' e.g. "He didn't like the feel of the gooey substance that scraped his left hand while climbing the tree." Similarly, the question "why is 'b-u-t – 'but' and 'p-u-t' - 'put'?' in "Chupke Chupke" gets no answer but laughter. The answer is that 'p-u-t-t' is 'putt', which when spoken, is pronounced to rhyme with 'but'. The word 'putt' means to make a light stroke, or to hit a ball lightly with a long stick/handle known as a 'club'. Those who play golf are well acquainted with this word and know that to 'putt' means to hit a ball with the exact quantum of force making it roll into the designated hole. The next time you put across these facts where English is concerned, watch your level of confidence climb great heights.

LESSON 350

Inclination

In a highly techno-savvy world today with everybody being so hard-pressed for time, how does one manage to arrange time so that one can enjoy and benefit from one's inclinations? The word 'inclination' means a slant or a gradual leaning toward an activity. An 'incline' is also a slope or a path going uphill. When related to our likes and dislikes the word 'incline' or 'inclination' is used thus: "I don't know where those days have gone when I had the inclination to listen to old Hindi film songs." When one has the inclination to do something that means it is more to take part in an activity that is to one's liking as a pastime. Sometimes, this pastime can also become a full time occupation e.g. "In the beginning, she was inclined toward gardening but now she is a successful landscape artist." To do justice to one's inclination one must have the time. As the joke/riddle goes: Q: "What did The Leaning Tower of Pisa say to Big Ben? A: "If you have the time, I have the inclination."

LESSON 351

Mention / Discuss

The word 'mention' like the word 'discuss' does not take the preposition 'about'. You will however note that many of us, constantly say, e.g. *"They mentioned about the picnic."* The correct sentence is "They mentioned the picnic." If you look carefully at the word 'mention' it is both Noun and Verb. The word 'mention' is used to indicate someone or something as a point of reference. The words 'in passing' can also be used e.g. "She was mentioned in passing." This means that the person was referred to without going into details. Even though the preposition 'of' is not used, its implication is clear e.g. (A) "Cruelty to animals? There was no mention." (B) "No mention was made of the cruelty to animals that takes place every day." The word 'mention' as Verb is used in the negative also, e.g. "Please do not mention anything of what happened last night." Before the now common, 'you're welcome' after 'thank you' the expression 'Mention not' was very popular. Nowadays very few Indians say, "Mention not" when someone says to them "Thank you." This expression was used in many scenes in the Hindi film "Upkar". Remember, as with the word 'discuss' the word 'mention' should never be followed by 'about.' You can easily remember the correct usage by looking at the following sentences: (1) "When mention is made of 'discuss' we should not use 'about'. (2) When we discuss 'mention' we should not use 'about'.

LESSON 352

Once / Twice / Thrice

"He has called **two times** for you." Here, the correct term for 'two times' is "twice". In English the numerical units *one, two* and *three* when associated with the number of times attempts, efforts, trials etc. are made, are generally spoken in a different form e.g. 'once, twice and thrice,' respectively. Of the three, the most common error is with 'twice'. When the action has been performed on two occasions, then 'twice' is used as we have already seen. When it is done on three occasions, then the word 'thrice' is used, e.g. "The students went thrice, but there was no teacher in the classroom." The word 'thrice' is similar-sounding to 'trice'. The word 'trice' means 'within no time, at great speed' etc e.g. "The dogs were next to her in a trice as soon as they saw the lady bringing their food." Remember, numbers beyond three have no such variations e.g. four, five and so on. These may be used as they are e.g. "The athlete was not allowed to jump four times." The words 'once, twice and thrice' are Adverbs of Frequency and they convey the best meaning when placed immediately after the Verb.

LESSON 353

The people of

"*Why you Indian people are like this?*" This is a common question asked by foreigners especially by those from Asian countries. This is the way a similar question is written also by students from such countries including India. Many Indians on their return from China, say, "*Chinese people have advanced a lot.*" When we use words denoting 'people' of a particular country or region, then the use of the word 'people' with it becomes unnecessary, e.g. "Indians eat a lot of curries." "The Nepalese have suffered so much in the recent earthquakes." It is always better to use 'the people of ...., and name the country, region, etc when using the word 'people' is unavoidable e.g. "The people of Europe have always been great explorers." "The people of Rajasthan wear loose-fitting garments because of the intense heat."

LESSON 354

Sacred / Scared

Many times while reading or speaking the word 'sacred' due to the letters 'c' and 'r' being next to each other in both these words, a common error occurs. The word 'sacred' pronounced 'say-krid' is mispronounced and read as 'scared'. The word 'sacred' is a synonym of 'holy' i.e. something which has great religious respect, e.g. "The shrine of Saibaba at Shirdi is sacred to Hindus." The word 'scared' means 'to be afraid of .....' e.g. "I am scared that I may not clear the test." The word 'scared' is at a level higher than 'afraid' showing greater fear, "She always takes a different route, at a safe distance from the cemetery as she is scared of ghosts."

LESSON 355

Handsome / Beautiful

Whenever we find the physical appearance of a woman appealing, we have a tendency to say, "She is beautiful." This indicates that we find the woman's physical appearance quite attractive. Where men are considered, we use the word 'handsome'. Did you know that the word 'handsome' was used in earlier days to describe a woman's physical appearance too? When novels were just begun to be written, women were described as being handsome. Later on, there came a clear demarcation of 'handsome' for men and 'beautiful' for women. No matter who you wish to describe as having some physical characteristics that are appealing, you may use 'handsome' for men and 'beautiful' for women. You must however remember to be polite and never use antonyms, for it is extremely rude to call someone who is not attractive as 'ugly'. Remember, the natural physical appearance of a human being is something over which we have no control. You can say instead, "I do not think she is beautiful." "I don't know why people call him handsome, I don't think he is." "I don't find him handsome at all."

LESSON 356

Novel

Many of us, wishing to show how good our knowledge of English is, say, 'I like reading English books, I have read all the novels of Shakespeare." Please note that Shakespeare did not write a single novel. That was because when Shakespeare (1564-1616) was writing his plays, novels had not even been begun to be written. The people of England had no idea of what a 'novel' meant. The word 'novel' is Noun and Adjective as well. As a Noun, the word 'novel' stands for a long story in the form of a book that is read for entertainment. The word 'fiction' is also used to describe a novel so that the reader can assume that the events described in the novel did not actually happen but took place only in the writer's mind. Sometimes, a novel is also written on actual events and incidents. Then it comes in the category of 'non-fiction. The word 'novel' as an Adjective is used to describe a strikingly different kind of idea that has never been thought of before e.g. "Leonardo da Vinci had this novel idea that it was possible for a man to fly."

LESSON 357

Eternal / Mortal

You must have heard of the word 'eternity' and its equivalents in other languages that promise 'life forever after dying.' The word 'eternity' is an Abstract Noun and its adjectival form is 'eternal.' When we speak of a time-frame referring to an eternity, it is impossible to even imagine the length of time or the period that the word implies. Closely associated with 'eternal' is the word 'immortal'. The word 'immortal' is used to denote something that cannot be destroyed or cannot die. The antonym is 'mortal'. When using these words, there is invariably omission of the letter 't' making the words 'immoral' and 'moral'. The last two have already been spoken about in an earlier Lesson. 'Mortality' is the aspect of the final ending of any creature on this earth. This word is also used to describe the rate at which death takes place in a particular segment e.g. infant mortality rate, male mortality rate etc . the word 'immortal' stands for 'life forever' or 'that which can never be destroyed or killed,' or 'that which does not die.' A single sentence containing both makes their use amply clear, e.g. "Man is mortal, God immortal."

LESSON 358

Like / Likely / Likelihood

The word 'like' in English has a number of meanings and according to the meaning, its uses are also many. The most common use of 'like' has to do with its use as a word showing comparison or resemblance e.g. "Your sister looks like you." In this sentence the word 'like' is Preposition and shows resemblance between this person and his/her sister. In the question 'Do you like me?" the word 'like' is a Verb. The answer is also a Verb e.g. "Yes, I like you." The word 'like' can also be used as Adjective, e.g. "I do not remember having read a like book." This means a book like the one now in front of me or the one being mentioned. A combination is also possible e.g. "The two books were quite alike." When used as an Adverb or Adjective the letters 'ly' are added and the word becomes 'likely' e.g. 'With the way you drive you are most likely to meet with an accident." Please note that the word 'liking' is a Noun. "Did you enjoy the food at that restaurant?" "No, it wasn't to my liking." The word 'likelihood' is also a Noun but an Abstract one. It means 'possibility' or 'probability.' "Do you think it might rain?" "There seems to be no likelihood of rain."

LESSON 359

Nobel - Noble

" *Who do you think will be the next Indian to win the Noble Prize?*" As Indians we feel extremely proud when a fellow-citizen wins this prestigious Prize. But, how many Indians can spell and pronounce the name of this Prize correctly? Very few. The correct spelling is "N-O-B-E-L" and the best way of remembering the correct spelling and pronunciation is by writing 'no bell' and removing one 'l' from 'bell' and then joining the two words. The word 'Nobel' is a Proper Noun and is the surname of the man who first instituted this Prize. The other word with which this word gets confused, is 'noble'. The word 'noble' is an Adjective and stands for a quality that makes its possessor above others as far as honour, values and principles are concerned, e.g. "His noble deeds earned him great reputation and admiration." In the earlier days, there used to be a rank i.e. nobleman in England. The Abstract Noun is nobility and can be used thus: "His nobility is way beyond question."

LESSON 360

Last but not least

The importance of the correct use of Articles in English can never be overemphasized. In addition to not using them, their incorrect insertion too is rampant and a matter of great concern. The best way to learn English is by counting the number of words in a correct sentence, closing the book and speaking the sentence out loudly, by counting out each and every word. If you find that the number of words spoken by you differs from the number of written words, you will more often than not, discover an Article has been added or omitted. The most glaring example is the idiomatic expression, last but not least. This idiomatic expression is spoken and also written by us Indians as *last but not the least*. Please note, there is no 'the' in this expression. This Lesson, being this book's last, in no way diminishes its importance or value. This Lesson too, like all the earlier Lessons of this book, will have served its purpose if it has given you food for thought.

Afterword

English is spoken in many languages in India. Use of the word 'languages' instead of 'regions', is deliberate and certainly not inadvertent. Whenever a conversation is initiated in English, it is well begun and one presumes it will presently be half done. Soon, however, one finds, to one's dismay and chagrin, the conversation, turning askew, has gone astray. That is because, after a few sentences, thanks to their wobbly grasp over English, the speakers have switched over to their mother tongue or the local language. Complicated scientific theories and complex financial terms (to cite two instances), are explained and elaborated upon, using non-English Indian languages. This is unfortunately true also of interactions involving those who have passed out from well-known English-medium schools. The term 'English-medium' is more of a status-symbol, for textbooks are written in English but very little teaching and consequently, learning, gets done using English. The answer to a question requiring a definition is, more often than not, given using a non-English Indian language. On being pointed out that a mixture (conscious or subconscious) of two languages results in a hybridized third language, the speakers stare at the scolder in resentful stupefaction. There have been instances when the person wishing the conversation to continue using correct English, is threatened with dire consequences.

It is high time hostility to English was done away with. The learning process where English is concerned will become easier if teachers, students and the general public graciously reconcile themselves to the fact that English isn't a foreign language. Our currency notes carry the signature of the Governer of the Reserve Bank of India with his promise above it in Hindi and English. We Indians must never forget that the Constitution of India too has been written in English. All rules, laws, acts, rights and duties are applicable and to be studied from the Constitution of India using English. Remember, as soon as you begin to unlearn incorrect English and learn correct English correctly you form part of that huge entity that occupies an important segment on the map of the world, and whose Constitution begins, "We, the people of India… " The English had enslaved India, English set Indians free.

While writing the Lessons in this book, I have carefully observed our Indian approach to the usage of English, and also the methods adopted to teach it. I have been through innumerable books on English grammar. It is well-nigh impossible to name them all, these having been read over four decades. Two books that stand out and whose influence over my thinking has been rewardingly overwhelming, are Fowler's *Modern English Usage* (1926) and W. Stannart Lee's *A Handbook of English Grammar for Asian students* (1938).

My interest in English grammar and an intrinsic desire to ensure that I'm correct when regularly using English have made my life richer. With this book, I hope to increase the wealth of information and insights related to English grammar in those who have a genuine interest in improving their English-related skills.

When, after having gone through the three hundred and sixty Lessons contained in this book, the focused reader is able not only to understand, but also has developed the capability to explain the Preamble to the Constitution of India using correct English, then, as a true Indian, I will consider that I have achieved more than the aim which I had set out with, when I first began to write this book.

Mine is a war against mediocrity and with this book, its first battle has just begun.

- Vinay Sethi

Search Guide

> Clearing Some Perceptions...

- 9. English – An Indian Language
- 113. Why English is so popular?
- 104 English – A 'Soft' Skill
- 80. Prioritise Books
- 300. True Education – Application of Knowledge and Skill of Comprehension
- 30. English in Job Interviews: Conveying your expectations(6)

> To Begin With...

- 47. 'Alphabet', 'Letters', Consonants', 'Vowels'
- 78. Basics of English
- 79. Parts of Speech
- 174. "D for Delhi', "B for Belly"
- 175. Intonation and Stress
- 200. Mother Tongue Influence – Just an Excuse(6)

> Confusions – Similar Words, Different Meanings

- 5. 'They're' – The Contraction of 'They are'
- 6. 'There' – An Adverb meaning 'in that place'
- 7. Their' – A Pronoun for Belonging
- 21. Contractions: 'I'll', 'He'll', 'She'll'...
- 22. Contractions: 'I'm', 'I've', 'We've', 'You're'...
- 23. Negative Contractions: Won't, Can't, Couldn't, Shan't...
- 24. 'Quiet' and 'Quite'
- 29. Homonyms: 'Complement' and 'Compliment'
- 49. 'Loose' and 'Lose'
- 58. 'Would': Courtesy and Possibility
- 59. 'Could': Ability and a Stronger Possibility

60. 'Should': Advice and Suggestion
63. 'Mediocre' and 'Average'; 'Awesome' and 'Awful'
73. 'Live' and 'Stay'
74. 'Expire' and 'Pass Away'
81. 'Accept', 'Except' and 'Expect'
98. 'Career' and 'Carrier'
102. 'Aks' and 'Riks'
108. 'Advice' and 'Advise'; 'Device' and 'Devise'
112. 'Boy' and 'Buoy'
114. 'Indeed' and 'In Deed'
133. 'Carton' and 'Cartoon'
134. 'Corpse' and 'Corps'
176. 'Wonder' and 'Wander'
178. 'Suit' and 'Suite'
181. 'Brake' and 'Break'
182. 'Wind', 'Rewind'...'Rewinded'?
184. 'Bath' and 'Bathe'
187. 'Reality' and 'Realty'
198. 'Stationary' and 'Stationery'
208. 'Improve' and 'Improvise'
255. 'Desserts' and 'Deserts'
256. 'Criterion' and 'Criteria'
271. 'Launch' and 'Lunch'
277. 'Through' and 'Thorough'
278. 'Minute (mi-nit)' and 'minute (my-newt)'
280. 'Picture' and 'Pitcher'
305. 'Saloon' and 'Salon'
325. 'Patrol' and 'Petrol'
332. 'Morale' and 'Moral'
334. 'Hospital' and 'Hospitable; (41)

Grammar and Rules – The Backbone of Language

8. Plural Nouns – with and without 's'
9. 'One of the ....'
12. Verb, Tense and Gender

14. 'Bear' and 'Bare'
15. 'Countable' and 'Uncountable' Common Nouns
16. 'Brought' and 'Bought'; 'Thought' and 'Taught'
17. 'Resume' and 'Résumé'
18. 'Do' - the grammar, the purpose
19. The Use of 'Have'
20. The Use of 'Make'
28. Plurals in Clothing: 'Jeans', 'Pants', 'Shorts' etc.
32. Irregular Verbs: Different Past Tense and Participle Forms
33. Regular Verbs: Usage and Pronunciation of 'ed'
34. Participle Form of Verbs: Use of 'has/have' and 'had'
35. Tenses: Introduction
36. Present Simple Tense
37. Present Continuous Tense
38. Present Tense for 'Near Future'
39. Present Perfect Tense
40. Present Perfect Continuous Tense
41. Past Simple Tense
42. Past Continuous Tense
43. Past Perfect Tense
44. Past Perfect Continuous Tense
45. Future Simple Tense
46. Future Continuous Tense
53. Articles: The Use of 'a'
66. Subject+Verb+Object
71. Regular Verbs not using 'ed'
75. 'If only I were...'
77. Preposition, Articles and Tenses
82. 'Most Happiest Day' – Use of Superlative
83. Nouns and Verbs: Inter-conversion
84. Nouns and Verbs: Some Basic Rules
109. 'Used to'
116. A, AN, THE
117. 'The' and Common/Countable Nouns
118. 'A', 'An' and Vowel Sound

119. 'The' Definite Article
120. 'The' and Proper Nouns
126. Conjunctions – 'And', 'But', 'Because'
127. Co-ordinating Conjuctions – 'And', 'But'
128. Subordinating Conjunctions – 'Because'
129. Subordinating Conjunctions – 'Although', 'Despite', 'In spite'
130. 'Either....or', 'Neither...nor'
137. Interjections!
192. Sentences ending with a verb – Indirect Speech
193. Sentences ending with a verb – Indirect Speech
194. Sentences beginning with a verb – only when Imperative
220. Suffixes – Typicality and Associations
261. The silent 'b' after 'm'
296. 'Won't'-'Wont' and 'Can't'-'Cant'
311. 'Been': A Unique Time-Frame
312. '...ing' – Proper/Improper Use
335. 'Hospital', 'Patient' and Use of Articles (55)

Prepositions

1. 'To' – Wrong Usage
2. 'To' – Incorrect Omission
3. 'To' – with 'hear' and 'listen'
4. 'Myself', 'Himself', 'Herself' and 'Themselves'
121. Pre-postions
122. 'On', 'At', 'With'
123. 'On', 'In', 'About'
124. 'Into', 'Between', 'Among'
125. 'On', 'Off' and 'Of'
268. 'With', 'To' and 'For': Associations with Verbs
301. 'Enough' and associated prepositions
336. 'Opposite to...'
337. 'Agree with' and 'Agree to' (13)

Correct Usage – For Correct English

10. Redundant Use of 'Colour'
11. 'Birthday' and 'Date of Birth'
13. 'Driving' and 'Riding'
25. 'Next Week', 'Last Night', 'Previous Evening' etc.
26. 'This Evening', 'Tonight', 'Day before Yesterday'...
48. 'Afraid of' and 'Afraid'
51. 'Cold' and 'Hard' Drinks
52. 'Sink' and 'Drown'
54. 'Disinterested' and 'Uninterested'
56. 'Weather' and 'Climate'
61. 'It' instead of 'them/they'
62. 'Cloths' and 'Clothes'
64. 'Hard' and 'Hardly'
65. 'Abroad' and 'Foreign'
67. 'I' and 'Me': Placing with Courtesy
68. 'Understand' and 'Understanding'
69. 'Make/Made' + 'Up'
70. 'Knock' + 'On'
72. 'Live', 'Alive' and 'Living'
85. 'My Uncle is Vegetable'
87. The use of 'Only'
88. 'Find' and 'Finding'
89. 'Taking a Test'
90. 'Answering a Paper'
91. Cousin Brothers, Cousin Sisters
105. 'Leave', 'Drop' and 'Pick'
110. 'Suppose', 'Supposed' and 'Supposedly'
115. Anybody, Nobody, Somebody, Everybody...
131. Matters of 'Heart'
132. The use of 're'
139. 'Work' and 'Job'
140. Terminology – 'Accurate' and 'Implicit'
144. Many Uses of 'Schedule'
149. 'Details' and 'Information'

158. 'Well' – Adverb, Adjective and Noun
159. Proverbs and Literature
160. Proverbs – the moral side
163. Rain Cheque
164. 'Back' and 'Ago'
165. The use of 'yet'
170. 'Declare' and 'Suffer'
177. 'Too' and 'Very'
180. Rather,..
185. Lakhs, Crores and Millions
186. 'Mutual' and 'Unanimous'
188. 'Hawker' and 'Vendor'
189. 'Buy' and 'Purchase'
190. 'Still' – as five Parts of Speech
191. Short(s)
196. 'Determine' – (Mis)Pronunciation
201. 'Husband' – the noun, the verb
202. Utterances – 'Say'
203. Utterances – 'Speak'
204. Utterances – 'Tell/Told'
205. Utterances – 'Talk'
206. 'Drawing' the Curtains
209. To answer your all questions...
210. 'Overlooking' and 'overseeing'
211. 'Look at', 'look into', 'look down upon', 'look up to', 'look up'
212. You see...
216. 'Watch' it
218. 'Complete' and 'Finish'
219. Flammable-Inflammable, Different-Indifferent
228. 'Economic' and 'Economical'
229. 'Economics' and 'Economy'
230. 'Finance' and 'Fiscal'
235. 'Alias'
236. 'Someone's in the lobby'
239. Disaster Management

240. 'Damage' – the noun
241. 'Down' – improper associations
242. At 'leisure'
245. 'Lifts' and 'Elevators'
247. 'To emigrate', 'Work Visa' and 'Tourist Visa'
248. 'Accelerate' and 'Escalate'
251. A pinch of 'Salt'
252. 'Salt' and 'Pepper'
253. 'Masala'
259. 'Medium' and 'Media'
260. 'Reach' – as Verb, as Noun
262. 'People' and 'Peoples'
263. 'Dedicated to...'
264. 'As' Simple 'As' That...
265. 'As' – as conjunction, as preposition, as pronoun
267. 'Weigh' your options
269. 'Move' and 'Shift'
276. Same word, different pronunciations
281. 'How're things?'
292. 'Grinning' and 'Smiling'
293. 'Stride' and 'Step'
294. 'Step On', 'Being in Step' and 'Keep in Step'
302. 'Valid-Invalid'
303. 'Fame' and 'Popularity'
308. Safe and 'Sound'
309. 'Discoveries' and 'Inventions'
310. 'Clever' and 'Intelligent'
315. 'Sympathy' and 'Empathy'
317. 'Bore' – different meanings, different forms
320. 'Rest', 'Restless' and 'Restive'
323. With a Sense of Humour
324. 'Tolerate', 'Tolerant' and 'Tolerance'
326. In a 'Spot'
328. For a 'Drive'
340. 'Use' and 'Utilize' (104)

Indianisms – Our Very Own

50. 'What is your good name, sir?'
57. 'I am very better...'
91. Cousin Brothers, Cousin Sisters
92. Addressing People – Mr./Miss/Mrs./Ms
93. 'Teacher' and 'Sir'
101. 'Postpone' and 'Prepone'
146. While Co-operating
147. Last-to-Last Week, Next-to-Next Week
150. Indianisms that Backfire
166. '...to sell my land...along with my wife'
167. 'I want to shave my son's head...'
168. 'Having' a headache
169. 'Male or Female...I am both...'
172. '...like anything'
195. 'Having' – the Indian version
231. 'He came by walk'
249. 'Doing a fight'
257. 'Publikcity' (18)

Manners/Customs

27. Wishing People: 'Good Day', 'Good Night', 'Good Evening'
76. Do we 'drink' soup or do we 'eat' it?
94. 'Respected Sir/Madam'
95. 'Thank you in Advance'
96. 'No, thank you', 'You're Welcome'
97. 'Excuse Me'
136. Abuse and foul-words
148. I Beg Your Pardon
161. How are you?
162. How do you do?
171. 'I would be highly obliged...'(11)

Idioms/Phrases

- 31. 'First Come, First Serve'
- 145. 'When the going gets tough'
- 151. Idioms and Proverbs
- 152. Negative Idioms
- 153. Positive Idioms
- 154. Idioms – For every emotion
- 155. Some Famous Idioms
- 156. The 'eye' of the beholder
- 157. Proverbs – Similar and Opposite
- 183. Something fishy...
- 207. 'Are you game?'
- 221. 'Breaking the Ice'
- 222. 'Trial and Error'
- 223. 'Tying the knot'
- 224. 'From the horse's mouth...'
- 225. 'Running neck to neck'
- 226. 'No news is good news'
- 227. 'Not my cup of tea'
- 233. Like a chameleon...
- 234. 'Springing a Surprise'
- 273. 'With due respect...'
- 275. '...between the cup and the lip'
- 306. 'White Elephant'
- 327. 'Raising the Bar'
- 339. 'A pat on the back' (25)

Vocabulary

- 86. Carnivorous, Herbivorous and Omnivorous
- 103. 'Day-dreams' and 'Nightmares'
- 106. 'Infant', 'Child', 'Youth', 'Adult'...
- 107. The 'Alleged' Crimes
- 111. 'Suppose', 'Supposed' and 'Supposedly'

135. 'Amateur', 'Professional', 'Novice', 'Expert'
138. 'Chores' and 'Errands'
141. 'Appraise', 'Apprice', 'Assess' and 'Evaluate'
142. 'Quotation', 'Estimate', 'Bill' and 'Invoice'
143. 'Cash', 'Credit' and 'Debit'
173. What's a 'Milch Cow'?
179. Where do we eat?
197. The multi-faceted 'Ego'
199. 'Insure', 'Ensure', 'Assure' and 'Reassure'
213. Sixth Sense
214. 'Superstitions', 'Omens' and 'Amulets'
215. The power of a rational mind
217. Watch on the Wall
237. 'Destruction' and 'Devastation'
238. 'Calamity', 'Catastrophe', and 'Apocalypse'
243. 'Left-handed' and 'Ambidextrous'
244. 'Assassination', 'Homicide', 'Suicide'
246. 'Diaspora' – the migrated ones
250. 'Relief', 'Rescue' and 'Rehabilitation'
254. 'Staple Diet' and 'Cuisine'
258. 'Publicity', 'Advertising' and 'Commercials'
266. 'Cleanliness is next to godliness'
270. 'Trivial'. 'Trifle' and 'Truffle'
271. 'Mares', 'Vixens', 'Stags' and 'Peahens'
274. 'Phobia'
279. 'Body Language' and 'Gestures'
282. 'Cynical', 'Pessimist' and 'Optimist'
283. 'Skeptic', 'Specious', 'Agnostic' and 'Atheist'
284. 'Rapport' and 'Vibes'
285. 'Beware', 'Aware' and 'Wary'
286. 'Loot', 'Plunder' and 'Pillage'
287. Synonyms and Antonyms – Some exact, some approximate
288. Synonyms and Antonyms: As per the Context
289. 'Compatibility' and 'Congeniality'
290. 'Potable' and 'Edible'

291. Anagrams and Palindromes
295. 'Scope', 'Periscope' and 'Kaleidoscope'
297. 'Chant', 'Prostrate' and 'Kneeling'
298. 'Breed', 'Bred' and 'Pedigree'
299. 'Fast', 'Feast' and 'Banquet'
304. 'Notorious'. 'Notoreity' and 'Goodwill'
307. 'Custodian' and 'Custody'
313. 'Heir', 'Inheritance' and 'Erstwhile'
314. 'Symptom', 'Syndrome' and 'Diagnosis'
316. 'Synchronisation' and 'Chronology'
318. 'Ignition', 'Dashboard', 'Rear-View Mirror'...
319. 'Illusion', 'Disillusion' and 'Deception'
321. 'Ghostwriters' and 'Psuedonyms'
322. 'Plagiarism' and 'Intellectual Property Right'
329. 'Clerk', 'Maidservant', 'Office-Boy' and 'Peon'
330. Child Labour and Superpower
331. 'Juggernaut' and 'Jagannath'
333. 'Scruples', 'Values' and 'Principles'
338. How's the 'ambience'? (60)

www.ingramcontent.com/pod-product-compliance
Lightning Source LLC
Chambersburg PA
CBHW020351170426
43200CB00005B/130